Keith Fa

'Ich habe genug'

a biography by
Julia Falkner

Thames Publishing
London

First published in 1998 by Thames Publishing
14 Barlby Road, London W10 6AR

A CD of some of Sir Keith's recordings
is planned for release in autumn 1998.

Printed and bound in Great Britain
by Lonsdale Press

Contents

For Ailsie and Jack Falkner

Preface

Sir Keith Falkner ... 'a singer who was that rarity who combined the gifts of a beautiful voice and interpretative insight ... makes for a musician who stands for the best in English music ...' [1]

Sir Keith, great singer of Bach, Purcell and Handel among others, was perhaps the outstanding recitalist of his time. He had the finest enunciation, quality, timbre of voice and was much admired and respected by his colleagues. He ended his career where he began it, at the Royal College of Music, as its Director. He was also a fine cricketer and sportsman.

This book is about the man, his training, his career in music and the rich life he lived with his life-long accompanist by his side – his wife, Christabel Margaret Fullard. Many will remember him with warmth and admiration. I am most grateful to all who have contributed reminiscences or helped in this endeavour. I wish to thank especially Wayne Turner, Kenneth Day, Mary Ketchem Larkin, Alex Falkner and John Keith Sutton and Professors Thomas Sokol and Raymond Jahn. I am indebted to all. Finally, to my parents for enabling me to share in their musical life.

Part III contains tributes which include facts mentioned earlier in the book. As these tributes were made at different periods of Sir Keith's career, it has been decided to include them unchanged.

Julia Falkner
April 1998

Throughout the book, direct quotations from Sir Keith are prefaced by ●

---

[1] In the early 1970s an article containing biographical material and a discography was written for the specialist magazine *The Record Collector* by Wayne Turner, himself a singer, also writer/collector, with an intimate knowledge of Sir Keith Falkner's work. This is printed at the end of this book.

Painting of Sir Keith by Sonya Mervyn

Introduction

The moment I began this book with my father, I knew it would be a voyage of discovery and a labour of love. He was heading for 90 and I, mid-50s. At first he was averse to the whole idea: an embarrassment perhaps and too late in the day. The afternoons rolled by as he ceaselessly mowed, albeit at a slower pace, his well-kept lawns. As he did so he could see me interviewing mother in the summer house. The temptation to be involved getting the better of him, he soon announced he was ready to begin. And so we did.

In a sense, we are born twice: our natal birth and that of our consciousness. This came early to me and so it was that in my eyes Keith became a knight in shining armour – the fact that he gained a KBE in his 67th year only confirmed to the public what I had known since childhood. He was as devastatingly handsome as mother was beautiful, and I adored him.

The young Keith Falkner, a natural sportsman, an all-rounder in fact, had had to make a career choice: cricket or singing. He could have done either with as great a success. From his chorister days at New College, Oxford, to his dying day, his choice of music gave him greatest satisfaction, though he never lost his love of cricket. He was indeed proud of his membership number at Lords, 475.

At 36, Keith was at the height of his singing career when I appeared on the scene, and he left my early months to the nursery. The smell of bay rum pervades, his red hair and cricket whites, the flashing smiles ('How jovial is my laughter') all come to mind. He was fun. There were indoor and outdoor sports; head-spinning tosses in the air, piggy-back rides, tidal waves at bathtime and endless walks with the dog. The best treat of all was to lie on the sofa while he practised. If we thought at all, it was that our parents' musicality was a 'norm'. It was not until later, during the war years, when we were sent to Cincinnati and New York City, that Keith's talents began to be impressed upon us. I can still see, and hear, an old 78 spinning out *King Charles*, and being greatly impressed by the Warner Brothers publicity film stills which stood about in leather frames.

The war years were devastating, not only for what they did to family life but also for the interruption of Keith's career, as for so many others.

Poignant letters tell of the heartbreak, especially for Christabel. The family home, Nettleden Farm, had been given over to refugees. We were reunited there in 1944, when life appeared grey, gloomily full of rationing after the largesse of the USA, with adjustments to be made all around. When home on leave, Pop, as he preferred to be called, entertained us richly. He was a man with varied interests and always held my rapt attention as we poured over my stamp collection, thereby teaching both geography and history, Or, finding my doing sums, he buoyed my interest by doing such fantastic calculations as to predict how many times one's heart might beat in a lifetime. He loved to show off by adding multiple columns of numbers, running a pencil quickly down the list and writing the answer, a trick learned in his banking days. I was fascinated also to learn that many years hence, when it would be the year 2000, he would be 100, I an ancient 63. This, at nine, seemed incredible, if not indeed impossible. Some nights he would take us outdoors for lessons on astronomy, pointing out the major constellations to our starry-eyed attention. Keith loved the elements, never fearing anything they might throw at him. Many times he and I would wander out into howling wind and rain to watch. Once a hurricane almost did us both in. Such captivating stories were told at bedtime that we hated to say the final goodnight.

In 1946, in the sunnier climes of Italy, we were separated again, being placed for the greater part of four years in boarding schools. As Music Officer for the British Council, Keith's work kept him busy until all hours. He and Christabel toured Italy many times in the name of music. So we much enjoyed our holidays together – Monte Circeo, Positano, Elba – always intrigued by Pop's endless sporting pursuits: swimming in January in the Adriatic or Mediterranean Seas; tennis and golf, when I endured endless rounds of caddying. Among his numerous talents he was a great raconteur of ghost stories. With a single candle guttering in the gloom, he would relate a seemingly endless repertoire. He loved maps and often sat with us to plan our next adventures, our next fantasy trip to the United States.

North America beckoned again, sooner perhaps than my parents would have liked for we all loved Italy. This time we would be together as Keith took up teaching – and performance – at Cornell University, in Ithaca, New York. We all found life very different after the halcyon Italian days. An accomplished pianist herself, Christabel continued to accompany Keith in concerts, entertain and take on piano students. Italy and England, with all our family and friends, seemed, in 1950, to be a world away yet on the whole we accepted this new life. Certainly upper New York State, in the Finger Lakes district, is spectacular and we continued our practice of picnicking along lake shores and waterfalls.

Another of Keith's talents now came to the fore, that of cooking. Weekly batches of bread emerged from the kitchen and his boiled dumplings were a treat. In season he made the best blackberry jam and his calorific trifles made with his own left-over cakes were lip-smacking. He enjoyed doing this and I am sure he was also aware it helped the family budget, if not the waistline.

A concern was our co-educational adolescent life, with all its possible pitfalls. Pop was most tolerant and understanding of these and guided us with a firm and gentle hand. We, on the other hand, treated him with apparent disinterest, for to us he was just an ordinary 'bloke'. No doubt we were a great disappointment, for when he offered to give us singing lessons we informed him we could get 'all that' at school. That he needed quiet before a concert we often ignored or, being unwilling to attend, caused distress. Could we but have those years again!

It was not an easy household, that of talented parents torn between public and private life. Our parents were very close, in tune with each other and their careers. Christabel always placed herself second to her husband, deferring, after discussion, to his decisions, desires and, yes, even whims – he could be moody too. As in all families with such committed parents, children perforce took second place. That we were forced to be apart for so much of our early life took its toll and caused resentment at this apparent lack of interest; it took some years to accept this and to understand how enriched our lives had been through travel, education and the musical scene. Now I was to discover and learn of his career, of his artistry through the process of interview. Therefore, as much as possible, I have let him speak for himself.

Keith continued to sing for family and friends well into his 80s but deplored the sound, remembering too well the voice at its apogee. This career, which took him away from British shores as music ambassador, made him a singer perhaps not the best remembered, but this happenstance gave the Royal College of Music a fine Director. In 1960 Keith and Christabel, past students themselves, sailed home to make the College 'the happiest place we could for students, professors and all concerned. No longer would our music-making be of importance: rather our lives would be devoted to others.' This they did wholeheartedly.

Once, talking about his knighthood, I suggested that Keith had earned this as much for his directorship at the Royal College of Music as he had for his work on the concert platform. 'Nonsense!', he replied. 'And should it have, I was only doing my job.' Would that there were more like my knight, Sir Keith.

PART ONE

Life

Chapter 1: The Early Years

... A small rather frightened boy was trying desperately hard to sing the right notes in a Bach Motet, for behind him 'the Doctor' (Hugh Percy Allen)[1]*, perched on three hassocks, was singing bass and conducting.*

He blew 'C' on his pitch-pipe to start in C minor, and it was the boy's job as the treble to start on E flat. Instead he sang E natural.

The small boy suddenly felt a punch from behind, followed by the words 'Shut up', sounding to him like the last trump. Later 'the Doctor' ordered him with fierce mien to write out the three creeds fifty times by the morrow; both knew that the other knew it was an impossible task. The next morning at rehearsal the boy hoped he would be forgotten, but to his horror there was 'the Doctor' walking straight towards him, trying hard to look as fierce as before. 'Have you done the imposition?' 'No, sir,' whispered the boy. Immediately the doctor put his arm round his shoulder and smiling said 'Well, redhead, do you know where you went wrong?' Then followed a simple explanation of the mistake and the boy's silent, but fervent, prayer that he might never make a mistake again.

This small boy was Donald Keith Falkner, born in Sawston, Cambridge, on 1 March, 1900, to John Charles and Alice Hannah (Wright) Falkner. 'Jack' was a descendent of the Falconer family Keith clan, part of the Sutherland and MacPherson. Some say the Falconers were connected to the Earls of Kintore near Inverurie but suspected to be from the wrong side of the blanket. Alice Hannah was also known as 'Ailsie'; her mother was a direct descendent of Sir Ivan Port, founder of Repton School in 1557. Her father came from Wrexham and was related to the painter Joseph Wright of Derby. The Falkner's last child was named after Lord Dundonald, to which they added Keith in recognition of the family's reputed connection with this clan. Certainly, as the youngster grew, he shared the Falconers' stature and complexion. Jack and Ailsie suffered the loss of three daughters to typhoid, while an elder son, Ivan, and daughter, Mercy, survived. They had married in 1893 and were appointed schoolmaster and teacher to what is today the John Charles Falkner Primary School, a post he held for thirty-five years. Tall

---

[1] See *Hugh Percy Allen*. Cyril Bailey, OUP, 1948.

and well-built with jet-black hair and moustache, he was known as an all-rounder, playing cricket for Sawston and Cambridgeshire:

- ... He was a magnificent specimen of manhood and a great sportsman. He had played water polo for England, was expert at rugger and grand at cricket, dismissing the great Jack Hobbs with a fine catch during the match in 1901 when the Sawston Church Institute defeated the Cambridge Liberals in a Junior Cup Final. He was also an inspirational teacher. His curriculum recognised the importance of organised games and drama but he also taught the importance of manners, insisting his pupils always raised their caps to every woman, of whatever age or class. He also believed in discipline, both at school and after it, resorting to corporal punishment on occasion. Parents who presumed to question his authority or his right to punish severely for any serious misdemeanour received short shrift at his hands. One father, himself a former pupil, so forgot himself on one occasion as to use foul language and was immediately knocked down by a powerful flat-hander. Slowly the man rose to his feet, took one sidelong glance at his old master and shuffled away in silence.[2]

The children's attitude to life was shaped by their father's belief that physical fitness was necessary for a sound mind. It was a hard life, free of luxury on a schoolmaster's pay yet full of enrichment: a good home full of loving guidance and protection.

At an early age it was common to see the barefooted, red-ringletted Keith propelling a pram through the village. Asked if he had a baby out for a walk, and always one to deal with matters in the way that seemed best under actual conditions rather than following a general principle, his invariable pragmatic reply was: 'No! It's a mangle-wurzel.' At this time, just before the ringlets were cut, Pears Soap Company was searching for the 'perfect' child, inviting photographic entries. Alice's entry arrived just after the deadline, though she received a letter stating that, had it arrived in time, 'we would have chosen your son'.

- These early years nurtured a love of both cricket and music, with my father and Ivan encouraging me in the former – I turned out to be a left-handed bat. My mother was a wise and serene woman with a passion for Shakespeare plays who directed numerous productions to high praise from the Master of Trinity. In addition to her teaching duties, she kept house and family, baking the weekly bread. In retrospect I realise how lucky I was to be the 'baby',

---

[2] Treviss Teversham, author of the *History of Sawston*, remembered his headmaster with affection in *Cambridge Weekly News*, 29 April 1992. Article by Mike Petty, 'An Eye on the Past: Figures of Authority'.

being shepherded through those early years by an elder brother and sister. I had my bath an Saturday nights in front of the kitchen fire. Afterwards, outside, Ivan always rinsed me down with a bucket of icy water no matter the weather. On Sundays, we all went to church while mother cooked Sunday dinner; the whole family went to Evensong. But it was my mother, who always called me Sonny, who encouraged me in music. She had a sweet voice and taught me many traditional 'airs'. Once she entered me in a garden fête competition, where I won first prize singing 'Robin Adair'.

There was talent here and Keith's father decided to enter him for a scholarship at New College Choir School, proudly noting in his log: 'The headmaster was absent today at Oxford in connection with the annual chorister trial for New College Choir. His son, Donald Keith Falkner, was successful in gaining a scholarship ...'

- So it was that I began a musical training. Not a little homesick to begin with, I found life at the Choir School primitive and tough. Lessons began in earnest, through example, of the basic skills so that in time rhythm, breath control, intonation, quality and the dynamics of singing became second nature. There were of course many hacks to my ankles in this chrysalis period [hence the story at the beginning of this chapter] for Dr Hugh Percy Allen was the organist. His influence was strong and he was both fierce and friendly, his rage often turning to laughter. What made him so dynamic was his zeal for the classics and contemporary music. Imagine a choir of eighteen boys and eight men performing all the Bach and Brahms motets unaccompanied on Fridays, along with new services like Pickard-Cambridge in B flat or trying out Robert Bridges's metrical setting of the Psalms. Eventually Allen decided I was ready for my first solo, *Remember now thy Creator* (Reginald Steggall). I had just played a hard soccer match and the full force of a heavy ball hit me where it hurts most. When I came to sing I was still feeling sick and faint and somehow managed to get through the performance but was never chosen for the big solos after that. I was often in the dog-house for high spirits, pranks and greed, upbraided in front of the whole school for disgraceful behaviour. Some forty years later, at an Old Boy's Dinner, the man sitting next to me said the only thing he remembered about me was that I could belch louder than anyone else in the school! Memories of these years stand out – such as the night in 1910 when we were told the King had died and because of this would be expected at an early rehearsal at 7am for special music. As it was, we sang the 'special music' at sight, as Allen turned up at the usual time of 8. Then, of course, on 23

November 1911 we ghoulishly thought of the execution of Dr Crippen[3] as the bells tolled for Matins. Outstanding was the Coronation service for George V in Christ Church Cathedral with the combined choirs of New College, Christ Church and Magdalen.

On our daily processions to Chapel we often passed Dr Varley Roberts, then organist of Magdalen, who was quite a character. He would always call out 'Good morning, boys' in his strong Yorkshire accent. A story went around that Magdalen had a bass choral scholar who would not moderate his voice so that Dr Roberts was forever saying 'Too much bass'. Finally at rehearsal one day he said: 'Gentlemen. I had a dream last night. I dreamt I had died and gone to heaven and the Almighty told me to join t'heavenly choir. There were ten thousand sopranos, ten thousand altos, ten thousand tenors and one bass. I was the bass. Almighty picked oop stick and we started. At once Almighty said "Stop! Too much bass !".'. On another occasion he was asked what he thought of one of the very first performances of Ralph Vaughan Williams's *Sea Symphony* conducted by Dr Allen. 'Plain muck!' was his reply. Another character was Dr Spooner of Spoonerism fame, who occasionally preached or gave out hymn numbers. 'Kinkering Kongs their Titles Take' had us giggling as we rose to sing. My favourite, as reported by Cyril Cyphus, then Decani head boy, was addressed to a student: 'You have deliberately tasted two worms and you can leave Oxford by the town drain!'

I was thirteen when, towards the end of term, my voice dropped doing vocal exercises. Taken down the bass clef to low E, I was elevated to the organ loft with Allen for the remainder of term. Life was to change abruptly from these four years full of choral music and I soon found myself, now over six feet tall, living at home again and bicycling fourteen miles a day to the Perse School, where I had been awarded a County scholarship.

Like his father before him, Keith was an all-rounder, always in demand. He had joined both a cricket eleven and Officers Training Corps when war was declared in 1914. The Corps, just returning from training camp, was fired up and went to watch the Cambridgeshire Yeomanry mobilise, many enrolling on the spot. With enthusiasm Keith, giving his age as seventeen, signed up for the Royal Army Medical Corps. He passed the medical but when his true age was discovered he was told to return at a later date. Meanwhile, Ivan was commissioned in the Canadian Black Watch and on his way to the trenches of Flanders was soon to be severely wounded on the Somme. For Keith, however, it was back to the Perse,

---

[3] Dr Crippen: American dentist who murdered his second wife and was apprehended in mid-Atlantic as he eloped with his secretary, Ethel le Neve.

where he acquired the nickname Bouncer for his raucous laughter and high jinks. Very soon he was dismissed from the German class for bad behaviour and so lost his scholarship.

- My parents took it in their stride and father was able to persuade Barclays Bank in Cambridge to take me on as a junior clerk. Here I experienced two years of discipline and hard work, continuing to play sports and sculling in winter at the boat house on Jesus Green. At the same time I began organ lessons with W T See, then conductor of the Cambridge Choral Society, who quickly persuaded me to join the basses. In my father's rather moth-eaten dress suit I had a first public performance in a *Messiah*.

Generally, however, music continued to be very much in the background, with work at Barclays continuing. But by 1917 Keith was more than anxious to join the Royal Naval Air Service so applied, was interviewed and eventually called up in 1918 to the College in Greenwich. The ground course consisted of navigation, meteorology, geography, engines and theory of flight:

- The two months spent at Greenwich were strict but enjoyable. After all, it put ten shillings a day in my pocket and there were nightly ceremonial dinners in the banqueting hall. There are no games; instead we ran two-mile runs on Blackheath before breakfast and I eventually earned my cross-country colours. Of an evening, I was often roped in to sing the popular wartime songs and ballads. My voice was beginning to settle so I soon found myself much in demand for songs like 'The Company Sergeant-Major' (Sanderson), 'Drake Goes West' (Sanderson) and 'Asleep in the deep' (Petrie).

At eighteen, in March 1918, Keith was 'passed out' and awaited posting to a Naval Flying School. In the meantime, the Royal Naval Air Service and the Royal Flying Corps amalgamated, eventually becoming the Royal Air Force. To the RNAS Probationary Flight Officers this caused consternation as their ground training had been for service with the Navy. Keith was sent to No 5 Training Depot Squadron at Stamford, where he was assigned his first flight instructor:

- My assignment to Lieutenant Capper did not last long for, in horror, I watched him collide with an aircraft during another pilot's instruction when the two DH6s collided at one thousand feet. Assigned another instructor, I had trial flights in a BE2, DH6 and RE8 but was not quick to absorb the airborne feeling. Eventually, and much to our satisfaction, us 'Naval types' were reposted to the RNAS Station at Vendôme. I was glad to be back in the Navy, where it was 'Show-a-leg' at dawn, mugs of ship's cocoa and flying instruction. For 'Trainers' we had Avros and Caudrons, with the latter being most popular as they were pushers, unlike the Avros, which had rotary engines and needed a 'rating' to swing the prop: 'Switch off', 'Petrol on', 'Suck in', 'Contact' and then 'Chocks away'. In a Caudron you could fly low and seeing a pretty girl waving, land, have a good time, swing your own prop and fly back to base. All this came later. My first solo occurred in an Avro 8657 when I was told to do three circuits and bumps. Before I had time to feel nervous I was airborne, loving the sensation of flight. After this, it was on to more advanced techniques such as loop-the-loop, sideslip landings and falling leaf.

The usual routine for flying solo was from Vendôme to Château Renault, to Blois and back to Vendôme. Late one afternoon, out on a 'Recce', the setting sun blazed into my eyes and I could see nothing. The cockpit in those days only contained a revolution counter, clock and compass but, with the sun, I couldn't read them. I changed course but had lost my bearings and decided to land, though the terrain appeared difficult. Still, I had to try. After almost landing in a swamp I spied a field and side-slipped into it round some trees. My momentum gave out just before I rammed into a hedge and ditch, from which a man suddenly appeared. He took off, mistaking me for a German, but I galloped after him to a farmhouse, where a gendarme appeared. Having explained the situation in faulty French I was escorted to a hotel for the night. At that hour there was no way to make contact with the base so we proceeded to dinner with the mayor, who soon asked me: 'Est-ce-que vous desirez jig-i-jig pour ce soir?' I declined the offer and next morning made contact with my instructor, who soon arrived with some mechanics. He was astonished that I had managed to land the plane in that particular field, exclaiming that he would never be able to get out of it. But he did. On another 'Recce', flying in formation, I got in trouble again for, flying over a town, I lost my 'prop'. With not enough height to restart the engine, I had to make another forced landing, earning a black mark: but I was learning my trade.

Eventually, as Flight Sub-Lieutenant, I was posted to Calshot Spit for flying-boat training in H12s with Rolls Royce 250HP engines. On 7 November 1918, I was passed out as a Second Pilot with special C & D categories (large flying-boats). A posting to the RNAS Station at Dundee followed and, on my way through London on 11 November, found myself caught up in Armistice Day. Arriving at Stannergate, Dundee, I found it to be a hub of activity, with ship and flying personnel crowding the station with all aircraft grounded during peace negotiations. Our days therefore were more social than anything else, and a Rugby XV soon formed. At Raeburn Place in Edinburgh I was in the scrum for the Northern area when, in no time at all, I was pushed aside by none other than 'Wakers' (W W Wakefield, later captain of Cambridge and England). I also discovered the pleasures of golf and played often at Monifieth, Barry and Carnoustie. Stannergate happened to have an attractive telephone operator and I summoned enough courage to invite her to a dance. The evening turned into a disaster for I am a poor dancer and she asked me to take her home at 11. Next day the station photographer asked if I had had a good time and showed several nude photographs of the girl. It was time I grew up! I also gathered that the O/C's wife had taken a fancy to me and one day, going on leave, I spotted her waiting for me on the platform. I avoided contact and took a later train.

It was at Stannergate that I earned a Bronze Medal for Lifesaving at sea.[4] Two friends, Macintosh-Walker and a Canadian, Tommy Vezina, and I, decided one day in February to go for a sail. Each of us thought the others to be sailors. About a mile off-shore there was a sudden gust: the ballast slipped, we keeled over and sank in the icy water. Vezina couldn't swim so, treading water, I got him on his back while Walker swam for help. Fortunately our predicament had been observed and after what appeared to be hours we were rescued. I was revived with a noggin and told I never would have made it if I hadn't been a rugby forward.

Musically, I continued organ lessons with C M Howe, with whom some years later I would sing *Elijah* with the Dundee Choral Union. Then in high summer I was re-posted to Killingholme, Wilberforce my new CO – his great grandfather the slave-trade abolitionist. Our duties were light, so there was lots of cricket in Yarborough Park, with matches in Grimsby, Hull and Yorkshire towns. At Withernsea I scored my first century. We played Bridge in the evenings when 'Yarboroughs'[5] appeared all too frequently.

With disarmament coming slowly, I had time to ponder my future. There seemed no immediate answer, though at one point I considered apple-growing in Tasmania. Eventually I was given a discharge date and detailed with a detachment of airmen to represent Killingholme in the Victory March in London. There were thousands of us: every country, every service, with detachments from the Fleet, regiments and air stations, the women's auxiliary forces. The route by way of Exhibition Road, Lambeth Bridge, along the South Bank to London Bridge, through the City and Fleet Street, the Strand, Admiralty Arch, the Mall, Buckingham Palace, Hyde Park Corner to Kensington Gardens, was lined with cheering crowds and well-known faces. I was demobbed next day and given a gratuity of £150,

---

[4] The medal, sky blue, was worn on the right breast and caused more interest than a DSO or DSC would have done!

[5] 'Yarborough': a Bridge or Whist hand containing no card higher than a nine. (After the second Earl of Yarborough, who is said to have bet 1,000 to 1 that such a hand would not occur. It did.)

which I spent courting a cousin I thought I was in love with. With the final £11 I bought my mother a carpet.

It was back to reality then and the supposed jobs promised to demobilised service personnel. I had no wish to rejoin the bank and went to an advice bureau with not much luck. Then Carleton, an old friend from Killingholme who was working for the Asiatic Petroleum Company, said he could find me a job. I was accepted and trained in necessary paperwork with the idea of sending me to the Far Fast. In the meantime I resumed voice lessons, this time with Joseph Reed, a fine lyric tenor. I was getting on nicely when, once again, Carleton stepped in to change my fate. He had heard that the Government was offering £150 scholarships to returning servicemen, and suggested I go along to The Royal College of Music and meet the Director, who was none other than Dr H P Allen, then the most dynamic and influential man in music in England. So, presented with this information, I took the step which would start me on a career as a singer. Here was the opportunity to meet Dr Allen again, the same man I had met and sung with what seemed a lifetime ago. I went.

Chapter 2: 1920–1930

The Royal College of Music in the 1920s was probably one of the finest in Europe, having a magnificent teaching staff: Holst, Vaughan Williams, Harold Samuel, Adrian Boult, Malcolm Sargent, Herbert Howells, George Thalben-Ball, to name but a few:

- I enrolled at the College in January 1920 to find myself in this world of awe-inspiring musicians. The Director, Sir Hugh Allen, had a great ability to put students on their mettle, find us wanting and then, by his own enthusiasm, zeal and encouragement, spur us on to greater achievement. The administrative staff were just as important to students. Shrewd in his judgement of character, John Hare acted as liaison officer between student and professor. He could encourage the timid, be sharp to the bumptious, serious with the earnest student and, with an imperceptible change of front, be any one of the foregoing to a professor requiring immediate attention.

The new student intake after four years of war included an unusual number who were destined to become famous: Constant Lambert, Michael Tippett, Ivor Gurney, Edmund Rubbra, composers; Herbert Sumsion, Thomas Armstrong and Boris Ord, organists; Angus Morrison and Howard Ferguson, studying piano; Marie Wilson, who was to lead the BBC Symphony Orchestra, John Pennington, leader of the London String Quartet, and Bernard Shore, viola; Thelma Reiss, the cellist; and Jack Thurston, 'the king of clarinetists' (though this might be disputed by fans of Goodman and Shaw). And the singers Tudor Davies and Trefor Jones, Vivienne Chatterton, Stuart Robertson, Martyn Green and Arthur Rees.

- My first voice teacher was the famous Alberto Visetti. He told me I had gold in my throat but I soon discovered he said this to all new pupils. A great teacher in his time, he was now approaching senility and in spite of his many kindnesses of extra lessons, I found I was not making progress. I changed to Albert Garcia, who agreed to take me on condition I studied with him for three years and gave up rugby. I had joined the Saracens earlier but was now told that as rushing about in the cold air made my voice hoarse, I was in no state to come for lessons. I switched to playing hockey for Southgate instead, though this too would come to an end for musical reasons. He was right, of course, and it is to him I owe the sound production and development of my voice. He taught the flat tongue, low-larynx method, whereas the tendency today is towards intensity of tone rather than quality: 'combustion' rather than 'warmth'. Garcia 'placed' my voice and I often returned for a refresher lesson even after I had moved on.

I studied piano with Thalben-Ball, later with Tommy Fielden; organ with W G Alcock; ensemble and musicianship with Harold Darke. My other activities included choral class, small choirs, football, hockey and umpiring the girls' hockey matches, where I was attracted by, and found myself somewhat embarrassingly attractive to, a number of girls.

There were exams too. In an organ exam, taken by Sir Walter Parratt, I played the Bach (little) E minor. After the Prelude and the first two bars of the Fugue he asked me why I played B and A rather than B and A sharp. With my response that it was in E minor he said: 'Fine! Now let's talk about cricket!' A man named Parker was employed to 'blow' the organ during examinations. On one occasion he 'blew' for a student playing the Toccata and Fugue in D minor, and gave him 898 pumps and stopped. 'That's what I give for that!', he said. 'He won't pass!' This sort of thing must have gone on a great deal, especially in Victorian times.

By now my voice was developing into a smooth basso-cantante and I was soon asked to join various quartets and ensembles. To be asked! The only singer to join a select group of composers, conductors, academic types and organists, presumably to provide a 'canto firmo' to the woolly sounds surrounding me, was very gratifying.

Word was beginning to get round and I was invited by Sydney Nicholson to join the Westminster Abbey Choir while one of the basses was away. With my chorister training I fitted in easily and was thrilled to sing with the Choir the Unknown Warrior service in 1920. This occurred again in 1970, when Dean Abbott and Douglas Guest invited me to sing with the Choir on the fiftieth anniversary of that service.

George Hiscock, studying with Garcia, became a good friend and we decided to share 'digs' together. We advertised and found ourselves bemused by one reply which stated: 'Comfortable room and meals. Husband out all day. All home comforts'. We soon found a comfortable room with breakfast and dinner for two guineas a week. We were always tight for money but in February 1922 managed to hear Chaliapin from the top gallery of the Albert Hall.

With a number of male singers back from the war, George and I appeared in the opening of the Parry Opera Theatre in a production of Act I of *Die Meistersinger von Nürnberg*. He was Nachtigall, I, Schwarz.

In February 1922 I tried out for a vacancy for Assistant Vicar Choral at St Paul's Cathedral. It was quite an experience singing *Thus Saith the Lord* with Stanley Marchant but, due to the awful echo, I kept hearing myself half a bar ahead of the organ in *For He is like a refiner's fire*. Nevertheless, I was appointed in March and found myself among a galaxy of bass voices: Harry Stubbs, Joe Farrington, Arthur Frith, Stuart Robertson and Stanley Riley. We had daily services with full choir on Sundays and Saints' Days. Each singer was allowed two free days and, being the junior bass, I had to take Wednesday and Thursday. I started to grow a moustache and caused amusement when a choirboy – I believe the future Sir Charles Groves – stage-whispered: 'I see you've got "eleven a side", Sir'.

In addition to the 'free days', deputies occasionally filled in for members who had other engagements. An official list of eight or ten basses could be called upon, with all solos taken by rota. Each of us had a 'solo' week every sixth week. It was Arthur Frith's turn but I noted he had sent in a deputy to sing a long solo duet for alto and bass. I was the bass and was horrified to see we had the two voice-parts in manuscript in alto and bass clefs with no accompaniment. That was a test if ever there was one! Occasionally I also deputised for absent lay-vicars at Westminster Abbey.

I became aware that the senior men had strong alliances with the City Companies and Masonic Lodges. I was soon invited to sing solos, ballads or join a male quartet to entertain them. My first engagement offered '2½ less 10': two and a half guineas less 10%. In the early 1920s the 'drawing room' ballad was still the stock repertoire for singers at such dinners. One of these party songs of the time, though I did not sing it, went:

> I called on my sweetheart, her name was Brown;
> She was having a bath and couldn't come down.
> I said. 'Slip on something oh so quick'.
> So she slipped on the soap and was down in a tick.

On 11 July 1922 came the first performance of Vaughan Williams's *Shepherds of the Delectable Mountains*, conducted by Arthur Bliss. The soloists: Archibald Winter, Leonard Willmore, Richard Kyle, John McKenna and – Keith Falkner. It would be 1923 before Keith came into contact with the composer and established a friendship he would come to value. Keith appeared in a number of this composer's works, namely the second performance of the *Mass in G minor* given by the Oxford Bach Choir on 17 June 1923 with Vivienne Chatterton, Constance Taylor and Trefor Jones; a shared performance with soloists Stuart Robertson, George Hiscock and Martyn Green of *Five Mystical Songs*; and in July 1924 as Constable in the première of *Hugh the Drover*, with Trefor Jones and Leyland White, conducted by S P Waddington. Then came the opportunity to sing the baritone solo in the *Sea Symphony*:

- Being a basso cantante and twenty-five, the F sharps at the top were not in the middle of my voice. I had a word with Dr Williams about this. 'Oh', said he, 'That's all right, me boy. What note would you like to sing there?' He quickly revised, taking out the F sharp, put a D there and C sharp in other places. For the rest of my career I sang this revised edition. To the composer it is often a minor detail. All of which goes to show that some singers are too meticulous about singing every note as written.

Having sung *The Songs of Travel* (Set I) often at the Proms, I was some time later engaged to perform the work in Belfast, Vaughan Williams conducting. I was nervous at rehearsal, wondering what the Doctor would think. Vaughan Williams picked up his baton, turned to me and asked; 'Now, how do these go, me boy? I haven't looked at them for twenty years!' I was instantly at ease.

Invitations came, the first to sing with the Tudor Singers. Another, to join The English Singers as baritone, was turned down for by now Keith was more bass than baritone. His engagements between 1921 and 1925 had been largely sporting and social, with some music. Following his association with St Paul's, more and more requests for his talents began to flow in.

A birthday letter from his mother on March 1, 1925 – Keith's twenty-fifth birthday – states in part:

My dearest Sonny ... Many many glad returns of it, my boy, bringing true happiness, splendid health and ever greater realisation of ideal ... I have lived over again in the last few days the balm and healing of your coming to us and the wonder at what God had sent us ... always remember, my laddie, that I gave you specially to God and asked Him to use you for Himself, and He has done. He has given you a voice that will be beloved all over England, in time, part of one of His own beauties, and the more you strive to reach the heights of spirit-level, commensurate with such a gift, the greater, richer, will prove your gift, and its inspiration to others ... you'll be the gladdest and among the greatest of our artistes yet ... Cheerio Sonnie! Face to the Sunlight! Part of my very self. How you are entwined deep in the depths of my heart where God laid you ...

On the evening of 3 March an entry in Keith's diary reads: 'Dinner: Miss Daymond and Harry Plunket Greene':

- This dinner was the turning point of my career. It came about because Sir Hugh Allen had chosen me to sing the name-part in Parry's *Job* at the RCM. Plunket Greene had sung the first performance of the work at Gloucester in 1892 so Dr Daymond asked him to help me, and help is hardly the word for it! He opened up a whole new world of declamation, colour and interpretation for me. I realised at last that the singing profession was a 'discipline' and not something to mix with other interests. Until then, like so many other young singers, I had been wasting my time between lessons. If I had not had his instruction and the warm friendship and guidance of Dr Emily Daymond at this critical period of my student life, I doubt whether I should have become a professional singer. He was the right spark at the right moment, leading me into thinking of a solo career.

Job took place in the presence of Dr Brewer, although I was unaware of this at the time, who would perform the same work at the Three Choirs Festival in Gloucester Cathedral later in the year. During the College performance I was so emotionally involved with the *Lamentations* and the final 'I know that thou canst do everything' that I had to lock myself in the lavatory for thirty minutes afterwards before I could see or speak to anyone. From that moment, I knew that singing was the joy of my life. The next day came the news that Dr Brewer had engaged me for the Festival performance on 9 September 1925. It would prove a great moment in my life, singing with Elsie Suddaby, Steuart Wilson and Horace Stevens. Dr Brewer conducted; with my father, mother and Emily Daymond – now known to the family as 'Schramm' – in the audience. We all stayed at The Dog at Over. In the bar the day following the performance the landlord read out the critique in the Gloucester paper. In broad dialect he called out: 'Ee called thee a tenor! Ee don't know t'ifference t'ween a sow 'n a hog!'

I left Gloucester to play cricket and journeyed with John Tillett of concert agents Ibbs & Tillett. He was friendly but brought me quickly down to earth saying only that he would watch my progress and perhaps, later, take me on the firm's books.

The *Job* performance at the College was not the first time I became emotionally affected by the magic of music and words. Sometime earlier I happened to stroll into an empty teacher's room for what I call 'vocal therapeutics'. On the piano I found a copy of Bach's *St Matthew Passion*. Until then I had neither seen a copy nor heard a performance of the work. I sat and played, singing through the bass recitatives and arias to emerge two hours later utterly stunned and excited by the sheer beauty and drama of the work. Within two years I would sing the Christus role in St Paul's with the Bach Choir.

Following his success at Gloucester, Keith now moved up into the 'first eleven', so to speak. Engagements became more frequent, more important. Invitations from Liverpool, Manchester, Glasgow, Edinburgh, Leeds Festival, the Royal Choral Society and the Bach Choir began to arrive with regularity. Now, Ibbs and Tillett took him under sole management.

- In 1926, increasingly in demand, I had to resign from St Paul's where I had experienced several years of sound professional training. I had had much criticism for the covered, woolly quality of my high notes, particularly from Garcia, who agreed it was high time I left. The acoustics of St Paul's, with the huge echo under the dome, required voices to remain dark and cavernous in the higher register. Garcia believed this was preventing the proper development of my voice in such arias as *The Trumpet Shall Sound* and *Thou Art Gone Up on High* from *Messiah*.

'Adam in Plus-fours': the London *Evening News* could not resist this headline following a performance in Haydn's *Creation* in Bedford, where Keith had to appear in his brown Harris tweeds. The stolen suitcase never did show up ..:

- ... with no evening clothes to be found, I had to walk on to the platform as though approaching the first tee! The conductor, a little man, announced: 'Mr Falkner *says* his evening clothes have been stolen!'

In the 1920s and 1930s, there were still many choral societies – church and chapel choirs – flourishing in the North of England. In winter, professional singers would most Saturday mornings make their way to Euston to travel to Lancashire or Yorkshire for a weekend of music engagements. These usually were a mixed concert on Saturday evening to sing-for-their suppers, followed by a party. Sundays saw a sacred concert in church or chapel, with excerpts from oratorios. Fellow travellers were often Norman Allin, Walter Widdop, Robert Easton, Roy Henderson, Tudor Davies, Heddle Nash and Dennis Noble. Keith's fellow singers were no longer students but the best in the country, a superb body of what he would come to call 'vintage' singers: Roy Henderson, Harold Williams and Arthur Williams were also great golf companions.

Apart from the choral societies, there were also the Boosey Ballad Concerts with F B Kiddle and S Liddle. These concerts were used to launch new songs, although this did not happen until the second half. Singers would be asked, beforehand, to look at a few new scores and asked which they would like to perform. At one of these concerts, Keith led off and sang the first performance of Michael Head's *Three Songs of the Countryside*: *Sweet Chance that Led my Steps Abroad*, *Money O* and *Nature's Friend*.

Head wrote to Wayne Turner: 'I have a vivid recollection of meeting Keith Falkner ... My songs (*Songs of the Countryside* to poems of W H Davies) were appearing at the Ballad Concerts ... I went to rehearse at his house as he was to give the first performances ... I remember the beauty of his voice, his keenness to get the interpretation to the satisfaction of the composer, especially the unusual *Nature's Friend*, and how delighted I was to hear my songs so beautifully sung. I remember his charming personality and also being amused that he should apologise for his voice being a little rough as he said he had got engaged the day before!'

- One of my first professional engagements had been in a performance of Bach's cantata *Du Hirte Israel*, conducted by Shepherdson. The aria *Beglückte Herde Jesu Schafe* is one of the biggest hurdles for a singer, as is *Esurientes* in the *Magnificat* for alto: long phrasing with no apparent places to breathe. I soon learned what I had to do to become a Bach singer. The discipline of long line and phrasing in the Bach *Passions*, the *B Minor Mass* and the Cantatas were certainly responsible for my advance in the profession. The same discipline is true of Handel. Many of the arias are formidable but, once mastered, provide satisfaction and pleasure of the most rewarding kind. The florid *How Jovial is my Laughter* from Bach's Cantata 205 became a great concert piece for me which I often included in recitals and broadcasts. I chose it for one of my first recordings for HMV. I also sang it at a BBC recital at 2LO with Elisabeth Schumann and a Dutch cellist, who muttered after my 'How Jovial': 'You must 'ave 'ollow legs!'

While still a student, Evelyn Barbirolli was asked to play some Bach obligatos for Keith. As she stated in 1990: '... Bach arias are very exacting both for the voice and the obligato, if the player of that obligato is a wind player. ... Naturally I was scared out of my wits and he couldn't have been kinder. We discussed the breathing for both of us, said what he was going to do and what I could do, therefore. Playing with him was an enormous excitement ... he was a wonderful musician. He had that marvellous musical line. The voice was very beautiful and he never seemed bothered by breathing in those long Bach arias. You were only aware of the music ... his singing always touched me. I was taken with the beauty of the voice, the musicality of it, the way he expressed, the way he phrased. He must have been the finest Bach singer of his time and, too, he was very handsome ...'

- All sorts of amusing and alarming things can happen during performances. One such occurred at a performance of the *B Minor Mass* with organ accompaniment at Eton Chapel. Henry Ley played the work with full and piano scores, while a boy turned the pages. We got through the first two phrases of the 'Quoniam' and had to stop for the organ was not playing the proper sequence in the aria. The conductor and choir looked at me. I looked up at the organ. Where were we? The audience, realizing the situation, roared with laughter as I sat down. I learned from Henry later that the boy had turned over the wrong page of the wrong score at the wrong time.

With the development of public broadcasting in the early 1920s , Keith took part in several experimental broadcasts organised by Stanton Jeffries, a former fellow student, in Marconi House in the Strand.[1] The public listened on tiny crystal sets. In October of the following year the BBC published Volume I, No 1, of the *Radio Times* with broadcasting coming from Station 2LO, Savoy Hill. Included was a programme of lyrics and part-songs by Hubert Parry and introduced by Sir Hugh Allen. The quartet: Dorothy Allgood, Dorothy Kitchen, Trefor Jones, and Keith Falkner:

- We were ushered into a heavily carpeted studio, curtained from floor to ceiling so that a dreadful hush hung over all. When we sang we could barely hear ourselves. Sir Hugh and staff shouted instructions, pushing us to and from microphones for balance tests. It was a momentous occasion.

    Another early broadcast was with Myra Hess. Harold Samuel was there to listen. Just before the 'On The Air' sign lit up, they both sat on the floor and played the piano above their heads. A way to relieve the nerves, the message being not to get too excited about it all.

    The BBC asked me to perform again, this time a half-hour programme of Russian songs, sung in English, by Balakirev. These were new to me and I arranged with Charles Groves that he come to the house to learn the repertoire.

The BBC also broadcast all the Bach Cantatas, one each Sunday, conducted by Stanford Robinson, for which Keith was frequently engaged. These and other broadcasts continued to enhance his reputation.

- During these years I often teamed up for joint recitals with Joan Elwes. In January 1928 we agreed to give one in Vienna which happened to coincide with Harold Samuel's 'Week of Bach' and a visit from Gustav Holst. The scenes at the end of each Bach recital resembled the enthusiasm given to pop stars today: people crowded onto the platform demanding encore after encore. During my stay Harold presented me with a volume of Schubert songs suitably signed, while Holst gave me his new songs: *Journey's End, The Thought, The Floral Bandit* and *Things Lovelier*. All Humbert Wolfe's lyrics.

---

[1] Keith's sister Mercy was also an early broadcaster: between 1929 and 1930 with SABC. She was a pupil of Paginelli.

Keith was also recording. The performance of *Hugh the Drover* at the RCM in 1924 had been recorded by HMV but by 1928 Keith was on his own. Two songs by Parry, *Love is a Bable* and *Follow a Shadow*, backed by Blow's *The Self-banished*, were not released. However, between 1929-30, several more were made and issued by HMV, among them Handel's *Droop Not, Young Lover* (*Ezio*), *The People that Walked in Darkness* (*Messiah*) and *What Tho' I Trace* (*Solomon*).

In 1928, Keith's father and mother retired from Sawston School and journeyed out to Capetown to visit Mercy's family. Ailsie, struck by an attack of pneumonia for which, then, there was no cure, died. It was a blow to the entire family but particularly to Keith. Gradually his deep sorrow began to lighten as he became increasingly aware of a fellow student studying piano, the beautiful Christabel Margaret Fullard.

Chapter 3: Christabel Margaret Fullard

Christabel Margaret Fullard was, in 1925, rehearsing the Dohnanyi *Variations on a Nursery Tune* with Adrian Boult and the College Orchestra when Keith Falkner first saw her:

- About this time I received an invitation from a certain Christabel Fullard, Secretary of the Christian Student Movement, inviting me to sing at a party. I declined. No sooner had I done so when I discovered she was the same beautiful pianist I had heard Adrian conducting. Asking around, it was hinted that should I find myself outside her piano teacher's room on a certain afternoon, I might just be able to run into this Miss Fullard. And so I did and, as I introduced myself, suddenly found that I was quite free to sing at the party after all, and quickly asked her to join me for an afternoon's cricket at Lord's.

Christabel was born in London in 1902, the second child of Maud (Diver) and Thomas Fletcher Fullard. Her brother Philip, born five years previously, became the high-scoring Great War fighter ace with 48 confirmed victories, earning the DSO Croix de Guerre avec palms with HC and Bar, ending his career as Air Commodore, CBE. Her father had read English at Oxford, going on to Exeter University for German and Russian, so that at the time of her birth he was a journalist and philatelist, secretary to Andrew D White, founder of Cornell University, when the latter was ambassador to Russia. A strict and musical family, the Fullards lived in a comfortable house in Wimbledon, Sunday evenings spent around the piano, the holidays in Hatfield. Christabel reminisces:

My earliest memory is there, where I was much fussed over by parents and relations, mother cuddling me on her lap as Philip stood in the background as, his nose very much out of joint, he demanded: Cuddle me too! Somehow I think this carried through all his life, though he was marvellously good to me throughout. I don't remember much of my father as he was away so much of the time. My life was uncomplicated until I was nine, when my father died of pneumonia; this, plus the fact that I had not seen grownups grieve before, was a terrible shock. This was soon followed by the shocking news of the sinking of the *Titanic*.

For a change of scene Maud took her young daughter away to school in Lausanne for a year before the family moved to Hatfield, where

Christabel was taught well at the local school, given violin and piano lessons, with a Bechstein bought for twenty pounds for practice. Life was idyllic until World War I, when Philip and all male cousins enlisted, most never to return. Rupert Brooke, who lived nearby, was one of the first to go. Philip was wounded in 1918 and sent home. Christabel's memories fill in more detail:

In 1921 Mother and I were back in France, where I attended the Lycée in Paris, easily learning the language and getting the proper lilt. It was impressed upon me about this time that it was more important to go through life being a friend rather than an enemy for it is such a waste of energy otherwise. We returned in 1922 to a comfortable house at 43 Bridge Lane, Golder's Green, and I enjoyed being escorted by my brother to parties and races for I was a true 'flapper'. I hoped to attend the Royal College of Music and went to play for Hugh Allen and was accepted. During the second term I was very lucky to win the Chapel Medal scholarship of £30, improving steadily over five years so that I was inordinately proud to win the Hopkins Silver Medal. I was also involved with the choral class and sang with the Bach Choir for a number of years. Then came the marvellous chance to play the Dohnanyi *Variations* with Adrian Boult. I don't remember being nervous, for if you know something well you get carried along with the excitement: I put my head down and went for it.

Of course I was very much aware of a fellow student, Keith Falkner, who was becoming increasingly well-known, having sung in *Hugh the Drover*, the *Pastoral Symphony* and *Flos Campi*. How odd it is that one is never aware when something momentous is about to happen. I was in College for my lesson and, on leaving the room, there was Keith Falkner. I smiled and was about to pass by when he asked if he could have a word. I was intrigued. Not only did he accept the invitation to the party but asked me to Lord's that very afternoon. I was translated, in Heaven to be invited by Keith Falkner, terribly excited to be in his orbit. At the Grace Gates, other folk seemed to walk on the pavement, I on air! Keith adored cricket; his favourite place was mid-off, though he loved to bat and bowl. I fear my mind and eyes were not on the game. We spoke of College, our families, his career and all too soon the game was over. He escorted me to my bus and shook hands. I thanked him and hopped aboard. Thus began our saga.

Keith takes up the story:

- From that moment I became her adorer to the exclusion of all others. Nonetheless, there was much competition from her brother's fellow officers. The next hurdle in my courtship came when I was invited to tea with

Christabel's mother. She was of the 'old school' of Victorian ladies with high moral standards, beautiful manners and a careful regard for etiquette. I sang for her after tea and wondered what impression I must have made, for I sang *Lord Rendal*, a Cecil Sharp arrangement of a very grim, melodramatic tale, followed by 'What shall we do with the drunken sailor?'. I soon gathered courage and asked Chris how much she thought a man should earn before he could ask a girl to marry him. £1,000 a year was her reply: I was making a meagre £700. However, we came to an understanding and agreed to marry once my career was truly established.

Christabel wrote ecstatically to her great friend Nancy Bernard Smith:

THIS IS ABSOLUTELY PRIVATE AND CONFIDENTIAL. *THE* most tremendous thing has happened. I am engaged to Keith but sotto voce (as) it's not official, simply because we can't possibly be married till about 1999! My dear, I can't tell you how tremendously thrilled I am and it all seemed too good to be true! because I've loved him for ages and I *never never* dreamt he could possibly fall in love with me. But he has and we're mad as hatters! Truly, love is the oddest thing – one does the strangest things without the smallest blush! Now, don't get nervous. We'll promise to behave when you're here ...

These were blissful years yet, as far as her own career, Christabel gave up her piano studies, though her teacher implored her to continue for her career could have taken off in its own right. The opportunity to go back to study with Dohnanyi came and went, though there were some lessons with Myra Hess. Christabel wrote:

It is so silly that when you fall in love all you can think about, or be involved in, revolves around the man you love. One should not stand still and I much regretted this in later years, though I played a lot for Keith but not publicly until after we married. I should have loved to have played more, especially Rachmaninoff, for his music is so rich and warm, as is Bach's, not like the modernists, who strike one as cutting open lemons. My advice to youngsters with any gift is not to waste a minute and by all means stick to it and make the most of it. The difficulty is that young people think they have got all the time in the world so, if you have a slacker, back him up and he will pull through.

With a four-year understanding, it was a frustrating time for both. The official engagement was made in 1929, when Keith bestowed an unusual fire opal, set in a platinum basket, upon Christabel's finger. The wedding day – 2 June 1930 – finally arrived, the ceremony held at Christ Church,

Chelsea. Johnny Johnston, erstwhile Succentor of St Paul's Cathedral, performed the ceremony, with Adrian Boult best man and George Thalben-Ball, organist. Christabel again:

> It was the happiest day of my life to marry such a good man who was so nice and easy, tall, straight and very good looking, with good manners in a fifty-fifty partnership in which I would be a backbone to build a home where Keith could rest, work and go on with his career, giving him the where-with-all to get on with life. You must serve your gift: never touch the principal, use only the interest.

And Keith:

- Chris arrived looking radiantly beautiful and we sang 'Jerusalem' with gusto as 'we swore to keep the watch of life together'.[1] After the reception at Adrian's, we hastened away to catch the boat train, arriving in Innsbruck the following morning, going on by car to the Plansee to settle to a halcyon honeymoon at 'Die Forelle' Hotel. On St John's Eve, bonfires burned on hilltops across the Lake as we lay together in the moonlight while I lustily sang Hans Sachs' famous line in his second monologue in *Die Meistersinger*, 'Nun aber kam Johnnistag'.

    Our first public recital together was for a Japanese Society dinner in honour of Prince Hirohito, where we had been invited to perform Japanese folk-songs. Two – *Imago* and *Hugagawa* – were much admired and would remain in my repertoire for years. We had a moment of panic when we discovered we had left the music in a taxi but the driver spotted the case and returned it in time, to our relief. Between 11 and 23 August we again performed together, for a two-week engagement at the Coliseum, three shows a day, as *Top of the Bill*.

The two would be apart for months on end during the war years, their children overseas as Keith gave all up for the war, enjoying the company of men. Of the separation, beautiful and alone, Christabel said:

> Keith once asked me whether I had ever had any 'experiences'. My attractiveness was not a handicap, rather it gave a sense of unapproachability which I used to good effect, able to say 'no'. If you look at a man he can quickly tell how you are likely to respond and I always looked straight into

---

[1] Quotation from W E Henley – *Love Blows as the Wind Blows*:

> In the year that's come and gone, in the golden weather,
> Sweet, my sweet, we swore to keep the watch of life together.
> In the year that's coming on, rich in joy and sorrow,
> We shall light our lamp and wait life's mysterious morrow.

their eyes. Men may look at you but you cannot be beguiled, you can stop anything with courage, otherwise it is very uncomfortable. I didn't want anything for I had a husband, wherever he might be. I enjoyed being good-looking and it is such fun! It is so easy to look beautiful, to arrange your hair, to dress well, if you have a good figure. If you have handicaps and can't see out of one eye as you get older, at least you've had a jolly good go. The twinge one gets seeing one's daughters looked at, instead of oneself, is very natural. You have to move on. It's similar to Keith having to leave the profession for he didn't want the reputation of singing after the bloom had gone. You have to make room for other people, which takes courage, but one is still beautiful in one's own way.

The Second World War over, we returned to two years of readjustment, attempting to regain a sense of family, of identity, the time apart having created a distance, the closeness gone, though we retained a feeling of admiration and respect. Mother was particularly high-strung and complex, at times very difficult and with ridiculously high standards but, as I grew older, I came to love and understand her better. Certainly she was the perfect mate for father, whom she adored. It was their nature and talent to be dedicated to music and each other. Christabel wrote:

> My mother also came to live with us; however, she was unwell, tired from the war, and died in 1946. This was the saddest day of my life. Having been so close to her throughout the years, I had never given thought of it happening. I continued to play for Keith throughout the years, rehearsing, accompanying him at concerts or playing at private party concerts, when Adrian Boult often turned over for me.

Keith made his feelings clear:

- As an accompanist, Christabel was the best of them all, and had been on the brink of a highly successful career in her own right. Yet she gave up her ambitions to form a partnership with me both in marriage and on the platform. We worked together, lived together, thought together and performed together. I could do what I liked for she sensed every whim or variation. Her playing of Somervell's *Maud* cycle was superb. We would broadcast this in the 1930s with Stuart Hibberd announcing. When he came to the song 'She came to the Village Church', he got in a terrible muddle over the words 'This is a little gem if ever there was one'. Before we went on the 'air' he rehearsed it over and over, undecided which words to accent: 'This', 'gem', 'ever', or 'is' 'there', 'was'. We had a laugh.

  We were both sensitive to each other's 'difficulties'. Once on a tour in which the first song in the recital was Schubert's *Liebesbotschaft*, the opening bar of which is a test for any pianist, especially on a strange piano, hall and audience. I was concerned. But I needn't have worried for she was there! Such songs as Vaughan Williams's *Roadside Fire*, and *Heimliche Aufforderung* by Strauss, she played superbly. Christabel was more than aware of my problems. This sensitivity for each other was the only thing to worry us in performance.

Chapter 4: 1930–1939

1930 was an important year for Keith personally, and for his career. As his reputation spread, he was in demand for recitals, choral works and concerts around the country. There were many solo broadcasts as well as those from the Proms. In August, he sang *Schlummert ein* from the great Bach solo cantata *Ich habe genug* (No 82). Included in the concert was *What Tho' I Trace* (Handel). A recording of the latter brought comment from the *HMV Monthly List*:

> The singing of Handel is a very exacting test of an artist's abilities, for it exposes any weak places that there may be in the technique. Listening to Keith Falkner rendering these well-known bass arias we feel proud that Britain has produced so fine a singer. The runs are so smooth and even, the breathing so well managed, and the phrasing and colouring so admirable that this record may well be held up as a model of Handelian singing.

Another Prom, in 1930, included the Hans Sachs monologues from *Die Meistersinger*, with satisfying press comments. At the Queen's Hall, in November, Keith sang Bach arias which included *Heiligste Dreieinigkeit* (Cantata 172). Two BBC broadcasts included the florid *Am irdische Schätze* (Cantata 106), *Gottes Zeit ist der allerbeste Zeit* – one of this composer's most formidable arias – and *Schwingt Freudig euch empor* (Cantata 36).

Keith joined the Bach Cantata Club in December for a performance of Bach's *B Minor Mass*. A few days earlier he was heard in Lincoln Cathedral in Ralph Vaughan Williams's *A Sea Symphony*. On the 14th, he performed *Five Mystical Songs* (RVW). He was with the Bach Cantata Club on Christmas Day for a performance of the *Christmas Oratorio*, of which HMV stated that he 'sang as if born to it', which sums up, in a nutshell, Keith's understanding of Bach.

New Year's Eve, Keith joined soloists Noel Eadie, Muriel Brunskill, Walter Widdop and the Royal Choral Society in the Albert Hall in Sir Malcolm Sargent's famous reading of *Messiah*. The *Musical Times* drew attention to certain failings in Handelian style, due, it seems, to a lack of homogeneity: 'Yet on the whole the solo singing was good and did not mar the effect of the fine choral singing …'

Early in 1931, Adrian Boult invited Keith to visit Washington with him. Myra Hess, with headquarters in New York, arranged an audition for Keith with Serge Koussevitsky:

- I attended this in Boston after completing a tour of New York State and Canada, and was hired to sing in the *St Matthew Passion*. Several years later we recorded it live in Symphony Hall, Boston. Of the three albums, some were splendid, some less so – inevitable when recordings are made during performance. But it provided excitement and great satisfaction. After a performance in 1939, Koussevitsky said: 'Next year ve do it as a sacred drama on stage'. Such a production would have been very moving and I would have loved to have done this but, as with so many other things, the war intervened.

Back home, Keith's calendar was full. In late January he sang the role of *Solomon* (Handel) with the Glasgow Choral Union. In February, among other commitments, came a broadcast for the BBC of the rarely heard *Requiem Mass* by Baron d'Erlanger under Sir Adrian Boult. In the same month, a performance of *Lamentation Davidii* from the *Symphoniae Sacrae* (Schütz), Bach's *Mighty Lord* from the *Christmas Oratorio* and *The Trumpet Shall Sound* (*Messiah*). A Queen's Hall Ballad Concert in March received good reviews. Also in March, a performance of Bach's *B Minor Mass* with the Royal Choral Society, under Sir Malcolm Sargent. Sir Steuart Wilson, with whom Keith sang year after year, as Christus to Sir Steuart's Evangelist, was also engaged, as were Muriel Brunskill and Dorothy Silk. Another performance of this work occurred in Liverpool on 21 March. The following day, Keith was at the Queen's Hall for *St Matthew*, giving the *Daily Telegraph* satisfaction. The *Daily Mail* remarked that an English musical festival was hardly complete without him.

- The after-effect of a broadcast performance of this work was marred by a vitriolic letter published in the *Radio Times* referring to Sir Steuart's faulty breath control and unlimited number of aspirates in the Evangelist's role, including 'Pi-hi-late's wi-hi-fe'. Steuart took the BBC to court, a daring thing to do! The case hung on the phrase 'faulty breath control'. At the time, Caruso was the most famous tenor in the world. Did he have faulty breath control? Played in court, a Caruso recording displayed frequent interlarding of the intrusive 'H'. With this and the fact that in Steuart's narration the words 'Pilate's Wife' did not occur, the whole case fell apart. In the end, Steuart received several thousand pounds damages, with a personal fine to the writer of the letter.

A performance of Bach's then rarely heard *St John Passion* was given towards the end of March in Southwark Cathedral. Frank Howes wrote:

> ... [Falkner] sang the reflective arias in the way we all know and admire but he brought to his characterisation of Pilate a suggestion of the kindly, puzzled civil servant doing his duty (just like an Anglo-Indian dealing with an alien religion), which was admirable for being no more than a suggestion.

In July there was a needed holiday at St Maxine, though Keith broke away for a concert in Paris on the 20th. He was back home in time for a Vaughan Williams concert in August, which included Part I of *Songs of Travel* plus Christopher Edmunds' superb song *The Bellman* and Parry's *Love is a Bable*.

Another recital, this time at St Olave's, in the City of London, included music by Parry, Bullock, Gibbs, Handel and Bairstow. In late August, Keith was heard at the Proms singing the *Meistersinger* monologues, with a number of songs as encores.

A performance of the *B Minor Mass* was given in September at the Three Choirs, where Keith's fellow artists were Dorothy Silk, Steuart Wilson and Astra Desmond. The *Musical Times* remarked that 'The *Quoniam* and *Et in Spiritum* were as good as anything heard during the week', a week, incidentally, which included Horace Stevens's celebrated interpretation of *Elijah*. In October there was a BBC recital which contained an unusually varied programme of Bach, RVW, Quilter, Peel, Parry's *Away, Ye Men of Rules*, Terry and German:

- Apart from 'plugging' two recently released record titles, the Parry song gained success of a different kind. I was invited by the famous Rules Restaurant to a free meal as they thought I had put a 'plug' in for them. Regrettably, a repeat performance of the song, in a subsequent broadcast, did not elicit the same response!

A Grotrian Hall recital, also in October, accompanied by Michael Mullinar, contained a formidable programme: *Bois Epais* (Lully), *Maidens, Beware Ye* (Leveridge), *The Self-Banished* (Blow), *What Tho' I Trace, How Jovial is my Laughter* (Bach), followed by the *Four Serious Songs* of Brahms. The second half consisted of folk-songs from England, the Appalachians, Hungary and Japan, and songs by Vaughan Williams, Gibbs, Edmonds, Bridge, Gurney and Parry. Press comments were all laudatory, *The Times* stating:

> Quite apart from his admirable enunciation it would be impossible to mistake Mr Falkner for anything but an English singer, or Scotch (sic) perhaps, as

one should say. Nothing pejorative is implied; on the contrary, his singing bore the true guinea stamp. But it owed more to those characteristics of sturdy tone and straightforward phrasing that mate so harmoniously with oratorio and native song than to effects of histrionics. Bach-Purcell-Handel ... could one find a better man to do battle for this mighty triumvirate. Perhaps, then, Mr Falkner is content to lord it in his own line; if so, he can snap his fingers at his rivals.

A performance of Dame Ethel Smyth's *The Prison* occurred in October. Keith shared the platform with the lyric soprano Elsie Suddaby under the direction of Charles Kennedy Scott, with the Philharmonic Choir. The *Daily Telegraph* commented: 'His marvellous voice seems to adapt itself with equal ease to the most varied styles ...'

- Visits to the United States and Canada became annual events. When in Boston, no visit was complete without attending a Boston Red Soxs game and, in particular, to see Babe Ruth when the Yankees were visiting. Once, crossing the Atlantic, I caught a bad throat infection and radioed ahead to say that I might not be able to sing with the Boston Symphony. Dockside, in New York, I was met by the orchestra manager, taken in hand and advised not to talk. Immigration and customs dealt with, the manager escorted me to Boston, where I was rushed to a throat specialist to ensure I would be fit to sing the *St Matthew* two days later. Such care and consideration were a new experience.

Many friendships were established with generous Americans, in particular Dr Lawrence and Dorothy Stanton and Miss Chittenden, patrons of the arts in New York. In Cincinnati, at one of his first May Festivals, Keith was 'adopted' by attorney Carl Jacobs and his wife, Frieda. Their combined generosity would, in 1940, manifest itself further.

1932 works included *The Canterbury Pilgrims* (George Dyson), a Robert Mayer Children's Concert, a Birmingham recital which included *Four Serious Songs* (Brahms), a performance in Glasgow of Handel's *Semele* in which, as Somnus, God of Sleep, Keith gave a sublime rendition of *Leave Me, Loathsome Light*. Later, a programme of vocal music directed by the Swiss composer Othmar Schoeck took place in the Aeolian Hall. It was the British première of his *Elegy*, a cycle of 24 songs. *The Music Lover* commented:

... a work of much beauty, with moments of real poignancy ... Schoeck expressed himself as wholly delighted with the performance by English musicians. He declared that it had never been better sung than by Mr Falkner.

With March came a performance of Verdi's *Requiem* under Malcolm Sargent, followed by parts as the Priest and the Angel in Elgar's *The Dream of Gerontius*, followed, in turn, by the *St Matthew*. 'Mr Falkner's singing of the Christus is now classical, beyond praise or blame,' stated *The Times*.

The rest of the year consisted of performances of the *B Minor Mass*, conducted by Adrian Boult, recitals and a solo broadcast by the BBC of works by Purcell, Arne, Handel, Quilter, Gibbs, Peterkin, Harrison, and two folk-songs: *Banks of Allan Water* and *Billy Boy*. Keith appeared thrice times for the Proms that year before he was back at Worcester for Haydn's *Creation*, Szymanowski's *Stabat Mater* and, of course, the *B Minor Mass*, 'where he did himself the greatest credit, widely different as the two tasks were', remarked *The Musical Times*. There was a repeat performance in November of the *B Minor* in Huddersfield, with fellow soloists Isobel Baillie, Muriel Brunskill and Francis Russell, conducted by Sargent.

- One evening, Jelli D'Aranyi, Adela Fachiri, myself and others went to the Albert Hall to hear the young child prodigy Yehudi Menuhin play the Elgar *Concerto* conducted by the composer. As far as most fiddlers were concerned, it was as though another 'Messiah' had arrived. Ethel Smyth's comment about string players brought some perspective and always amused me: 'It's all the same fingering to me!'

1933 opened with a January BBC recital. This included Numbers 1 to 7 of *Dichterliebe* plus four songs by Parry. Other BBC recitals for the year were of interest: one began with *Mein traut Gesell* (Monch von Salsburg), *T'was in the Cool* (Bach), *What If I Seeke for Love of Thee?* (Jones), *The Inn* (Toye), *The Vagabond* (RVW), *Seven Meadows* (Gurney) and *Sigh No More* (Aitkin). Another was comprised of music by Handel, Wolf, Wood, Sharp, Denis Browne, Howells, Shaw and Mussorgsky.

- During this Brahms Centenary year, I sang two performances of the *Deutsches Requiem*. One, with Isobel Baillie, was conducted by Sir Thomas Beecham in the Queen's Hall. During the 'Behold all Flesh is as Grass' chorus, he loudly stated: 'Melancholy piece, this!'

Of the now familiar *St Matthew* later, the *Daily Mail* wrote: '... the outstanding impression is that of Mr Keith Falkner's beautiful delivery of Christ's words in the narrative held forth by Mr Steuart Wilson.'

The remainder of the year contained appearances of *Canterbury Pilgrims*, d'Erlanger's *Requiem*, a recital at the Royal College of Music when Keith sang songs from Butterworth's cycle *Love Blows as the Wind Blows*, and a recital in the Grotrian Hall accompanied by Michael Mullinar which was broadcast by the BBC later in the year. Press comments were full of praise, with the *Music Lover* commenting: 'The Editor wrote of another artist some months ago that he wished that for once, just once, that artist would do something not quite perfectly, it being in the end almost wearisome to have a catalogue only of perfections. Well, I feel the same about Mr Falkner. There is no singer to whom I would sooner listen. The perfect ease of production, the impeccable diction, the beauty of tone and above all his intelligence as a musician, render him apparently proof against all or any of the shortcomings which we are only too accustomed to expect from others of the genus singer.'

- I came closer to opera in 1933, though it was not my forte. On the 50th anniversary of Wagner's death the BBC broadcast excerpts from *Meistersinger* directed by Adrian Boult, with Miriam Licette, Gladys Parr, Frank Titterton, Jan van der Gucht, and myself as Sachs. I sang the *Flieder* and *Wahn* monologues as well as the formidably taxing *Panegyric* in the Finale.

Remarkably, the *Radio Times* produced a short article on Keith's preference for food on concert days:

> ... varies his diet too, but according to the type of concert he is giving. If it is a recital, he eats a huge breakfast of prunes, porridge, bacon and eggs with honey and toast. He has a large lunch of steak and boiled pudding (he is a large man!) but after that he eats very little – possibly a lightly boiled egg at tea-time – and nothing more until after the concert. However, if it is a big work to be sung, which to him is far more fatiguing, he has a 'high tea' about six o'clock, for which he usually chooses bacon and eggs ... after the concert he has a hot milk drink and sandwiches – unless it is a Gala Night, when he demands stout and oysters!

Though *The Dream of Gerontius* was not a Keith favourite, he sang both the roles of Priest and Angel of the Agony at the Three Choirs Festival that year. Sir Jack Westrup commented: 'To hear a singer thrust himself into the very heart of the music like this is an experience that occurs but rarely and, when it does, leaves an imprint on the heart and mind.'

1935 opened with a recital with Dorothy Silk in the Aeolian Hall. A quote from the *Musical Times* shows insight into this bass-baritone's development:

> ... Every new year his tone gets more instrumental. He is rapidly shedding his oratorio manners ... 'Bright is the ring of words when the right man sings them' ... Mr. Falkner brought this home forcibly to us. . . He shows what care and cultivation can do towards the enrichment of our beautiful language. And all that he gives the language, it gives him gratefully back again. He sings for it. It sings for him. Since his tones have become more concentrated, the upper-middle and higher notes have developed a fine bronze-like character which imparts to the whole voice a new virility ... Let him give up trotting about the country singing 'Messiahs' and Bach Masses ... let him go further and flaunt it in the face of the foreigner. Let him show them what an English singer can do. He could if he would!

Significant perhaps that Keith would soon be on his way to America again, followed later in the year by a tour of South Africa. While preparing for these concerts, Sir Hugh Allen asked him to join the Associated Board of the Royal Schools of Music (ABRSM). This adjudicating body came into being in 1889 to raise the general level of music-teaching in Great Britain and throughout the British Empire. It has been a major force in the development of music, especially of performance, since its inception.

- I protested that I was not qualified to judge standards in so many different instruments. Allen, however, suggested it would be my job to judge standards of performance, not to criticise methods and technique. My own experience and common sense would see me through, he said. So I agreed and soon found myself working alongside the Board's local representative resident musicians, who organise examinations and give years of loyalty and enthusiasm to students, examiners and Board alike. My first candidate was a small boy who, as he walked in, asked me to tune his fiddle. After momentary panic, I suggested he ask his teacher, for an examiner is not allowed to assist a candidate. My last candidate, years later in the 1980s, was also a small boy, Grade I Piano. After each scale, each test, each piece, he would pause to turn and ask, 'Sir, have I passed? Sir, have I passed?' Exasperated, I asked him what he was so worried about. 'Sir! My father has promised me £1 if I pass, £2 if I get Merit and £5 if I get Distinction.' I felt inclined to ask him to give me £2 and call it a day!

Invitations to adjudicate other competitive festivals began to come in. The first was the Feis Coil but, before taking up these tasks, Keith sailed for New York, arriving early January for an engagement with the Scola

Cantorum in Carnegie Hall for the first American performance of Walton's *Belshazzar's Feast*. The *New Yorker* commented that it was the loudest work heard in 1935.

- It was a marathon for in addition to the Walton work, there were important bass roles in Nabukov's *Ode* and Handel's *Solomon*. On the 22nd I gave a recital in New York's Town Hall accompanied by Coenraad von Bos. My agent, Annie Friedberg, then informed me that a Hollywood 'scout' wished to arrange a film test for Warner Brothers. Intrigued, I went with Coenraad, who insisted on accompanying me, gratis. Made-up, I was made to stand far too close, in embrace with a very pretty girl, while I sang my piece, *One Alone*. It was not until I was about to sail for commitments in England that I heard from Warners, asking me to fly immediately to Hollywood for further tests, with a view to making musicals.

It is possible that Keith might have added another string to his bow for, with the voice and good looks, he could have become, say, an 'English' Nelson Eddy. However, with a full list of engagements he felt unable to break, Keith sailed for home. The 'scout' never did understand how anybody could turn down such an opportunity. A few years later, three films would be made for Warner Brothers in England.

On return, Keith's commitments included a *St John Passion* under Sargent and Elgar's *The Apostles* in Nottingham conducted by Sir Hamilton Harty. From May to October he was away, for his first adjudicating tour of South Africa. Home again, he was in demand as much as ever.

- In January 1936, Julia Christabel, our first daughter, arrived on the scene. I never did know what to do with babies! I remember telephoning Christabel while I was at the Bethlehem Bach Festival and, forgetting all about the 'new arrival', enquired after the dog!

At this festival in May 1931, Keith was soloist in an afternoon performance of Cantata No 195 *Dem Gerechten*; in the evening, in the Cantata *Sehet, wir gehn hinauf gen Jerusalem* (No 159) and the *Magnificat*. The next day came the *B Minor*. Then he was off to his first Cincinnati May Festival for Bach, Handel, Haydn, the narrator's part in Prokofiev's *Peter and the Wolf*, and Brahms's *Four Serious Songs*.

- I found the Brahms set was even more satisfactory in the orchestral version, for you felt on completion that you had done something really big. I had been more than surprised to see, on arrival, a street banner proclaiming: 'FALKNER SINGS BRAHMS!'

Next, it was on to the Ann Arbor Festival for a performance of Elgar's *Caractacus*; fellow soloist was the fine American bass-baritone Julius Huehn. Keith went on to appear with the St Louis Symphony before returning to New York, sailing home to sing at the Norwich Triennial Festival, where Sir Thomas Beecham conducted the seldom heard *Hercules* (Handel), with Keith in the title role. Later, Dr Heathcote Statham conducted a performance of the *Magnificat* in which Keith was said to have given a virile performance of *Quia fecit mihi magna*.

The annual Three Choirs Festivals were extremely popular from the mid-1920s to 1939, providing Keith with regular engagements from 1925 to 1939. Apart from the music, they were great social affairs.

- Two hostesses were famous for their luxurious hospitality and generosity. One, Mrs Gwyn Holford of Gloucester, was a delightful eccentric who wore large hats at both breakfast and luncheon, and had strong convictions regarding the Anglo-Catholic religion. She was also a stickler for social etiquette. One evening at dinner, a guest seated on her right poured the remains of his sherry into his soup, announcing that he always did so. The retort was swift: 'Then this will be the last time you dine in my house!'

  The hospitality of Mrs Holland Martin was equally gracious. On one visit my fellow guests included Sir Hugh Allen, Sir Walford Davies, Elsie Suddaby, Mary Jarred, Joyce Grenfell and Steuart Wilson. After dinner, Sir Hugh produced a copy of the 'notorious unintentionally comic' oratorio *Ruth* by George Tolhurst. We all stood around the piano with Allen and Walford playing four hands while the rest of us sang the various parts. It was hilarious and at moments we all became quite hysterical, breaking many times for laughter and repeats. Joyce pleased us enormously with her resonant voice and sense of fun.

1937 was a busy year. With their growing family, the Falkners could no longer burden Christabel's mother, and set out to purchase a home. They eventually bought Nettleden Farm, near Berkhamstead in Hertfordshire.

- Once settled, my old teacher Albert Garcia, still active at the RCM, came down, bringing the newly-arrived New Zealand bass Oscar Natzka. They were an enormous help as, together, we laid a concrete drive to the garage and seeded the lawns.

In December, Warner Brothers approached again, this time with a contract, and Keith soon found himself on the set at Teddington Studios for the first of three films. *Mayfair Melody*, with Chilli Bouchier and Joyce Kirby, was directed by Arthur Woods. The songs – *A Song Doesn't*

Care, *Wings*, *San Diego Betty* and the delightful *Without the Moon*, were
written by Kenneth Leslie-Smith and James Dyrenforth.

- Upon their release, I took Christabel and Julia to see them, bemused,
  embarrassed and somewhat irritated to have Julia suddenly exclaim: 'There's
  Daddy!' Heads turned. *Mayfair Melody* was being shown all over London
  and in spite of its being, in my opinion, a bad picture, people seemed to like
  it. The two other films, released in 1938, were *The Singing Cop* and
  Thistledown. In the first I played a policeman who poses as an opera star in
  order to expose a prima donna as a spy. My fellow stars were Marta Kabarr
  and Chilli Bouchier. In one scene I appeared as Mephistopheles and sang the
  famous *Serenade*. In the last, I played the part of a Scottish laird who
  believes his continental wife is unfaithful. Songs were *Music and Mystery*,
  When You Say Good Morning, I Don't Know Much About Music and *There's
  Magic in a Song*, all composed by Kenneth Leslie-Smith.

Arranged by the British Council, the Falkners were, in January 1937, on
the road to Eastern Europe, where the pianist Cyril Smith joined them for
recitals in Vienna, Prague, Budapest, Zagreb, Belgrade, Bucharest and
Czernowitz (Cernauti). It was a responsibility as all three were musically
representing Britain. The *Belgrade Politika* and the *Bucuresti Gazeta*
stated that, with Falkner a master singer, they hoped he would soon
return.

- After the concert in Budapest, I was presented with a copy of Kodaly's Opus
  I, *Enekszo*. I sang the work often at concerts, broadcasts and, on one
  occasion, at a recital at Balliol College, Oxford, where Thomas Armstrong,
  then Choragus of the University and organist of Christ Church Cathedral,
  played for me.

Home again, there was a performance of the *St Matthew*. A Verdi
Requiem followed. The performance of *Stabat Mater* with the Leeds
Philharmonic was a March highlight. Between mid-March and mid-May,
Keith and Christabel were in America, where performances took them all
over the Northwest. Home, Keith appeared twice at the Proms that year.
He sang again at the Three Choirs, where he and Mary Jarred sang in the
first performance of Kodaly's *Budavari Te Deum*, conducted by the
composer.

- Kodaly was very gracious, saying how pleased be was that I had introduced
  his song-cycle to English audiences, inscribing my copy of the *Te Deum* 'To
  Mr Keith Falkner – gratefully for his beautiful singing'.

Then it was on to Leeds for a *B Minor* and Verdi *Requiem*. A *Missa Solemnis* (Dettinger) and a *St Matthew* were heard in October. From October 11-20 he was involved in the filming of *Thistledown*.

To this point, with the exception of his mother's death, Keith's life had been free of travail, free of illness except for the usual concern for his vocal chords. In November his father, John Charles, was in a car accident, dying from injuries on 5 December:

- Though very distressing, in some ways the news of his accident did not surprise me for he, like me and Julia to follow, was fey in the 'aware' sense of the word. Before leaving for a performance in Ireland, I had put him on a train for a visit to Norfolk. Boarding, he said he didn't want to go – having some premonition. He was right. The funeral was held in Sawston, a very sad ending to a wonderful and busy year. I did manage two *Messiahs*, a performance of *Five Mystical Songs* and King's carols before the close of the year. My sorrow was lightened by the arrival, in February 1938, of our second daughter, Philippa Margaret – Pip – 'a playmate for Julia', as the announcement in *The Times* stated. I am convinced she was conceived during our happy time at the Jacobs's residence during the Cincinnati May Festival the previous year. Now, returning from Gloucester following a recital with Herbert Sumsion, I returned on the breakfast train and arrived at Broadcasting House for a morning recital. I grabbed a moment to telephone the nursing home and was told the baby was a lovely girl, with no trouble at all. Herbert Howells met me in the lobby and we rejoiced together.

February was as busy as ever. Keith sailed for America again early in March, a voyage he described as 'Hell'. He docked for a round of meetings and concerts before going on tour, returning in time for a performance with Ernest Lush at the Wigmore in April. Performances in Kendal and Chester followed an *Easter Oratorio* for the BBC and another *St Matthew*. Throughout all, the summer being fairly quiet, were the usual sports. In late summer there were two programmes for the BBC, one of Bach and Purcell, the other of lieder, with two Proms followed by a *B Minor Mass*, Verdi *Requiem* and other engagements.

Performances for early 1939 included the Mozart *Requiem*, Haydn's *Creation,* the *B Minor Mass* with concerts in Glasgow and Hereford, followed by a *Messiah* in Hanley. On March 3, accompanied by Christabel, he performed the Kodaly *Opus No 1* for the BBC. There were further concerts in Bedford, Jersey and London. A visit to America included the Brahms *Requiem* under Koussevitsky. It was on then to Cincinnati:

- Here, I sang with the greatest singer I was ever privileged to sing with. I had heard Kirsten Flagstad almost drown out the orchestra in the closing scene from *Götterdämmerung*, and feared for our duets together in Haydn's *Creation*. In the event, she sang with such great purity and control that I might have been singing with Elsie Suddaby or Isobel Baillie. It was the most satisfying 'Adam and Eve'' performance I ever experienced. Though not a sociable person, our work together was smooth and friendly. Ivor Newton's affectionate tribute to her goes a long way to dispel the idea of an 'Iceberg soprano'. We returned to New York, and Christabel sailed for home while I stayed on for tennis in Forest Hills, with the composer Bruno Huhn. His song 'Invictus' has been sung by every baritone and bass the world over. Then it was on to the Bethlehem Bach Festival. The conductor was Ifor Jones for performances of Cantata No 69, *Lobe den Herrn, meine Seele*, with the aria 'My Redeemer, Dearest Master'; the motet *Komm, Jesu*, and Cantata No 71, *Gott ist mein König*, with bass aria 'Day and Night are Thine'.

Ich habe genug followed, which, by this time, he had virtually made his own, and solos in Cantatas No 104, *Du Hirte Israel*, and the *Magnificat*. The following day he was a soloist in the *B Minor Mass*.

Keith returned to England in late May with very favourable press comments to his credit. Despite ominous rumblings in Europe, he filled his summer with cricket and concerts. Highlights in June were a Malvern Charity Concert with Christabel; a *Messiah* for the Foundling Hospital in London, founded by Handel; Mahler's *Kindertotenlieder* with Hubert Foster Clark (conductor), introduced by Neville Cardus for BBC Manchester. On the 26th both Keith and Nancy Evans performed at a Merchant Taylor's Company Dinner in London. She writes:

It was during the early 1930s that I first heard Keith Falkner sing. Fortunately my home-town, Liverpool, was a fine musical city ... (and) I heard all the leading soloists ... I was studying singing then, so it was a tremendous inspiration to hear singers of their high standard ... Keith Falkner was a particular hero! Beauty of voice, impeccable diction and, in addition to his fine musical gifts, a very attractive presence and personality ... his singing of *O Ruddier than the Cherry* remains wholly vivid ... It was a special occasion when my partner was Keith Falkner. A very happy evening was made even happier when he treated me to supper at the Savoy Grill: the only time in my life hat I ever tasted 'Black Velvet', a mixture of Guinness and champagne!

The month was rounded out on the 29th with a BBC Empire broadcast and a concert at Kingswood School in Bath. In July came a concert of

Quilter songs and, for the BBC, Schubert's *Die schöne Müllerin* cycle. The 20th saw Keith bent for South Africa:

> It was my second visit for music examinations and concert tour. The voyage aboard the *Arundel Castle* was athletic, as Santha Rama Rau, then an RCM graduate student returning to India, and I played endless deck cricket, quoits and tennis. There was a brief stop-over for tennis and a swim at Reid's Palace Hotel, feeding proffered gins to sunning lizards. We crossed the equator in stupefying humidity so I took the liberty of appearing for lunch in shirtsleeves. The steward accosted me quickly to say, with the Captain's compliments of course, would I please go and get properly dressed. In Cape Town I was reunited with my sister before moving on to the tour which took me to about thirty-six towns. I was in Fauresmith, staying at a club, when war was declared on 3 September, appalled to hear a member shout: 'Thank God! Hitler will make Germany rule the world!'

The *Rand Daily Mail* announced the forthcoming performance of *Elijah* to be performed on August 18. The tenor soloist would be the American Richard Crooks, with Dorothy Clark and Margaret Roux:

> • I had spent the week before in Durban at sea level. The performance was in Johannesburg at 6000ft. As I made my way across the platform I was awed and pleased to see Richard Tauber in the front row. It was a normal performance until I came to the middle of the bass aria *Is Not His Word Like a Fire*, marked *allegro con fuoco*. Suddenly my heart began to pound and my breathing became erratic. I was near panic as Richard stage-whispered: 'Take it easy! Take it easy!' Under great stress, I continued, learning afterwards that this sort of thing happened to singers and athletes if not acclimatised. I went on to other concerts but due to 'restrictions' the tour itself had to be cancelled. By October 20 I was homebound with one other first-class passenger. No sooner out of Table Bay, we were called to see the captain, who handed out field glasses with instructions to take regular daytime watch for submarines. We spotted none and put in at Sierra Leone before making for Southampton, sailing well out into the Atlantic before turning for Britain.

At 39, Keith was in his prime. During the voyage he considered his future, deciding the first thing to do was to rejoin the RAF. At his age this turned out to be difficult.

Chapter 5: 1940–1946

It is twelve o'clock in London. Hitler has spoken and Lord Halifax has replied. There is no more to be said. Or is there? Is the tongue of Chaucer, of Shakespeare, of Milton, of the King James translation of the Scriptures, of Keats, of Shelley, to be hereafter, in the British Isles, the dialect of an enslaved race? ...

Words falter. There are no phrases for the obscene ambition that attacks, for the magnificent mobilization of a people that defends, unshaken and unafraid. We can only pray that soon the time will come when the vultures no longer defile the British skies and the cry goes out from John O'Groats to Land's End: 'Twelve o'clock and all's well!'

(The New York Times)

- 'Peace in our time'! Rather, 1940 looked pretty grim. Back home I applied to the Air Force but, hearing nothing, carried on with concerts and the usual spate of *Messiahs* in Hanley, Liverpool, Royal Choral in London, Manchester with the Hallé, Glasgow and a recital with Howard Ferguson – *Die schöne Mullerin* – at a Myra Hess National Gallery concert. On the 30th of May I was in Winchester and had just sung Herbert Howells's song *Mally O!*:

> 'Will ye go to Flanders, my Mally O!
> And see the great commanders, my Mally O!
> You'll see the bullets fly
> And the soldiers how they die!'

when, during the interval, I heard that the Hampshire Regiment were returning after the battle and miracle of Dunkirk. I felt extreme embarrassment and tried again to enlist. Meanwhile, cables from generous friends in the States began to arrive offering safe haven. However, Christabel and I had other ideas as we felt duty-bound to stay and do what we could, but we accepted for the girls, now four and two.

Christabel wrote to their friends the Stantons on June 18:

Keith and I ... don't hesitate for a moment about sending them for I'm sure that whatever plans are made for their welfare will be good and as fine as we could expect under the circumstances. They are both splendid small creatures, and I do not intend to have their physique ruined by shattering noise and the possibility of undernourishment.

- There had been no response from the RAF when I had lunch with Lord Ponsonby of Shulebrede and told him my dilemma. Now wheels turned and I was soon requested to present myself at the Air Ministry. In a letter to the Stantons on 26 June I wrote '... I may be doing my bit very soon now. I am glad to say, that since last week, and France's lamentable plight, we here have become stronger in spirit and determination. Our great enemy is the rumour-monger and hysterical type of person who delights in spreading bad news ...'

Eventually I was passed for ground duty but, with a number of engagements on the calendar, I requested and was assured of a posting to an RAF station near London. When my orders came, they were to proceed to Wick, some 730 miles away, where I would be Intelligence Officer to No 3 Fighter Squadron 'resting' from the Battle of Britain. It was from here, and a red telephone box, that I said goodbye to the girls, who sailed from Liverpool in late July.

Christabel recalled the awful experience:

> ... the sudden and overwhelming separation ... (Julia) was magnificent. Only once on that last morning did she say 'Mum, I don't think I want to go to America.' It nearly unhinged me. King George (VI)[1] was hurriedly brought into action and so we went on with that ghastly morning in Liverpool ... Given the same options again, I would never have parted from them ... the war and the separation changed our lives irrevocably.

In a letter to the Stantons:

> The children went off in grand style ... I felt very proud of them ... it is such a grand experience for them to be launching out as pioneers at their time of life that I cannot grudge their going ... how I should love to see them walk down the gangway! I am purposely not mentioning when the boat sailed or its name ...

'Daddy' monitored our progress via the 'ops' room, and some time later Marshal of the Royal Air Force Lord Trenchard wrote to *The Times*:

> ... In 1940 a spontaneous and generous offer came from thousands of people in the United States who were willing to take into their homes children from this country ... many went to friends. For the many more who had no such friends there, the United States Committee for the Care of European Children ... formed the necessary liaison between them and the American Committee

---

[1] King George VI: often brought into action as on an evening when, refusing to stay in bed, Julia was threatened with a spanking by Keith. 'Oh!', said the four-year-old, craning over the bannister: 'And what would King George say to that!'

in New York ... over 800 children were sent ... More would have been sent had transport been available, but the sinking of the *City of Benares* by enemy action brought the scheme to an end ... It is not possible to express in words the deep sense of gratitude which we feel for all those who made possible this great social movement.

Keith wrote on August 6, 1940:

- ... It has been a great wrench – it is extraordinary how precious our 'whippersnappers' become as soon as one had to say goodbye. But it is all as nothing compared to the gratitude we feel for you both ... I rejoined the Air Force (and) music is necessarily in the background – all I can hope for is an occasional broadcast to augment my pay. It remains to be seen if I shall retain sufficient voice to do another tour in the USA when the war is over! Perhaps a university appointment may be possible.

How prophetic!

Keith and Christabel were together at Wick in late September/early October, and it was from here on 26 September that she was requested to journey to Edinburgh for interview for the censor and posting to Inverness. They were now very worried there might be another baby on the way, which would have caused difficulties all around: what justification would they then have had in sending their daughters to the States only to produce another child in wartime? As it was, they needn't have worried.

- I soon found myself re-posted to the Operations Room at Naval and RAF Kirkwall to learn control of aircraft by radar and VHF. Then I was off again as Intelligence Officer to a new airbase at Skeabrae, where living conditions were primitive. The winter was so bitter we often had to fill buckets with snow to boil a kettle. All the maps were out of date so I journeyed to the RAF Map Depot at Harrow. With a hundred-weight of maps I proceeded to Euston Station during a bombing raid and felt extremely vulnerable under the glass roof. Yet the moment I was in my sleeper I felt safe and slept soundly. I arrived late at Thurso to find no boat to Stromness until Monday, so tackled the SNO on the urgent nature of my 'baggage' and was provided with a tug. The Pentland Firth is notorious for its turbulence and the crossing was a nightmare but I soon found my sealegs and watched with exhilaration as we made our way into Scapa Flow. Once on land I was given 'restoration' in the form of pink gins and so made my way back to base.

[Letter to the Stantons:] ... An interesting series began on our radio on the USA – historic explanations of your policy and people which go a long way to a fuller understanding of the USA and your people by our 'man in the street'. It is a source of regret that so many English people get their impressions of America from the movies; and, vice versa, from the rather snobbish attitude of so many English people abroad ... It's only that having known and received such friendship in the USA, we can't bear that there should be false impressions ... It is a blessing the children are away from this 'Beelzebub'! Strange to say, my interest in life and things now is more vivid than ever. I cannot account for it ...

On Christmas Day, as the men's Xmas dinner, traditionally served by the officers, was in progress the 'maroons' went off. Dropping my plates, I ran for my moped and raced towards a German Heinkel III, known as the Milktrain, which had been shot down. I arrived in time to prevent the uninjured pilot and navigator from destroying the plane and, with a guard, took them in custody.

[Letter written 15 January, 1941:] ... so glad to hear you are getting a lot of music. Is the Bax very difficult? I'm told he is very badly affected by it all, has become more of a recluse than ever, music the only approach to him. Yes! The news of the defeat of the Italian army, following upon the success in repelling the Luftwaffe, has had a great tonic on us all. (But) we still have a lot of leeway to make up (for), we have yet to defend this island; at the same time, any minor campaigns that can be waged successfully are vitally important in these days of world-wide propaganda.

With occasional 48-hour leaves, the winter passed not unpleasantly, with long walks over the moors with their Jack Russell 'Bee', a wedding present from Edwin Fisher, then Chairman of Barclays Bank:

- One day, as the dog chased through the heather, we came across a small tarn surrounded by myriad daffodils. Weeping with the beauty, I found myself singing Quilter's setting of 'Fair Daffodils'.

Chris wrote to the Stantons on 31 May 1941:

Keith had a broadcast in Glasgow on May 8. I was not allowed to play for him as he did not wish two of us to be (there) at the same time. So I went off to Kendal, where he had two concerts at their Festival ... after that we went to Buttermere ... for hours we completely forgot the war ... it was all rather a superb dream ... Times are so uncertain yet one must make plans, otherwise life would be intolerable. Half one's joy is in the future – sometimes all of it ... we are all shaken to the core by Hess ... You will rejoice with us over the battleship *Bismarck* but at what a cost! Crete is holding out by almost supernatural means ... Today I heard that all the Curtis factories (USA) are foregoing their summer vacation, which means an extra 200-odd planes and 170 propellers. That's the spirit!

Christabel was much amused by an incident which occurred in Inverness at a tea party for Polish pilots. The opening gambit was 'Are you married? Do you have a family?' Two responses were: 'Yes, my wife is impenetrable' and 'No, my wife is impossible!'

- So, this first year of war I served at Wick, Kirkwall (Sector HQ), Castletown and Skeabrae. In February I was sent to Harrow for a Fighter Controller Course, of which the best part was riding a tricycle fitted with VHF and radar round a big field, being 'vectored' on to another tricycle acting as the enemy. The week was pleasant for I stayed with Henry Havergal, then Music Master at Harrow School. Each evening, strings and woodwind gathered to perform Bach Cantatas. One evening we were without an oboe and so I sang *Ich habe genug* accompanied by a clarinet! After the course, I returned to Skeabrae and was then posted to Middle Wallop, where I took control of 604 Night Fighter Squadron from the ops room and from field radar equipment at Sopley. One night, a friend, Keith Geddes, was controlling and urged me to go outside to observe a night fighter in contact with a German aircraft bombing Southampton – my first 'visual' of a bomber being shot down in flames.

    Middle Wallop was luxury after Skeabrae, a peacetime station with fine buildings and Mess. The dew point was always a worry, due to the proximity of the river Test, causing mist and fog. Despite flares on either side of the runway, it was hazardous for night-fighters to land if ground mist had settled during their absence. Generally, life here was social with frequent cricket, tennis and music provided by John Hunt, Denis Matthews and the Griller String Quartet. There were often musical lectures and once I was asked to introduce one given by Eric Fenby on Delius. Richard Rickett, my red-headed friend, and John Hunt were interrogation officers of German aircraft shot down in the area, while the artist Sir William Rothenstein became a good friend. He was 'in residence' to paint some of the night-fighter pilots famous for their successes, namely Group Captain John 'Catseye' Cunningham, Rory Chisholm, Edward Crew and Keith Geddes. Geddes had been Provost of the Royal College of Art in the 1920s, when often he and Sir Hugh Allen would meet to watch the two colleges play soccer and hockey. I was extremely flattered when Rothenstein asked if he could propose me for membership to the Athenaeum, seconded by Dr Percy Buck. Many years later I was told that when my name came up for election a member asked what else I had done besides being a fine singer. Dr H C Colles is reported to have replied, 'Well, I know he got a hundred at Lord's not long ago!' I was elected without further ado. He did not specify that it had been on the Nursery Ground.

    It was an interesting posting in the company of Bee. One day I returned from a long walk on a very hot day and left him in my room to recover with a bowl of water while I went about my duties. Sometime later the CO, Group Captain Elliott, went into my room, intending to refill Bee's bowl. For his efforts he got a nasty bite on his wrist but fortunately bore no grudge. The Mess was short of cash so cases of wine were offered from its splendid cellar. I bought one of brandy and two of Dow's 1908 Port, the final bottle corked in 1992 in a family celebration.

Writing to the Stantons on 9 August 1941:

- Our news is very good ... and a long letter from the Jacobs in Cincinnati, with twelve photographs of the children. They look absolutely grand! ... Philippa now 3½ ... Julia goes to kindergarten but has not learned much. I do not mind this as one could not expect her mind to work on too many details. Also her heart may have been a bit sore ... '

The summer and autumn of 1941 dragged on, with Keith's diary recording sporadic visits with Christabel, the occasional broadcasts – some in the middle of the night, such as on 26 September to the USA, which included Samuel Barber's *Dover Beach* with string quartet. We were able to pick up a somewhat garbled 'Hello, Julia and Philippa', then the concert began and, with increased interference, faded out. But we had heard his voice! Keith wrote to the Stantons in September:

- ... I suppose the good times will come again and each day is one nearer the end of this strange life .... I don't know how we could take it without you all behind us ... I am no longer 'Intelligent', my job more responsible and operational, which makes life more vital ... We had a lovely weekend together in London in July, behaving like 'rubbernecks', not telling any of our friends we were there, just lazing, lunching and dining out, seeing some shows and walking in the park. A lovely interlude to this life of 'je ne sais quoi'! We ended with an air raid on the last night, but were too tired to do more than turn over in bed. So blasé does one become ...

- In November I was posted to the Scilly Isles – St Mary's to Portreath Sector HQ, where we tracked the south-west approaches for intruders and our own aircraft. I was able to take a week's leave with Chris in Drumnadrochit, but on 7 December we listened with trepidation as the news of the Japanese bombing of Pearl Harbour came through. Apart from the horror of the devastation, we wondered about our children's fate and could only feel that, at last, America would be fighting with us. I did manage a 'bunch' of *Messiahs* at Bradford, Leicester and Halifax before settling in for the winter. Though warmer than Orkney, it was rather primitive, an isolated existence with little social life, walking and tennis the only form of exercise. Interest focused on the daily arrival of the *Scillonian* from Penzance, the coming and going of local fishing boats, with the occasional flying boat en-route from Portugal. Half a squadron of Hurricane fighters were stationed here, the airstrip on the side of a hill, so it was amusing to watch a newcomer trying to land: overshooting the crest, he went straight into fields of early spring daffodils destined for London. All this unnecessary activity caused much animosity among the growers.

Singing was now almost impossible and, in any case, I was not satisfied with my performance in the occasional concert I did have. I could not get in enough practice and had no real incentive, though I did manage a *St Matthew* with the Bach Choir in March 1942, a broadcast and a concert of English music (Purcell to 1930) at the National Gallery.

Writing to the Stantons on 7 March 1942, Christabel said:

> ... Just for the time of war blinkers are a blessing perhaps ... At the moment we seem to be retiring to specific lines – which is all bunkum – but they must say something to soothe us, only it does not ... Keith had 48 hours last week (his birthday) and went to London for singing lessons ... He has been tucked down on those Islands long enough amongst strangers. We are planning some leave together soon if I don't die of excitement before then ...

Also in March came a sudden request that other arrangements be made for us. The Stantons offered sponsorship and on the 27th Keith wrote to them:

- We really did not wish to ask your direct help ... but further arrangements seemed to be badly held up. We therefore presumed upon your previous kindness and friendship ... Our only fear is that your household will be too upset by two small children ...

In April, Keith was posted to RAFNI in Belfast and during the next two years served at the field radar stations Ballyhalbert, Ballywoodan, Ballinderry and Ballydonghy, making his way up to Squadron Leader by the end of hostilities in Europe. Christabel somehow managed a transfer to Belfast, which made their lives bearable. Her loving husband wrote to her on 2 June 1942:

- 'Twelve years after', 11:45
  My dear 'Bride of yesterday',
  Let me see, you were on your way in the Daimler with Uncle Will clearing his throat, and I was dividing my attention between Adam (Keith's father's nickname), who was to have the silk hat, and with Adrian if every stone had been turned. I remember feelings very rushed the last half-hour and feeling that there was now no escape, I was caught in the net. And by jiminy I was and still am. Your arms, thank God, still hold me to you as no one else

in the world could possibly hold me. I seem to have absorbed part of you, so that I could not if I would think or plan anything without your part in it. In fact, after twelve years I may say that I can give you a splendid recommend. In the 'Be your age', a particularly nice part is about the charmer who grow up fresh and beautiful and blossom slowly into full maturity. I think you are such. You have given me such a long crescendo of delight and love and now you are just on the crest of the wave of full love and happiness for me. I can't tell you how different is your love now from 10 years ago, but there it is. Your barriers are down. To have my advances welcomed and 'taken care of', is the finest tonic for my adoration of you that can be. The times and hours I spend away from you, thinking of you, are legion. Please go on marrying me – goodness knows what heights of ecstasy we shall arrive at. If you give me such perfect ravishment and intoxicate delight as you did last Friday and particularly the previous Sat. and Sunday – if you can recall them in every detail, as I can – then you will hold me to you with iron bonds.

The sooner we can all four be together the happier I shall be. You talk such arrant nonsense about not being a good mother – I could shake you. You have been a wonderful matrix. You gave them the finest start I've ever heard of, each nine months' perfect care and nutrition, whilst you denied yourself anything that could possibly injure or affect them, and I think they do you proud. What if you did feel irritated by them, isn't that natural? Don't those you love irritate and at the same time thrill you more than anything else? Go on, you are the woman for me and my daughters and just you remember it. You stick to me as close as possible.

On 18 June, Christabel wrote to Dorothy Stanton:

Your first letter, the children with you at last ... my first letter from Julia in my life ... Are they really beautiful? Is it in the bone, or just nice baby faces ... how lovely that Julia is interested in the piano ... Keith was invited to play cricket in Dublin so into mufti he leapt and went South ... played well and met many friends and felt pre-war again. Indeed one can in that country we now refer to as 'that melancholy exception'.

[4 July:] ... nothing could give Keith or me greater happiness than to know the children are having a 'home life' with you as long as you feel equal to it and it fits in with the professional atmosphere of your home ... in England they were always part of us ... Julia came and lay on the sofa during the early mornings whilst K and I rehearsed and so imbibed a great deal ... So please keep them as close to you as you feel able ... I remember in one of your first letters you stressed that you wanted them to feel secure and my heart warmed to you greatly because that is so essential in a youngster's life ... It is lovely to hear of Julia's passionate interest in music and Keith's singing (and) how good of the Doctor to play to them on his cello. When J was very small I called her 'Baa'. One day she said to me, 'Baa do love Mum, Baa do'. This was most undermining, hard to think about even now. I am an 'austerity Mother' a pure war product!

[July 29:] You mention Miss Chittenden and the little book she has so kindly dedicated to the daughter of England's greatest singer. You can imagine me just bursting with pride at my husband AND my daughter ... I hope it is published ... What do you think of the news? I feel exhilarated although the PM has just said we must realise we are still only at the beginning ...

• Apart from the fact that we were at war and our children overseas, we were as content as anybody could be getting leave together when we could. Then I began to get communications from 'above' suggesting I prepare myself for posting to Burma. I had been in Ireland nearly a year and could hardly think I would be allowed to remain so near Christabel for much longer. However, Burma did not claim me and life continued much as before, my work not arduous as the crew grew adept at 'reading the tube', a process of assessing height and direction of aircraft, then manoeuvring 'an attacker' into position. There were only occasional hostile aircraft with diminished German raids, the war at last having turned against them, more intent now on the development and firing of V1 and V2 rockets. One operation which left me shaking in my boots occurred just after the Greenland 'summit' with Roosevelt, when Churchill was returning to London. For some unknown reason his flight was interpreted as hostile, and a section of fighters was sent to intercept. I advised them to proceed with caution, and thank God I did, for the aircraft was indeed friend, not foe. I don't care to think what might have happened had I had to deal with a trigger-happy pilot.

Only on the fringe of the war, the station was, nonetheless, on twenty-four-hour alert, crews on a three-watch basis with much inter-service sport in the form of cricket, soccer, shooting and athletics. I once requested by telephone that the Sergeant of the Watch come to see me and was amused to hear the exchange operator on the open line say: 'Sahn't! 'Ole Man wants ta see yer!' The Air Vice Marshal made regular inspection visits and on one I took him along to meet the outspoken and forthright technical officer, an American, a law unto himself. He was sitting with his feet up and made no attempt to rise. The AVM, taken aback, demanded: 'Is this what you are paid to do?' 'I ain't paid for what I do', came the response, 'but for what I know!' Wagner, an electronics expert, predicted there would be no future for singers after the war as 'electronics' was progressing at such a pace that 'it' would be able to produce sounds much better than anything live singers could do!

Bee [the dog] had enjoyed the country life 'ratting and rabbitting' but at fourteen was getting slower. One evening during a terrific gale, a horrifying screech suddenly pierced the house were I was billeted, wind tearing past windows, billowing the curtains. Not a second later the maid rushed in hysterically, pronouncing the screech to have been the 'Banshee', the spirit whose cry is believed to forewarn death, never more true than in Ireland. I wondered. Within days Bee was bitten by a rat and soon lost all his vitality and had to be put down. Had the Banshee warned? I was distraught and wept my heart out.

Sport continued to play an important part in Keith's life and he became a temporary member of the Ulster Club in Belfast. But of singing there were only two occasions during his stay there: a recital comprising Finzi's cycle to Hardy's poems *Earth, Air and Rain*, accompanied by Christabel, and a broadcast of arias such as *Arm, Arm Ye Brave* from Handel's *Judas Maccabaeus*, with a brass band.

- But, I was not pleased with my voice and I soon picked up a throat infection which resisted cure. I was sent to the resident specialist, where, in a queue of officers, my turn soon came. Without looking up the resident ordered me to sit down and open. Mirror over one eye, he had a look and exclaimed: 'Good God! Where have I seen this throat before?' He was, of course, Ivor Griffiths. As we chatted, he inquired what I was doing there. Then he asked 'Why aren't you singing? If you don't keep it up, your throat will atrophy and once that happens you'll have a hell of a time getting it back into form!' I took this to heart, thereafter getting in daily practice, even if it had to be while walking or driving.

With two refresher courses at radar stations Neatishead (Norfolk) and Northstead (Durham) behind him, Keith was posted as CO to the permanent radar station at Patrington (Yorkshire), where he worked with a Polish squadron at Church Fenton, taking over the administrative and liaison work with Sector and Group headquarters. Involved with the physical and mental welfare of the station, Keith supervised and played hockey, soccer and cricket, while free use of the church organ gave him opportunity for practice and performance with singers from the local Army and RAF detachments.

- Conducting a performance of *Messiah* I almost felt back in the 'profession'. Afterwards, I wondered if I should have been a conductor for the feeling of power and control over a big work is exhilarating, giving a false impression of one's abilities.

For Christabel's birthday [18 November 1943] Keith wrote:

- ... Here is a tribute to you by Spencer and my own thought for you on your day:

> Coming to kisse her lips, such grace I found,
> Me seemd, I smelt a gardin of sweet floures
> That dainty odours from them threw around
> For damsels fit to decke their lovers bowres
> Her lips did smell lyke unto Gilly floures
> Her ruddy cheeks, like unto roses red
> Her snowy browes, like budded Bellamoures;
> Her lovely eyes, like Pynks but newly spread;
> Her goodly bosome, lyke a strawberry bed;
> Her neck, lyke to a bunch of Cullambynes;
> Her breast like lillyes, ere their leaves be shed.
> Her nipples like young blossomed Jessemynes;
> Such fragrant flowers doe give most odorous smell;
> But her sweet odour did them all excell.

With that I close, a fitting tribute to the 'pains I feel' ...

Keith wrote to the Stantons on 27 January, 1944:

- ... I am glad I was able to assist in the Christmas celebrations with the Oxford Group songs ... do you hear Cornelius's *Christmas Songs* in New York very much? I think they are beautiful, especially the 'Three Kings'. For several years in the 1930s I broadcast the cycle around Christmas Day ... your vivid description of the Christmas morning descent with candles to the dining room for stockings was joyful to read. It brought back to me how splendid you are to us and our girls ...

Christabel also wrote in January, happy she could now contemplate the return of her children:

> ... I do hope I shall not be too great a disappointment to either of them. Somehow I do not feel a very exciting woman ... living a life of a troglodyte does not make one glamorous. I have been talking to Keith about setting up house again ... I so much incline towards our re-union that I am apt to forget that the Atlantic is not cleared of all U-boats. But at any moment it may be! ... I am pleased to say we have found a piano and it is now on its way to Keith, so he can do lots of work in his off-duty time.

> [17 February:] Keith has had a nasty week of tonsillitis ... I contented myself by sending a few oranges, which have suddenly appeared on the market from a cargo which came interspersed with bombs from Spain! We await the second front and wonder where it will be ... there is a tense feeling in the air ...

Spring and summer passed and, with late autumn, we sailed home in convoy to dock in Liverpool. What a birthday present for Christabel! Full of excitement, we disembarked early with our 'nurse' and placed ourselves under a large 'F', sitting on our luggage. It was like Bedlam as families and friends rushed towards every letter of the alphabet. Philippa, pointing, exclaimed: 'Don't *they* look funny!' Sudden recognition: 'They're Mummy and Daddy!', I shouted, and ran.

- And, lo and behold! There were our two girls, full of life! Julia growing beautiful, Philippa full of life and excitement! And we had them home in time for Christmas.

Christabel wrote to the Stantons on 3 April 1945:

Keith did a brilliant broadcast last month and has had such a fan-mail. After one year's silence we feel so pleased ...

Keith was still on duty, of course. Then, on 5 May 1945, came worldwide jubilation, and immediately after VE-Day he and a number of controllers and technical officers were sent to Veile, on the west coast of Denmark, to examine a German-equipped radar station at work:

- The operation was routine and quite recognizable, while a dummy air-raid was laid on by Bomber Command. Only one innovation existed, that of a direct line to Hitler in case of invasion or other vital news. The next day the demobilised Germans set off for home carrying or pushing their belongings in anything on wheels. I was demobbed finally on 24 August at Uxbridge and given my 'hand-out' tweed suit, something received by all service personnel. I had expected to be chosen for a mobile radar unit for Normandy on D-Day, but suspect I was 'by-passed' for I was now forty-five. Looking back, Christabel and I were extremely lucky to have been posted fairly close for much of the war. To be back on 'civvy street" was sobering, rather like coming round from an anaesthetic. And so, family life resumed at Nettleden Farm.

Christabel to the Stantons on 26 November:

... [the children] are very well and preparing busily for parents' day ... Yes! Keith is expecting to go to Cincinnati for the May Festival BUT transport does not seem to be available. Cunard say they can do nothing unless and until K produces something from the Ministry of Information (!) to say his journey is really necessary. K has told Cincinnati ... but it would be grand if he could do the Christus in St Matthew, than which he does nothing better ... [nothing came of this] ... he is getting back into his stride, doing about two concerts a week, recitals and teaching ...

- I accepted an invitation from the Director of the Royal College of Music, Sir George Dyson, to teach one day a week and also took some private pupils at the Wigmore Studios. Singing engagements began to come in, however, but the concert world was not yet back to normal; conditions were still frightful, rationing still in force and train travel ghastly. What performances I had included a recital in Eastbourne with Eric Gritton, a Verdi *Requiem* in Leeds conducted by Sir Edward Bairstow with the tenor Peter Pears, the only time we sang together. There were also recitals in Durham, Bridlington and Tunbridge Wells, where it was nice again to meet up with Douglas Ian Akers, a fellow Free Forester. There was a *Messiah* at Harrow School, followed by a recital in Macclesfield with Pauline Juler.

The *Irish Press* on 28 January 1946 commented on a symphony concert with the Radio Eireann orchestra conducted by Captain Bowles. The soloist on the occasion was 'that admirable singer, Mr Keith Falkner. He gave a beautiful rendering of *Was durftet doch der Flieder*, from Wagner's *Die Meistersinger*.

- As I found these sporadic performances unsatisfying professionally, I applied for the job of Concert Manager of the Liverpool Philharmonic but without success. Wondering what the next move should be, I had lunch early in 1946 with Eric Gillett, whom I had not seen since the cricket tour with Clifford Bax's Old Broughtonians before the war. Having discussed the effect the war had had on our professional lives, I told him that, although I was beginning to pick up the threads again, my heart was not in 'it' in quite the same way. I had, after all, missed out five years, five years of what should have been the apogee of my career, not to mention the loss of family. I needed stability now, a family life. Gillett mentioned the British Council was anxious to appoint a Music Officer for Italy and urged me to talk with Seymour Whinyates. I hurried to do so. The first thing she asked was whether I would be interested in the position. Would I?! I was thrilled at the prospect. My old cricket crony Richard Rickett was also stalking the streets of London in search of occupation. Though a member of the Political Division of the Allied Commission in Austria, it was a temporary institution which would cease upon a state treaty being signed – in point of fact it was not until 1955.

Rickett recalled:

Keith and I eventually established a routine by which we would meet for lunch at a modest café appropriately situated near Wigmore Hall and exchange hopes and experiences. Keith's coup in securing an interview with the British Council seemed well out of my reach, but emerging from a maze of devious enquiries and rejections I found myself one day being encouraged by another British Council official, who assured me that, far from being irrelevant, membership of the Austrian Commission was a very valuable asset, whether I was interested in music or not. It would present the Council with a direct link with the Austrian Commission to which the Council was not officially affiliated. Whether I had any qualifications in the practice and administration of music was not of essential importance: what was needed was familiarity with Vienna and 'knowing the ropes'. So it was that, after satisfying administrative requirements, Keith and I found ourselves in the same boat, he in Rome and I in Vienna, which at that time was enmeshed in the tangled web of Allied Four-Power Occupation. The café by the Wigmore Hall seemed a long way off to both of us.

- There was much to sort out – Nettleden to be sold, which I shall ever regret, having bought it for £1,200 in 1937 [at today's prices probably worth some £300,000]; furniture stored; any number of family arrangements to be made. Meanwhile, I travelled daily to London to prepare for this new job, being introduced to the mechanics and administration of Music Officers abroad. On May 26 I met my new boss, the poet Ronald Bottrall, sensing my job would be under close scrutiny. Before I left for Italy I met with Professor Edward Dent, who gave me introductions to eminent Italian composers and conductors, giving sound advice when dealing with them. This was the spark that set my mind alight for my new job in sunnier climes.

Chapter 6: 1946–1950

Keith continues the story:

- On 4 July I set forth, leaving Christabel to pack and study Italian with the girls. The war barely over, remains of battle littered the countryside, unsafe tracks and temporarily repaired bridges making progress southward slow and difficult. Thus I arrived in Rome five days later, warmly greeted by Clive Robinson, the Administrator for the British Council. Other personnel were Ronald Bottrall, the Representative; Ian Greenlees as No 2; Ashmead Bartlett with Portraits and Books; and Beverly Reed. The Council had close association with Roger Hinks, Director of the British Institute, and Ward Perkins, Director of the British School.

  The four years we would spend in Italy were the most creative of my life so far for, up to now, I had done what I was trained to do: sing. This had provided great satisfaction, but contained little initiative beyond interpretation in song. Now I had to use my imagination, which led to musical activities of a much wider nature: friendships with administrators, composers, critics and performers would broaden my whole outlook on music.

  The family joined me in August and we settled briefly into the Hotel Excelsior before moving to the Villa Manzoni – the Manzoni of the Verdi *Requiem* – north of Rome. We chose an Italian school for the girls, where they quickly became proficient. Lessons were imperative for me in order to establish contact with musicians and to explore resources, though I never became fluent as my excellent bi-lingual secretary, the tiny Hilda Colucci, took control.

  For the most part the job went smoothly, with only occasional 'blockages' from on high, such as the time I received a memorandum informing me that a well-known English pianist was coming to Rome and that I must immediately arrange a recital for her. I felt unable to do so as, having passed her prime, she was unsuitable. A retort came down: 'You were asked to do something, *not* to give your opinion!' When such things occurred, I donned my Free Forester tie to remind me of better days.

Exercise was vital and Keith soon found it on the squash court of the British Embassy. Golf and cricket also appeared in the repertoire.

- I made a speedy trip to Allied headquarters at Caserta to learn what they were doing musically and ran into an old friend, Richard Tilney. Back in Rome, HMV gave me unlimited opportunities to meet conductors Serafin,

Molinari and Bellezza; the tenors Gigli, Lauri-Volpi and the new find, Di Stefano. Gigli particularly wanted to hear what threat Di Stefano might pose and so took his wife to the opera. After the first act he rose to go home, saying there was nothing to worry about.

In the *RCM Magazine*[1] an article entitled 'British Council Music Officer in Italy' appeared in 1947, summing up Keith's first year in Rome:

- In spite of the desperate economic position, opera was in full swing in the open air at the Baths of Caracalla when I arrived in the hot weather ... opera is as important to the Italian as football to the Englishman, and is treated in the same spirit.

  Opera apart, I was amazed by the intense vitality of music in Italy, though surprised to find so many English people who decried it, and disappointed that so many Italians just smiled at the mention of English music. It was a queer sensation suddenly to be among people who knew little of our music ... after a year here I am convinced that Italy stands second to none in practically every branch of music. How much is heard in England of Italian music outside opera? Yet in Italy orchestral and chamber concerts are as flourishing and certainly of as high a technical standard as anything we can show. With composers of the calibre of Malipiero and Pizzetti of the older school, and Dallapiccola, Petrassi, Tommasini, Cortese, Tocchi, Turchi, Zaffredi, Tosatti, etc, of the young and not-so-young school, there can be little wrong with Italian music. Here, of course, it is all taken naturally without much publicity. This is to be expected, for music in Italy has had a clear run for centuries.

  What has been done for English music? What is the British Council doing to assist it? ... It is impossible to assess the amount of good done by personal contact; by the number of letters written on or about English music; by lectures; by concerts; by articles in the press.

A very important part of the job was to arrange visits for English musicians and conductors, and to do this one had to deal with the concert agent Camus. With her help, and despite a paucity of funds, Keith was able to arrange tours for Sargent, Boult, Goossens and Barbirolli. Lady Barbirolli and Sir John were impressed:

Keith did marvels yet with almost no money, not to mention a difficult Chief. He always bemoaned that he only had something like £200 per annum to work with. It must have been very frustrating ... I recall him saying, 'If only I had more, I could do so much more!'

---

[1] For full text, see *The RCM Magazine*, Vol 43, No 3, 1947.

Before Sir John's first rehearsal with the Santa Cecilia Orchestra at the Argentina in 1947, I drove him around the Square as loud speakers, set up at my request on the American Services Network, blazed forth his recording of Elgar's Second Symphony. He was impressed. At rehearsal it was pure delight to observe his nurturing of the four string leaders as though they were a quartet, almost playing with them. He was a most dynamic figure and when he conducted there was no doubt he was Italian. There was also enjoyment when he was in Rome which, for Sir John, was a time of reunion. After a concert he would disappear into the kitchen to prepare delicious pasta, and once told the story of the invention of 'Tortellini' by a master chef of Bologna in the 17th century. One night, as he told it, the chef had a vivid dream of Venus and was allowed to examine her beauty in detail so that on waking, he rushed to his kitchens to form pasta in the shape of her navel!

Sir Malcolm Sargent visited frequently and, as I was often busy elsewhere, Christabel would be sent to meet him. 'Where's Keith?', he would demand. Informed that I was in, say, Venice, he would then ask where the reception committee was, but he was never objectionable. Sargent never travelled by public vehicle, as testified to by Herbert Howells, who met him waiting outside the Albert Hall one day and asked why he didn't catch a bus. 'Go on a bus?! I haven't been on a bus for twenty years! That's the fun of being a success!' And, his concerts were always so for with a delightful personality, immaculate dress and trim figure, punctilious in detail, he was an ideal conductor. Sir Malcolm was also noted for his risqué stories, often relating one about an Eastern potentate, guest of a city company, who ended his speech of thanks with, 'And I thank you, my Lord Mayor, from the bottom of my heart. My wife thanks you also from her bottom.'

My old friend Serge Koussevitsky soon followed with the young Leonard Bernstein in tow, to conduct the Santa Cecilia Chorus and Orchestra in the Verdi *Requiem*. At a break in rehearsal he demanded that I sing, for he didn't like the bass. Naturally this was impossible and would have caused a 'Turbo' chorus, while I would have been drawn and quartered.

Sir Adrian's visit was memorable, especially as his visit would have a bearing on the future. Eugene Goossens came and we spent some days in Naples with William Walton and his wife, sharing the hospitality of Jim Barber, Director of the British Institute. Sir William came to my office in Rome to introduce himself at a time when I was secluded in my office discussing the latest cricket matches with Clive Robinson. We were so engrossed that it was some time before I glanced at the visiting card deposited on my desk by the porter.

It was the habit among Italian critics to stand at the back of the hall during concerts, talking among themselves during performances unless there was something special to listen to. When Ben Britten and Peter Pears gave their first concert I was apprehensive but, after a few bars, the critics turned towards the stage, silent as they experienced something new and special. Eventually, I persuaded the Rome Opera to put on Purcell's *Dido and Aeneas* and Britten's *Rape of Lucretia* as a double bill. The latter was met with acclaim, much cheering and shouting from the 'Gods' during the rape scene. When I tried to persuade Dr Antonio Ghiringelli to do the same at La Scala, I was informed that it could not put on an English opera done elsewhere in Italy, but he would consider Bliss's *Olympians*. Though the performing material was produced, nothing came of it. In the end, La Scala put on a production of *Peter Grimes*, and sometime later I persuaded the RAI to give a studio performance of it with Previtali, astonished to watch him conduct the orchestra with separate conductors for chorus and soloists. It was efficient but amazing.

In mid-September 1946 the International Festival of New Music was held in Venice, a grand holiday for the family. The Grand Albergo was home while La Fenice was the site of the Festival, with conductors Gregor Fitelberg and Hermann Scherchen – Keith's first experience of the 'football crowd' attitude of Italian audiences as the whole house took sides to shouts of 'Bravo'' or 'Basta' with the atonal music.

Contact was soon made with the Accademia Musicale Chigiana in Siena, and a firm friendship formed with Count Chigi Saraceni. From this association, Keith was able to direct many English students to the school. He often transported musicians to Siena in an old Army pickup, and one winter offered to drive Gaspar Cassado and the conductor and pianist Maestro Zecchi. The route was rough going through the Sabina area, past Monti Sabini, on into Viterbo, up the hairpin bends of the high pass, to Aquapendente:

- On one occasion and having arrived at Aquapendente, the old PU had had enough, requiring temporary repairs. With Conte Chigi promising a car for the others (my last glimpse of Mo Zecchi was in a trattoria with his feet in a bucket of hot water as he was afraid of catching cold), I made my way back towards Rome with the 'rumblings abdominal' increasing alarmingly the further I went. Suddenly, the off-side wheel rotated madly ahead of me and bounced into a ravine. There was nothing for it but to set off on foot, so I hid my suitcase in some underbrush and set out. Around 3 am a farmer on his way to market offered a lift, and as we came down Via Cassia I jumped off and climbed over the high gates of Villa Manzoni, just managing to get indoors before attack by the Schnauzer guard dogs.

The music critic Paoli, sent to visit, England wrote: 'L'Inghilterra e l'anticamera del Paradiso!' And, indeed, so we found it in the summer of 1947, despite restrictions, when we returned for a short holiday. Christmas was spent in Positano, with its unspoilt charm, in 'Buca di Bacco', the cliff-hugging hotel. Throughout the four years, spare time did not really exist, though there can be no complaint about the pleasure of it all. Hundreds of picnics, spent in the company of Britten and Pears, Lord Harewood and his wife Marion honeymooning, Eugene Goossens, Rudolph Bing and others, in plentiful sunshine, good food and wine surrounded by the people, and language, made us feel Italian.

I had settled comfortably into my job when, to my surprise, I was invited by the Arts Council to appear for interview for the post of Music Director, to succeed Steuart Wilson. As I was too much involved and excited with work yet to be achieved in Italy, I refused this and other enticing invitations which came. I chose to wait for the 'one and only'.

A letter from P G Hurst now appeared in *Gramophone*, though nothing came of his request:

British singers of the first class are not so common in these days, and it is of importance that their work should be adequately recorded .... in my opinion, the work of Keith Falkner stands alone among British baritones today, although his appearances have never kept pace with his merit. His musicianship is above average, and his vocal technique and equipment surpass, as I believe, those of any baritone we could name. His power of interpretation is in a class apart, and he colours his voice to match his music, which is a rare enough accomplishment; and he can let us, if we wish, hear his words without breaking the vocal line, which is if possible rarer still. The traditions of oratorio are falling too much into decay, and it is too lightly assumed that the task of singing it can be undertaken without special training and study. We need Mr Falkner to correct this impression. Will the recording companies kindly note?

- I had great regard for Italian musicians, while Mo Glinski had great interest in the promotion of English music. The critics Mo Bonnocorsi and Mo Colacichi took a real interest in my work, as did Mo Razzi, Director of the RAI, and Mo Siciliani, Artistic Director of the Maggio Musicale in Florence and Perugia, giving friendly cooperation. I much admired Mo Corti, Director of the Santa Cecilia Orchestra, who often wrote to me after I had left, always asking whether my charming daughters still spoke classic Italian. The warmhearted and brilliant composers Dallapiccola and Petrassi often visited my office to discuss performances, while Pizzetti, the GOM of Italian composers, was friendly and generous, though he said once, after I had given a lecture on English music, 'An interesting talk about something that doesn't exist!' This reminds me of a critic who demanded, after a performance of Delius's *Walk to the Paradise Garden*, 'Quando commincia la musica?'

I particularly appreciated the conductors Guido Cantelli and Victor De Sabata. The latter once begged to hear Toscanini's recording of a Beethoven symphony so that he could learn how Toscanini had managed to get it on three or four double-sided 78s. We did so, and halfway through the first movement he 'knew', going off happily to do his own recording. The young composer and Mendelssohn Scholar Stephen Dodgson was a great addition as he helped with concerts at the British School and elsewhere. Giacomo Ghedini was another to be admired, especially for his edition of Carissimi's *Felicitas Beatorum*, heard at the Perugia Festival. He gave me a score and parts; we later performed the work for him with the *Collegium Musicum* when he came to lecture at Cornell in the 1950s. The pianist Alfredo Casella was also in Rome and he, Ward Perkins, the critic Rinaldi and composer Francesco Malipiero, all became good friends.

In due course a 'round the table' quintet was formed with singers Joy Hoodless and Vera Terry, Australian sopranos; Christabel, alto and piano; James Eagleson, American tenor, and Keith as organiser and bass. As cars were still difficult to obtain, he acquired through diplomatic channels a Fiat 'Millecento' for the eventful tours:

● Our first concert was for the Anglo-Italian Association in Camerino, the programme ranging from madrigals to solos, to Ernest Walker's *Songs of the Helicon*, to part-songs. Joy had flaming red hair and was always hailed by a barrage of admiration and catcalls each time she appeared to the packed theatre. Our hotel there was so cold that we all clamoured for hot-water bottles. 'Si, Si!' was the response, 'Il Prete!' What did we want with a priest, we wondered, but in this case 'Il Prete' turned out to be a long-handled copper bedwarmer.

It was on to more prestigious towns then, such as Perugia, Firenze and Siena, where the *Songs of the Helicon* were a great success with Conte Chigi, who demanded we record the cycle. In parting, he begged us to return next year, 'especially La Signora!' In Livorno we gave a concert to a full house. Beginning our last item, *Ilkla Moor baht 'at*, the chandeliers began to sway wildly amid ominous rumblings and shakings. The audience, in panic for it was a 'Terremoto', began to rush to the exits as the lights went out. With presence of mind, Jim lit his lighter while we resumed singing, calming the audience. As we finished the song, they applauded and left the hall to face a mass exodus of cars and carts leaving the city. We packed up and headed for Rome.

The 1948 summer holiday was spent enjoying the clear blue waters of the Mediterranean. Composer Jacques Ibert and his wife, a keen subaquean observer, were also in residence and it was, according to Keith, a daily delight to see only the bottom of her anatomy floating in the bay:

- When we first met at a dinner party in Rome, Mrs Ibert came up to me to say she understood a music officer had been appointed to the British Council. 'A nice man, I hear', she said. 'Do you know him?' I could only say yes, that of course I did.

On 28 August, Keith and Christabel teamed up with Gaspar Cassado, 'violoncellista', and Giulietta Gordigiani Mendelssohn, coll. al pianoforte, to present yet another concert at L'Accademia Musicale Chigiana. Keith's songs ranged from Monch von Salzburg, Dowland, Tobias Hume to Vaughan Williams, Britten and Korbay. A Dallapiccola cello solo followed, then the artists joined forces in *Six Studies in English Folk Song* by Vaughan Williams.

Life continued as busy as ever. A concert on 7 December for the British Council 'Concert Series of Italian and English Music and Musicians' had Keith and Christabel sharing the programme with Thomas Matthews (violin) and Eileen Ralf (piano). The Falkner contribution was *Celia has a thousand charms* and *What power art thou* (Purcell), *Non lo diro col labbro, I feel the Deity within*, and *Arm, arm ye Brave* (Handel).

- With Sir Victor Mallett's appointment as Ambassador to Italy, life became more social but greatest personal satisfaction came from lecture and recital tours presented between 1948 and 1950 with Francis Toye – a godsend for he knew everyone and spoke classic Italian.

Of these tours Francis Toye wrote in his book *Truly Thankful?*:

The two long series of tours undertaken in conjunction with Keith Falkner and his wife were perhaps the most interesting, as they were certainly the most enjoyable of all. Keith was – is – a dear friend who in the past had even worked as my pupil, an admirable singer and a fine musician ... we set out to illustrate English Song from Elizabethan times to the present day ... the lion's share of our success should be given to the Falkners ... I do know that the songs were liked and from chance remarks overheard I should say that this was a matter for surprise.

A lecture recital for the British Council Centre in Naples on 5 March 1949, presented a typical programme: *There is a Lady sweet and kind* (Ford); *What if I seek for Love?* (Robert Jones); *The Self-banished* (John

Blow); *What pow'r art thou?* (Purcell); *Advice (Maidens, beware ye)* (Richard Leveridge); *The Vagabond, Songs of Travel* (Vaughan Williams); *She came to the Village Church, O let the solid ground, Birds in the high Hall garden,* from *Maud* (Arthur Somervell); *Mally O!* (Herbert Howells); *So sweet Love seemed* (Robin Milford), and *Rollicum Rorum* (Gerald Finzi).

- Francis [Toye] would occasionally 'turn over' for Chris, though his arm was often in the way so that she had to butt him in order to read the notes. Our most enjoyable tour was to Sicily, visiting Palermo, Messina, Taormina, Catania, Siracusa, Agrigento and back to Palermo. At a social luncheon here, Francis was in a boisterously cheerful mood, arguing history and dates with an Italian duchess who became more and more exasperated. 'Well! How old do you think I am?' she demanded. 'Oh, ... about a hundred' he replied. 'No! Ma Guarda!' she exclaimed, and with laughter exposed her fine-looking bosom. On another tour to Trento, Toye discoursed in perfect Italian on English Song. When he spoke his native tongue afterwards, there was amazement that he could speak English so well: a great compliment. He spoke Italian so fluently that in 1951 he was invited to deliver the oration at La Scala on the 50th anniversary of Verdi's death.

A move, in 1948, to a large apartment in the Parioli made it easier to entertain visiting musicians. With the increasing traffic, a Lambretta, similar to the more popular Vespa, was bought to get to the office in record time.

- Though I had not played for a number of years, the Anglican Church asked me to be its organist. The loft in this huge edifice appeared suspended from on high, the congregation miles below. Julia often 'turned over' for me, though on one occasion Clive Robinson did so. As he turned the Psalms, I had an awful sensation for I suddenly had no idea which verse I was playing.

Early in January 1949 Keith set off for Naples with Eugene Goossens to meet with the Waltons to discuss changing the order in performance of *Façade*:

- My first performance of this work was in Florence, conducted by the American Newell Jenkins. Over the years *Façade* became a favourite which I performed many times. Following my meeting with Walton we all went to the opera to hear *Zaza* (Leoncavallo). The house boiled with excitement as Carlo Tagliabue and Giacinto Prandelli neared their top Cs.

  In April the International Society of Contemporary Music held its Festival in Palermo, with England represented by Constant Lambert, Humphrey Searle, Edward Clarke, Elisabeth Lutyens, and Frank Howes, *The Times* critic. Lambert conducted a piece by Searle but was in poor health, a pity to observe his physical decline; Frank's huge faded panama hat was much admired.

The summer holiday was spent on Elba, across the bay from Porto Ferraio. One guest was the cellist Joan Dickson, studying in Rome, who recalled her visit in 1991:

> ... the island was as romantic as it sounds, and was then completely unspoilt, as it had been forbidden territory in Mussolini''s time ... meals outside under the pine trees looking across the bay ... bathing from the private beach, rowing lazily in the bay and long walks on the very hilly terrain covered with rock-roses, an amazing variety of pines, visiting small villages and hamlets. Fascinating conversations with Keith as we toiled up some of the very steep hills, clambering over rocks ... we set out to climb Monte Cappanne ... Somewhere on the way I remember saying to Keith 'You would make a wonderful Director of the Royal College of Music!' I can picture that spot still ... no one was more thrilled than I was when his appointment as Director was finally announced some 10 years later.

- In September, Seymour Whinyates and *The Times* music critic Dyneley Hussey arrived by train in Siena to pay an official visit. The platform was mobbed and as I saw the Husseys trying to step out, Mrs Hussey's large hat was pushed off her head. Mr Hussey jamming his trilby firmly about his ears, drove into and through the scrum in true Twickenham fashion, making a passage for his wife. Seymour quietly emerged when two officials arrived to produce order. From my diary: Heard later *La Senna Festeggiante*, one of the thirty-three Cantatas by Vivaldi ... two delightful sinfonias and several splendid soli. Two for bass remarkably fine. Cesare Siepi possesses one of the best bass-baritone voices I have heard for some years – the only emotionally thrilling moments came from him, (though) he is inclined to bellow a little and missed chances of expression and contrast. The voice is rough-edged but it was sheer joy to hear a voice rich and even throughout its range F to F sharp. In the right hands, and given the intelligence, he could become a singer of real merit. Opera will probably swallow and spoil him.

In March 1950 the Istituzione Universitaria Concerti began its series of lecture-recitals. *Il Momento* (Rome) commented:

> ... a very good lecture on Purcell by Keith Falkner, Music Officer of the British Council in Rome. The lecture was followed by examples sung by Mr Falkner and the sopranos Vera Terry and Joy Hoodless, while Mrs Falkner accompanied on the piano.

Mr Falkner's lecture was a pleasant combination of learning and humour. Referring to the Westrup book on Purcell, he mentioned Byrd's first influence on the composer and the subsequent influence of Carissimi, Stradella and Lully; he then examined the characteristics of Purcell's style, and made a survey of the different types of his musical production. As a conclusion, the lecturer pointed out how too often England is referred to as 'the land without music'. The musical programme which followed convinced us that England is not a land without music. In this programme we heard alternatively some intensely dramatic arias and some gay ones, and the audience was greatly impressed by the beauty of them all.

The performance was magnificent. All artists showed a great love and intelligent mastering of the music. Mr Falkner had a great personal success, specially after the aria *What pow'r art thou?*, from *King Arthur*, in which his warm bass-baritone voice was at its best advantage, and after the 'rural' duet *Let us wander*, in which Joy Hoodless, a young Australian singer with a beautiful dramatic soprano voice, joined in a serene and unaffected rendering.

The final tour of the Madrigal Quintet took it, between 28 March and 2 April 1950, to Viterbo, Camerino, Perugia, Livorno and Siena. A review by *Il Mattino* on 9 April under the title 'At the Chigiana Academy in Siena – Concert by English Madrigalists' in part read:

> ... it is, in fact, common belief that English singers rank not among the best, and this prejudice was somehow chilling the enthusiasm with which we had accepted ... we must make honourable amends and admit that we had taken for granted an incorrect statement. We were drawn to admire and applaud the ensemble which performed in Siena, both for the accomplished art of the singers and for the spontaneous musicality and the joyous, attractive content of their 'conversational singing' .... We must admit that concerts are not always welcomed ... but this particular one ... was a charming exception, also because it was entirely devoid of pompous artifice ...

The 1950 recession called for cuts in the British Council's budget, with the arts the first to suffer. Keith's position would be scrapped at the end of August. What to do? A position with an Australian conservatoire was recommended by Eugene Goossens, while Sir Adrian, on tour in Italy, suggested a possible appointment with the BBC. His tour over, Sir Adrian went on to give a series of concerts with the Boston Symphony, staying with Doc Davison, then Head of Music at Harvard, who knew Keith well as they had met many times during the 'thirties. They discussed Keith's availability, Davison mentioning that Cornell University wanted to set up a voice department:

- I first knew of Adrian's recommendation when a call came from John Kirkpatrick asking if I would come to Cornell as Visiting Professor for two years, with a decision needed by early June. In the meantime, Ben Britten had booked me to sing Bach's solo Cantata No 56, *Ich will den Kreuzstab gerne tragen*, at the Aldeburgh Festival with the oboist Joy Boughton, Trevor Harvey conducting.

Under the headline 'Keith Falkner's Return', the *East Anglian Times* wrote of the –

privilege of hearing this famous bass-baritone again for the first time for many years. His singing of the solo part, one of the most exacting in the repertoire of vocalists, had all the old flexibility and authority. His control and phrasing are as fine as ever and his singing has, above all, that spiritual quality which makes him an interpreter of Bach's music par excellence.

Frank Howes, for *The Times*, wrote:

His singing ... had his own but now uncommon combination of warm tone and firm line and another rare combination of flexibility and certainty of intonation ...

All very well and good, but decisions had to be made. In the end it was the sportsman in Keith who decided the issue. While in Aldeburgh, Keith had taken a long walk along the salt flats towards Thorpeness where:

- I ran into Bruce Boyce, also singing at the Festival, who took one look at me and demanded why I was looking so worried. I explained and mentioned the choices. 'There's only one choice!', he exclaimed. 'It has to be Cornell!' Bruce had studied at Cornell and told me the golf course was next door to the music building. That settled it! I sent off a cable immediately, accepting the position for the Fall semester.

New adventures were again on the horizon but for the summer much remained to be done. After a final two-week holiday in the Tyrol, where Keith and Christabel had honeymooned twenty years previously, it was back to Rome, to pack and say goodbye:

On the night of 31 August we made our way to the Rome terminus for the night train to Genoa. I was very moved as members of the Council staff and many friends came to see us off, a host of regrets and well-wishing correspondence from critics and musicians all over Italy. We were sad to go as we would have been quite happy to spend the rest of our lives here.

Ten years later Frank Howes wrote about Keith's work in Rome in an article for *The Musical Times*, describing how he had brought out Britten,

Pears and Barbirolli among others, and had succeeded in getting English operas performed. He remarked on Keith's warm acceptance by the Italians:

> ... they liked the unfamiliar mixture of honest Englishman and sensitive artist, or cricket and music, so to speak ... The chance visitor from England who saw them (the Falkners) at work could be proud that his country was represented by two such personable and proficient ambassadors.

- Francis Toye hosted a final lunch party to wish us 'God speed', asking what I would do finally. I told him that I would love to go back to the Royal College of Music, in any capacity. We laughed as he replied: 'They'd never make you Director for you're not an organist!'

The Times reported on 8 September that Mr Keith Falkner would take up his two-year appointment, having since the war been conspicuously successful in commending English music to Italians, not least by his own singing.

In his autobiography Francis Toye wrote:

> ... In him I lost the oldest, in a sense the only, intimate man-friend I had in Italy. We had known one another for years; in the remote past he had even worked at his voice with me; latterly ... we made many joint tours of musical propaganda all over the country. It was a sad day indeed when I said good-bye to him at Genoa, whence he, his wife and family sailed for the States. There ... doing, I suspect, more rather than less for the cause of English music. The charm, warmth and simplicity of his personality should in America carry even greater conviction.

Chapter 7: 1950–1960

One could only wonder what awaited at Cornell, one of the finest universities of the Ivy League, an association of eight universities in the northeastern United States. In many ways it was fortuitous Keith's contract with the British Council came to an end in 1950, as four years in Italy was quite enough; it gets under your skin and unless outside volition is used, difficult to make up one's mind to leave. Yet we would have been content to stay had there been the possibility of eventual pensioned retirement for Keith.

So it was off to a close university faculty life with, again, an unlimited scope for creative ability. Sailing from Genoa in a freighter, cavorting dolphins escorted us as far as Gibraltar; then we passed out into the hurricane-swept Atlantic and the future.

The *Maria 'C'* docked on 22 September in Brooklyn, where John Kirkpatrick, Chairman of the Cornell Music Department, met us to escort us to Ithaca, situated at the foot of Cayuga Lake in up-state New York. We settled into a 'sabbatical' house, the first of five during the tenure, counting our blessings for the warm welcome.

Twelve years later Morris Bishop, in his *History of Cornell*, wrote:

> The Music Department outdid itself with its performance of the *St Matthew Passion* in 1950. To the stellar group of performers and scholars in the department was added the famous British singer Keith Falkner.

> When I first saw the building which housed the Music Department ... I couldn't believe my eyes. 'What?' I said, 'do you mean to tell me that this little house is the Music Department?' 'It's true,' they said. 'But,' said I, 'It's not a building – it's just a house!' 'That's right', said the upperclassmen. So I started up the twenty-three stone steps that lead to the porch ... the old house welcomes you, asks you to stay for a while, and to share in its riches of records, scores, practice rooms, listening rooms, and people ... warmth and intimacy infuses 320 Wait Avenue.[1]

• Within hours I reported for 'duty', the Cornell Music Department a refreshing challenge, buoyed up by the generous faith it had in me. I would be one of fourteen academic and performing musicians, required to teach

---

[1] *Cornell University Music Review* (Vol 2, No 1, Spring 1959) by Betsy Northrup ('58), a pupil of Keith's.

sixteen hours a week, the rest of my time to be spent developing music activities as I saw fit, with a date fixed for my first recital. The faculty was comprised of Chairman John Kirkpatrick, a fine pianist not only the classics but a splendid exponent of the American School as well; Donald Grout, a most sensitive performing musicologist, whose accompanying was superb in a lecture I illustrated for him of Schubert's songs. Later, in 1957, his conducting of the *St Matthew Passion* recalled performances I had sung with Vaughan Williams at Dorking and for the Bach Choir: a performance of great feeling and intensity. Bill Austin had a brilliant musical mind, able to transpose at sight, reminding me of Gerald Moore. Though our paths did not cross often, the composer Robert Palmer became a good friend. There were Harold Samuel, the organists Chuck McClain and Jack Carruth; Monroe Levin and Cameron McGraw with their splendid four-hand piano performances (Cameron went on to write the invaluable tome *Piano Duet Repertoire* (Library of Congress 1981); Vivian Laube, secretary and concert manager, who became good friends with Isobel Baillie when she succeeded me; Floyd O'Grady, the caretaker of Sage Chapel, a man dedicated to his job, ever-ready to help when we staged performances such as Honegger's *King David* in the Chapel; and the composer Gilbert Weeks, President of the Friends of Music, whose wife Ann provided lavish hospitality and encouragement. Gil wrote *The Triple Foole* for me, which I sang both at Cornell and Wigmore Hall in 1955.

In up-State New York, winter can arrive with lightning speed. The budget did not allow a car, so we walked everywhere and on one mild evening made our long way to Bailey Hall for a performance of *Elijah*. We emerged, hours later, to howling winds and a blizzard of snow. Winter had arrived.

- On 9 December, I drove to Syracuse to hear Sir Thomas Beecham conduct the RPO. Backstage he demanded to know what I was doing there. 'Come and sing the *Messiah* next month for me in London!' This, of course, was not possible with my new duties.

My routine was soon established. A main concern was that most of my students produced the same open American 'AAH' sound to all vowels. I mentioned this at a faculty meeting, saying I could not get a beautiful sound until the basic vowels were established. A professor asked what I considered to be beautiful sound, he preferring the Chinese Far-Eastern way of singing. Western singing demands the universal vowels to produce beautiful tone to interpret Western music. I was advised to see the linguistics professor, who was not much help: 'Tharn't no pure vowels! Say "Orange" for me.' I 'oranged'. 'Yes', he said, 'you've got a southern English accent' and proceeded to show me a map of the United States which showed where all ethnic groups had settled. 'All I have to do is ask a student to say "orange" and I know exactly where they come from.' I went back to work and gradually began to find singers keen and able to prepare simple classics for our student concerts. Quality and content increased.

Over the decade Keith sang in a number of concerts and recitals, most in the 'Sunday Afternoon Series', the first occurring in February 1951 to a packed house. With Christabel as his accompanist, the programme consisted of folk-songs of the British Isles. In March he re-established contact, made before the war, with Wells College in Aurora, giving a similar recital.

The Cornell campus hosted many sporting activities, though few colleagues were interested except for some students and Robert Hull, conductor of the University orchestra. On a number of occasions William Campbell, University and Marching Bands Director, would 'sneak' Keith through the back door for basketball games, varsity football and other intermural events:

- Campbell called my attention to band music by such English composers as Walton and Gordon Jacob. He also told me that on my arrival on campus he thought I was just another 'boiled-shirt' Englishman but had since changed his mind, saying: 'Now, I know you're not!'

  I enjoyed singing even more now that I no longer had to think of it as my main source of income. I was content with my job, the encouragement to sing as much as I liked, happy to have ample time to work on my voice, but the $2,500 pa was still a worry. Fellow faculty members suggested each of us find a summer job, so I placed an advertisement in *Time Magazine*, offering Chris and myself as butler and cook, two teenage daughters as waitresses. There was only one reply, which asked: 'Why not come South to Carolina? Pick my apricots, share proceeds. Daughters can sell ice-cream on the Highway'.

This suggestion was not taken up and the senior Falkners spent that summer clearing woods around Dorothy Stanton's new home in Connecticut. In ensuing years, Keith's income would be supplemented by summer-school work at Cornell and three tours for the Associated Board.

- Eleven years had passed since I had sung with Koussevitsky. I was now approached by the manager of the Boston Symphony Orchestra to see whether I would be interested in singing the *St Matthew* under Pierre Monteux. I auditioned for the 'Christus' and Monteux appeared pleased, though I heard no more for some months. Then came a telephone call informing me of dates of rehearsal and performance but, as this conflicted with the Cornell performance and recording of Handel's *Alexander's Feast* on 16 March in Rochester, I sadly had to refuse.

The violist and long-time friend Bernard Shore, HMI for Music in England, came on an official visit early in April 1952. July was busy with a move into the home of Morris Bishop, on sabbatical; and there was a song recital whose programme consisted of songs from the 16th, 17th and 18th centuries, when the temperature was 92°:

- I was in the long runs of 'How Jovial' when a large black fly buzzed around my head, to hover just below my nose. With the next intake of breath I would have sucked it straight down my throat. So I stopped to bat it away, and continued with 'my laughter'.

The *Ithaca Journal* reported:

> ... Aiding Mr. Falkner on his highly successful program was Mrs Christabel Falkner, who, always in excellent form, provided sypathethic and most proficient accompaniment at the piano. Elements of mystery still concern at least a few of us of the jam-packed and appreciative audience – did Mr Falkner ever catch the fly who, obviously no respecter of Bach, attempted to horn in on a cadenza ... ?

After a lone break at Eaglesmere, Pennsylvania, for golf and study, Keith was back on campus to teach and finalise plans for a tour to Bermuda with John Hunt, arranged by Ibbs & Tillett. They arrived on 6 October for performances, interspersed with golf and dinner parties:

- I was well pleased with the result of the new resonant approach to my production, as it carried me through much better than recent experience. I was conscious though that I had 'given' too much, strain evident in the voice, although the bloom was still there, just the thickness to be avoided. Contact with the audience on the 10th was better. John played Chopin beautifully.

In November, Christabel made a trip to England, her first in two years. John Hunt had been appointed to teach at Cornell for a semester and in this same month presented a programme with Keith, the complete *Dichterliebe* cycle; this was recorded. Of the concert, the music reviewer for the *Cornell Sun* wrote:

> ... The consummate musicianship of Mr Falkner and Mr Hunt gave a searching quality to the Schumann Lieder, a searching that penetrated deep to reveal a personal and profound meaning in the score and in Heine's text.

Hunter Johnson told me that this was the greatest performance of this cycle that he had ever heard.

During Thanksgiving break, the two went off to Keene, New York, in blizzard conditions, to walk the Little and Big Crows and to climb Noonmark. Several days later they drove to Saranac Lake, where Donald Grout gave a lunch party for the Klemperers and Galkin, all making music together. Christabel returned in December to be followed in January 1953 by the Griller Quartet, for a series of concerts.

Also in January came an invitation from Earle Moore, Director of Music at Ann Arbor, who had conducted Keith in Elgar's *Caractacus* at the Ann Arbor Festival before the war, eager for Keith to consider an appointment as head of that University's Voice Department. On the heels of this came an invitation from Dean Clarke, at McGill University in Montreal, asking Keith to consider the position of Dean of Music. Then Yale offered a similar appointment:

- Any one of these jobs would have been of considerable financial benefit, but the regimented timetable was a very different life to the free artistic development allowed at Cornell. Furthermore, I had been appointed Associate Professor and was content to stay.

Federico Chisi, the Florence University musicologist, now came to give a series of lectures and attended the performance of his realisation of Carissimi's motet *Felicitas Beatorum* sung by Keith's students.

March saw another recital; accompanied again by John Hunt, the whole programme was devoted to Schubert and Beethoven. On 22 March there was a performance of the Mozart *Requiem* with Keith's students. Spring recess was again spent at Keene; then in April came a student recital, and the final recording of *Dichterliebe* was made. Throughout the spring there were the inevitable cricket matches.

- The Associated Board took me off for a two-month coast-to-coast tour of Canada beginning in May, examining with Douglas Hawkridge. We were in Winnipeg when I listened to the broadcast of the Coronation, tears rolling down my cheeks. In Vancouver an amusing episode occurred after we examined our last candidate, a Chinese girl most elegantly and beautifully dressed. Her performance for the GRSM Diploma was fine, Douglas and I thinking in terms of 'Distinction'. The invigilator approached afterwards, exclaiming, 'You've no idea what that girl said as she left! She said she'd like to spend a weekend with one of you, the rest of her life with the other!' Douglas and I looked at each other, speculating on our qualifications.

With Keith away, Christabel spent part of the summer with 'Fannie Farmer' of cookbook fame. The Fall semester began with teaching and preparing a programme entitled 'Words and Music' in conjunction with Morris Bishop. Accompanied by Christabel, this was presented on 22 November. The concert was identical in content to that given later in the Wigmore Hall in January 1954: *O Willow willow* (anon), *Farewell my Lute* (Gerstman), *Sweet Kate* (Jones), *Sweet, stay awhile* (Dowland), *The Triple Foole* (Weeks), *To Althea* (Parry), *Have you seen but a white lily grow?* (Delius), *Ethiopia saluting the Colours* (Wood), *Birds in the High Hall Garden* (Somervell), *The Clock of the Years* (Finzi), *Severn Meadows* (Gurney), *So Perverse* (Bridge), *All day I hear the noise of many waters* (Goossens), *Old Sir Faulk* and other excerpts from Walton's *Façade*.

For the 1953 Christmas concert with the Sage Chapel Choir, Keith sang *The Three Kings* (Cornelius) before he left for England to present two recitals with John Hunt in Wigmore Hall, the programme as mentioned above, given on 7th and 12th of January, 1954. On the 20th, he was soloist in a performance of Mozart's *Requiem* in the Albert Hall. From letters to Christabel and diary:

- [22 December:] ... I never by any chance, day by day, let you know how much I love you and depend on you ... Just please remember that you have been my life for so long now that I can't show my emotion all the time ... anyway I pray for you to be near me all my life ... Walked into Conraad Van Bos, then into the Laurelton Hotel, where I found Myra (Hess) ...

  [25 December, aboard the *Queen Mary*:] ... The further I get from you, the more I realise how much I love you. It is so sad that this sort of thing has to happen to make me alive to the fact that my life has revolved around you for twenty-eight years and that I can't conceive of it without you for long. Already I'm looking forward to the return trip ... Cherbourg tomorrow, then Southampton ... O dear, I wish you were with me ...

  [29 December:] ... John Hunt's for rehearsal of most of English group ... Nice to see my name on the Albert Hall boarding once again ... Lunch with Adrian (Boult) and 'the Master' (RVW) and his new wife ... went to Kingsway Hall to hear a Decca recording session of the 'Wasps' overture. Please ring and tell Donald (Grout) that I believe I shall be able to persuade him (RVW) to do an American tour next Fall and to use his ingenuity to see if 'ways and means' can be found ...

  [New Year's Eve:] Mein traut Geseel, mein horchster Hort, iss dass dir wienschen meine wort. Auf den Tag so dass Jahr aufacht, etc, etc! ... There's no one like you ... It's so curious that it should give me great satisfaction to sing of unrequited love in *Dichterliebe* and to have the most blissful time of my life with you! ... So thrilling and exhausting being in London again. I find myself stepping out each day with the thoughts and attitude of the '30s – then I catch sight of myself in a mirror and am at once shocked into 'Be your age, you silly old fool!'

[7 January 1954:] ... John and I are going to do our Schumann programme at Balliol at Oxford on the 24th ... this is the day ... your cable just in ... I'll do my best for you tonight ...

[While from the diary:] ... All very heartening but frightening. Hall manager Brickell said it all sounded beautiful. Said Herbert Howells had been to buy tickets and recalled the wedding work he wrote for C and me ... nearly full house ... all the colour seemed to work ... given a wonderful reception, all very moving and exhausting. Emmie (Tillett) said: 'The old magic was there and you made me think of Kathleen (Ferrier) ...'

[7 January, 10.40 pm:] My own true love ... OH! I do wish you could have been there ... just to hold my hand and catch my eye. I should be shouting from the house-tops that so much of musical London was sitting like a mouse at my feet – but it was nerve-wracking in an entirely new way. To see so many old colleagues and revered people was a stimulation and a help – RVW, Epsteins, Bullock, Steuart, Roy Henderson, Robert Easton, Suddaby, Bruce Boyce, Howells, Lush, Lofthouse, Clives - a host of people ... I felt the sympathetic feeling at once and the stir that comes ...

[11 January:] ... Such stimulating letters have come in from so many people – I can hardly wait to get back to get down to hard work. My mind is anxious to explore all the possibilities for us for our next go! I must go on singing and find my salvation somehow from the technical problems ...

[Following the second concert, on 13 January:] we thoroughly enjoyed ourselves and the audience did too. I do wish you had been there and in many ways sharing it with me on the platform. John, being an outsider so to speak, has given me a new lease of life but don't ever forget my sweet there is no one in the world who can play for me as well as you do .... The programme held together. Sang 'Sir Faulk' twice, 'Roadside' and 'Mally' (and) heard RVW was tickled to death ... The Genoa Consul General was there – a host including Isobel Baillie, who insisted on taking my autograph ... It's been wonderful and I'm all moithered. I've got to go on singing, quite obviously. There's so much work to do and so little time ...

'Keith Falkner's Return', reported the *Daily Telegraph*, on the 13th:

Keith Falkner and John Hunt gave their second joint recital to a warmly appreciative audience at Wigmore Hall last night. The pianist played German classics and then accompanied Mr Falkner in an anthology of English songs ranging from Robert Jones and Dowland to Gurney and Walton.

For long an absentee in foreign parts, Mr Falkner – a leading oratorio singer 20 years ago – has retained admirers here who are delighted to welcome him back. His warm-toned voice is indeed a pleasure to hear and his selection included many gems. The audience was much impressed by Finzi's sombre Hardy song *Clock of the Years* ...

[16 January:] ... wonderful letter from RVW. 'You were magnificent the other night. Christopher Finzi was bowled over by your singing of his father's song ... or rather *we* were bowled over – we certainly were.' All very thrilling ... I hear the queue on Tuesday stretched nearly to the end of the Hall, waiting to come round to the Artists' Room ... Reminded me how important to take in your audience for that second before getting serious and starting ... Myra's dictum: 'All the qualities of giving a good party'.

The performance of the Mozart *Requiem*, on the 20th in the Albert Hall, consisted of a small choir, the Philharmonia Orchestra, and Colin Ratcliffe, Pauline Brockless, Norma Procter, David Galliver and Keith as soloists.

- [From the diary:] ... a good house. Refreshing performance without much finesse – very good blend, quartet fine. The trombone led me a dance, taking the 'Tuba Mirum' so slowly that I nearly didn't hold it out! Nice to be back in the Albert Hall, apart from the usual nerves.

Letter from Bruce Flegg to Christabel dated 14 February 1954:

... Keith will have told you what a tremendous success his whole visit was. I doubt if he told you how superbly he sang at his second concert too – but he did and, he will have told you, packed full of musicians. This final long group was most interesting and full of lovely things. John Hunt played for him and for himself very finely too. Keith must feel very happy and gratified over it all and he gave us, with John, a really splendid party before he left ..

- At a luncheon on the 23rd at the RVWs with the Finzis I brought up the subject of America again, hoping to persuade RVW to visit Cornell in particular. Ralph said he would love to, enthusiastically recalling the fall colours on a previous visit. Cables sent to the Music Department and Myra Hess turned wheels, with enough money found to offer a Visiting Professorsbip for the Autumn term of 1954, followed by a lecture tour through the United States so that Ralph could see the Pacific and Grand Canyon.

[Letter dated 27 January:] ... *Dichterliebe* – our best performance to date! .
Much relieved and thankful to the Almighty for making everything so
splendid for me for these concerts ... To Elmer Cotton's athletic store to see
if he could provide a cricket mat second-hand. I said, 'You won't remember
me – Keith Falkner.' 'Good Heavens! Of course I do', he replied. I
remember you getting a century against Oxfordshire at Fenners.' What better
thing could he have said? I expected 'Oh, you are a BBC baritone.'

[2 February:] My Darling, I'm nearly on my way longing to get home to you
and only wish we could have a few days without interruptions! ... I hope you
will fill my arms before many nights are over ...

All in all, it had been a most successful venture and Keith returned home
on the 8th, eager to get on. The rest of February was a busy month with
student examinations, recitals, visits from the Stanley and Hungarian
Quartets, not to mention an Heptagonal Track Meet. On March 12 he was
in Rochester for a Philharmonic concert, travelling on to Montreal, where
he sang *Ich habe genug* with the McGill CMS. He was there again on 4
April, this time for a broadcast of *Façade* in a French programme for
CBF and Mutual Broadcasting System (USA). Back at Cornell, Keith
was narrator in Honegger's *King David* on March 25th, with John
Kirkpatrick conducting his own translation of the work. Monroe Levin
recalled the experience recently:

> ... Nobody I have talked to who was there has ever forgotten that
> performance ... the main reason was Keith's speaking voice ... It even
> overcame the limitations of translating simple French words into English.
> John Kirkpatrick's choice for David's farewell to life, 'Cette vie était si
> bonne!' worried me: 'This life has been so wondrous!'. Keith leaned into the
> 'N' sound just the way a French actor would have done, and Sage Chapel
> was reduced to tears.

Throughout May there was much cricket and another student recital.
Another performance of *Façade* came in Montreal on 21 July for CBC
Television before a short holiday, again on Nantucket and notable for two
reasons: hurricane Carol roared up the Eastern Seaboard, and a telephone
call from the Cornell golf pro:

- He told me that Sam Snead had been doing some camera shots on the course
  when, returning to the clubhouse, he saw sticking out of my bag a hickory-
  shafted putter circa 1925. He took a fancy to it, telling the pro that if he could
  have it I could have any club I liked in exchange. Nothing doing: the putter
  a most prized possession.

The 1954 fall semester began, with the anticipated arrival of RVW on campus on 24 September. He was, of course, enormously popular with the students, who flocked to his lectures:

- One of my students told me how wonderful he was. 'Next time I'm going to get there early, if only to sit and look at him!' A number of amusing happenings occurred during Ralph's stay. At a party arranged with the Folk Song Club, RVW sat in a large chair with two girls perched on either side. In all innocence one asked whether he knew the song 'Greensleeves' – he who had composed myriad variations of the tune. Kindly he said that he did and why didn't she sing it for him. On another occasion Ralph suggested the composition students might like to show him their works, an offer enthusiastically taken up. One young lad, a composer of brass band music, came along with a lengthy, dissonant score. To save time RVW suggested the student play a reduction on the piano. At its conclusion he observed: 'If a tune should occur to you, my boy, don't hesitate to write it down.'

It was a full semester. In October, Kubelik was also on campus with the Concertgebouw. On the 26th, Keith was again in Montreal, for the first public performance in that city of *Façade*, conducted by Alexander Brott. The *Montreal Gazette* reported:

... the *pièce de résistance* of the evening was William Walton's *Façade* in its original form. Keith Falkner paid us a very welcome return visit, but this time as a speaker of Edith Sitwell's verse instead of his better-known role as baritone. Here was distilled the very essence of the 'twenties in highly concentrated form. Standing at a desk vaguely reminiscent of a Presbyterian pulpit, Mr Falkner declaimed with urbane gusto the tongue-twisting, ear-tickling impertinences of Sitwell's poetry. He became in so doing the very embodiment of that epoch of country houses and travel on the Continent ... Mr Falkner is indeed a versatile man to be able to excel in this rather specialised field ...

Keith was back at Cornell in time for a Vaughan Williams lecture which he illustrated in song. Then on 9 November, under Robert Hull, the Buffalo Philharmonic, Cornell A Cappella Chorus and Sage Chapel Choir presented a Vaughan Williams Concert, with the composer as guest conductor. On the 14th, accompanied by Christabel, Morris Bishop and Keith presented a variation to their previous *Words and Music* programme on the theme *The Seasons in Poetry and Song*. The recital included *Menelaus* from *Four Last Songs*, which RVW had given to Keith, and concluded with an epilogue, *So the Year's done with* (Ernest Bryson).

The first performance in America of *Sancta Civitas*, conducted by Josef Krips, was given in Buffalo on the 22nd, before which RVW conducted the *Tallis Fantasia*. In her biography of her husband, Ursula Vaughan Williams commented on the *Sancta Civitas* performance:

> ... It was a work which Dr Krips knew well and the choir, trained by Hans Vigeland, sang as if they had known the music all their lives, and Keith was magnificent. Ralph said it was one of the best performances he had ever heard, and, as it was his own favourite of his choral works, he was very happy ...

Thanksgiving came, and with it a round of parties before the Falkners joined Ralph and Ursula in Rudolph Bing's box at the Met for a performance of *Aida* on the 30th. 1 December found them at Yale for a lecture and recital of folk-songs:

- Ralph liked to find Ursula in the audience, so that she could indicate that everything was going smoothly. As I got up to give several examples – *Bushes and Briars*, *Searching for Lambs*, *Souling Song* and *Seventeen come Sunday* – not being able to locate Ursula, RVW whispered: 'Where is she?' 'She's at the back of the hall,' I whispered back. Years later, at a rehearsal of the Glee Club, Mr Schiller, the conductor, told me he had a recording of this lecture and said he was mystified by some strange sounds on the tape. These, I told him, were the whispered exchanges over the whereabouts of Ursula.

Preparing to return to England, RVW wrote on 2 December:

> But it is *you we* have to thank for your wonderful hospitality to both of us. Owing to you and Donald [Grout] we had a wonderful time – and if I have been of any good to the cause of music you know how proud I shall feel – and then you crowning your good by bringing my dry bones to life by your wonderful singing at Yale. We sent a cable to Walton in the name of us four.

Keith was back in Montreal on 5 December for yet another performance of *Façade*, this time for CBC television. There was another student concert on the 8th and on the 12th *Messiah* was sung in Sage Chapel before the Christmas recess. 1955 began with a performance of *Ich habe genug*, which Keith sang again in March. On the 24th, with Evangeline Bicknell, a faculty wife, he sang a concert performance of Purcell's *Dido and Aeneas* conducted by Robert Hull:

- Evangeline had a beautiful mezzo voice and gave a splendid performance of *When I am laid in earth*, though it was touch-and-go, for two days later she gave birth to a daughter, who was, of course, named Dido. Another student of mine, a faculty wife who shall remain nameless, wished to be introduced to lieder so I gave her Schumann's *Frauenliebe und Leben*, which she refused to sing. 'No decent American woman', said she, 'thinks like that about a man!'

The final part of *Messiah* was performed in April with students and Keith. It was followed in May by a performance of the *Deutsche Requiem* (Brahms) in which both Helen Boatwright and Keith sang. On the 19th he left for London to sing in the series of six concerts for the Arts Council of Great Britain's on 'English Song', held between 26 May and 30 June. For the first, on the 26th, Keith shared the Ralph Vaughan Williams programme with Nancy Evans, Richard Lewis, accompanist Michael Mullinar and the Hirsch String Quartet. His contribution: *The Vagabond*, *Let beauty awake*, and, *The infinite shining Heavens*, from *Songs of Travel*, and *Lovesight* from the *House of Life*. He also gave the first performance in England of RVW's *Menelaus: On the beach at Pharos*.

For the Council's fifth programme, on 23 June, he appeared with Sophie Wyss, Flora Nielsen, Wilfred Brown with the pianist Eric Gritton and harpist Marie Korchinska. Accompanied by Gritton, Keith sang *Seven American Poems* by Arthur Bliss, settings of poems by Edna St Vincent Millay and Elinor Wylie.

Around this time, Keith was invited to apply to succeed Sir Ian Hunter as Director of the Edinburgh Festival, but was too happy with life at Cornell to even consider it.

Naturally, Keith was at Lord's for the Test Match during June and on the 30th joined Hilary Macklin, of the Associated Board, for the Henley Regatta – Cornell versus the Russians in the semi-final of the Grand.

On 21 July he set sail for South Africa to adjudicate for the Associated Board:

- The tour was arduous but I enjoyed travelling up and down the country by train, attending the social and sporting events in Johannesburg and Capetown. Solomon gave a splendid recital, the last time I heard him in public. I visited my sister's family before returning via Rome, in late September.

The fall offered a number of interesting concerts. On 9 November, John Kirkpatrick put on a unique performance of the *Messiah* in its entirety.

- As important as its music, every word was sung, with some 'da capos' omitted, making it possible to perform as a single concert. It was fascinating and gave me the opportunity to sing the middle section of 'The trumpet shall sound' and the rarely performed 'Thou art gone up on high', the whole effect of text unfolding. My fellow performers were Helen Boatwright, Margaret Tobias and William Tanner.

The *Ithaca Journal* reported:

> ... [a] musical high-point of the present concert season in Ithaca. It would have been good were it done with a professional orchestra and a chorus like the Bethlehem Bach Chorus; done with Cornell and Ithaca musicians and the Sage Chapel Choir, it was magnificent ... A serious attempt was made to recreate the kind of performance that Handel's audiences heard ... the soloists did wonderful work ...

- The splendid composer and conductor Karel Husa had recently arrived to be part of the Department and we made music together as often as possible. Tom Sokol also came to take over the Sage Chapel Choir and Cornell Glee Club, which to date had been rather isolated from the Department. Under Sokol it would achieve national importance. We became great friends, both on platform and golf course, which by now sported eighteen difficult holes.

A performance of RVW's *Fantasia on Christmas Carols* was given on 18 December with Keith singing 'splendidly', though the *Cornell Sun* found the choice of work unimpressive. On the 27th, Keith sang *Where'er you walk* at my wedding.

It might appear that Keith was largely pursuing his own interests and career while at Cornell. Not so, for while he *was* involved in this, most of his time was taken up with students. He was in fact able to develop the voice department gradually, eventually providing all the adult soloists for *Noye's Fludde*, Bach's *Magnificat* and the *B Minor Mass*.

- It was slow going to begin with, the first lot of students disappointing in that, used to helping young professional singers, I had to adapt to students for whom 'applied music' was only one phase of their university training. All were a delight to teach because they loved to sing. One of the most interesting students in the first years was John Bergsagel, who not only had a pleasing baritone but was a composer and fine musicologist as well. He went on to Oxford to specialise in Medieval Music and returned to Cornell to pass the 'Viva' for both Masters and Doctorate on the same day. Graduate student Barbara Lee worked with me throughout the ten years, undertaking my teaching schedule during my sabbatic year. There were so many I remember with affection.

  Only once was I sadly disappointed. At a faculty meeting I was asked for a report on a student who, while she had a nice voice, hadn't done a stroke of work. Thanked for my comments I was told similar reports had been coming in from all her professors, so that she had to go. I felt sorry for if I had spoken less harshly she might perhaps have been reprieved.

Some students gave amusement,such as the lad who rang to say: 'Hey Prof! I'd like to take some of that vocal tuition of yours!' In class, I noticed other students eyeing him with adoration. It turned out he was in the 'Top Ten' and had earned over $100,000 the previous year. I was suitably impressed. At his agent's suggestion he told me he needed some training as his next records had to be lyrical. So he sang for me, yodelling, without any sense of quality or control, leaving me tempted to ask if he could teach me how to earn $100,000 per annum! Another, captain of the Lacrosse team, presented himself to talk 'private like', his problem a matter of holding a tune. Singing Cornell songs returning from away games, the team always told him to shut up. But he was a one-note-man, with D below middle C his base, and nothing would shift him to C sharp or E flat. Finally I asked if he had a girl friend. 'Sure! She's a music major', he replied. I suggested she probably could teach him better than I. Sometime later, I saw him on campus and asked how he was getting on, 'Oh! Just fine, Prof!' During my last years Elly Applethwaite, a law student, developed into a fine mezzo of rich quality. She came to see me in 1990 and recalled that her mother had been greatly concerned about our relationship:

'I first met Professor Falkner in the fall of 1956 ... in the 1958/59 academic year he and I sang Bach's *Wachet auf* in St Paul's Chapel at Columbia University with Tom Sokol and Choir ... I believe I was the only black singing that evening. The audience, however, was highly integrated because my mother had brought out the troops. A year after my mother died in 1964, an aunt tells me that when we came out at the beginning of the second half, my mother turned to her with a sigh of relief and remarked: "Thank God! He's an old man!" I had been writing home about my pleasure and excitement of studying with Professor Falkner and had talked about him even when at home. My mother had come to the conclusion that her daughter was in danger of being seduced, going regularly to church to pray for my virtue. Her prayers were answered. I came across a letter recently that he sent me after one of my recitals. It was a critique ... I don't know whether he was too soft-hearted to give correction in person or whether, knowing me, I simply didn't take to correction well. Whatever the reason, I was sent a letter in which I was complimented, then told in some detail how it could have been improved.'

Early in 1956, Keith's students performed the solo parts in the *B Minor Mass*. In April he was on the platform to sing *Three Psalms* by Edmund Rubbra, dedicated to Kathleen Ferrier, with the Ithaca Chamber Orchestra and Cornell A Cappella Choir.

Seven years had passed and it was time to plan for sabbatical leave, during six months of the 1956/57 academic year, to adjudicate for the Associated Board in New Zealand. Leaving Ithaca on 20 May, the Falkners flew to Panama to board ship bound for Wellington. The *New Zealand Herald* published an article on 19 June under the heading 'Man Whom Many Young Musicians Will Face':

> A man who means a great deal to young musicians began yesterday to examine some of the many young performers he will meet in New Zealand between now and December ... Professor Falkner has been examining musicians for 20 years, and during that time has been to many parts of the world in a sphere where race or language does not matter. A keen singer himself, he will, while in New Zealand, take part in several recitals together with his wife and Dr C Thornton Lofthouse, the other examiner.

All in all, 2,500 candidates were heard, 1,800 theory papers marked, some 90 Diploma candidates judged. In addition, Christabel and Keith gave six recitals and five illustrated talks on 'What is good singing?' for NZBC. On 3 October there was a performance of *St Matthew* given with Keith and Wilfred Brown, Charles Lofthouse, harpsichord, with James Robertson conducting the National Orchestra. On 20 November, in Wellington, Keith narrated *King David*. After a recital on 12 December the *Christchurch 'Press'* reported:

> ... Mr Falkner, ... one of the greatest baritones England has ever had ... What he can give to talented young people of the United States will do them more good than most of the other things that are being quietly filched from England. In his singing, all the essential of technique can be clearly heard. They seem easy, but are very hard to master. However, if they can be heard all gathered together – clarity of enunciation, purity of vowel differentiation, breathing that supports and is always at one with the voice, a placing that can produce ringing tone and also the pianissimo that has character and will carry a wide range of dramatic colouring, and all the rest of it – then the fortunate student can know what is his goal, and can be inspired to go through all the gruelling labour to try to reach it.
>
> ... In the programme there was one item of outstanding interest ... hearing a new song (*Menelaus*) by Vaughan Williams is enough of itself to mark out an evening.

• I recorded *Façade* for the NZHC on 18 December with Robertson and was then free to take a welcome Christmas break. New Zealand was great fun as we saw it under ideal conditions; the clean air and space appealed to us, the travel breath-takingly beautiful yet awesome, our time spent at the Fox

Glacier Hotel was a fine reward for all the hard work which renewed our energy for sailing back to pick up the strings. Before we sailed, we received a telegram informing us we were grandparents to Jeffrey Keith. We were delighted, though as I said to Christabel, it's not that I mind being a grandfather, but I do object to being married to a grandmother!

It was 1957 as we made our way home aboard the *Rangitiki*, trade winds blowing: 'Day-long, night-long the cool and pleasant breeze' (Masefield) from *Saltwater Ballads*. Chris and I parted, she to fly on to England, I to return to Cornell, where I was invited to stay as faculty guest at the Telluride Association, founded in 1910 by Lucien L Nunn. It was a new experience living with some thirty stimulating, friendly and intelligent young men who were the trustees of a four-million-dollar endowment, responsible for the direction and administration of programmes. It gave me the chance to help entertain visiting house guests such as Sir Jack Westrup and Aaron Copland. An amusing incident occurred when John Denison, then Director of Music for the Arts Council in Great Britain, came to visit. One enthusiastic 'gramophile' asked Denison whether he had heard the amusing recording of Wagnerian heroines sung by Anna Russell (*Anna Russell Sings?*). 'Yes', he replied, 'she was my first wife!'

There are no further entries in Keith's diary until late March, when, during spring break, he came to meet his three-month-old grandson and whisked me away for a long weekend in Atlantic City. Back on campus, Jack Westrup gave, in April, a lecture on the dramatic elements in Bach's *St Matthew Passion*, quickly followed by a performance of the work conducted by Donald Grout. As usual, Keith sang Christus, fellow artists being Adele Addison, Carol Smith, the Met tenor Eugene Conley as Evangelist, and Norman Farrow. The *Cornell Sun* reported: '... Bach has given these few and slightly ornamental lines a striking poignancy and intensity. Falkner understood perfectly this role, which he has sung many times before, and gave it great depth of feeling and musical beauty.'

- Many years later, in 1989, when I returned to Cornell for Donald Grout's Memorial Service, I met two, by now, middle-aged professors who had been graduate students in 1957. They recalled my 'Christus' and argued whether I had sung it from memory. I told them that yes, I had, but held the score to prevent sight taking over from sound. I once sang with a tenor, who shall be nameless, in a performance of *Messiah* who followed the music from his score but for each of his solos stood up, ostentatiously closing his copy, placing it on his chair as though to say, 'I know my part if no one else does!' It appeared to be turning oratorio into opera, asking for visual as well as musical approval, and I vowed never to perform in such extravagant manner.

On 7 May Keith took part in a faculty concert, his contribution a group of Purcell songs accompanied by William Austin, harpsichord, and John Hsu, cello. He took a weekend break before returning to Cornell for a student concert on the 14th, after which he gave a farewell party at Telluride. Examinations were held on the 17th, with cricket at Princeton the following day. Auditions for Menotti's *Amahl* were held on the 21st, a final cricket match against Rochester on the 26th. Now, at last, he was free to fly to England, only to find his consort in very poor health, though they managed a short holiday at San Mamete.

- In England, I stood in for George Hiscock on 31 August as his daughter Mary married Forbes Taylor, both in the theatrical world, and happy to share their day with a wedding breakfast at 'Rules'. While in England I was asked by the BBC *Music Magazine* to record a programme with Frederick Stone to honour Francis Toye, to be broadcast on his 75th birthday on 27 January, 1958. The programme included *The Inn*.

Back on campus, the Falkners' last move was made to a house on Turkey Hill which provided country walks. Rehearsals for *Amahl* continued, the performances held in November. Elly Applethwaite, then in her junior year at Cornell, recalls:

... I sang three of the five performances as the mother, particularly happy to be cast as this was the late 1950s and, while I had sung many recitals at Cornell, I had not been on stage in any dramatic productions ... the reason was, quite simply, that the only roles anyone seemed to be able to picture me in were as people's maids [and] I was not going to play that kind of role. I particularly wanted to sing [in *Amahl*]. I don't know what discussion took place, I'm sure it did not happen without discussion ... I have credited Professor Falkner with my ultimately being chosen to sing the role. Needless to say, he taught and coached me in it. He provided a very warm and supportive atmosphere for me and for his other students ... more than anything else, he made me want to sing and for that I will be eternally grateful ... also, he made it possible for me to study, offering me the Martha Jane Dale scholarship, which I held for three years.

The 1958 spring semester had the usual compliment of students, exams and recitals. For his part, Keith presented a lecture with Cesere Siepi in January; sang the Beethoven cycle *An die ferne Geliebte* in February; took students to the Met in March; was a soloist in a concert of contemporary chamber music, his contribution a diptych for voice, viola and piano by Rubbra: *Two Sonnets* (Alabaster) consisting of *Upon the*

Crucifix and *On the reed of our Lord's Passion*. Spring brought the usual round of cricket matches and, though professing not to like Gilbert and Sullivan, he was counsellor for the Savoyards, assisting in the production of two performances of *Princess Ida* in April with students in all roles. On 11 May there was another performance of *Wachet Auf*, this time in Sage Chapel; only now was he able to look forward to a trip home with Christabel.

Away from 28 May until 26 August, Keith spent the summer adjudicating in Scotland and Wales, in June attending the Test Match and on the 22nd in Aldeburgh for the Festival:

- I drove down with Emmie Tillett to hear Ben [Britten]'s new work and first performance of *Noye's Fludde*. It was a superb afternoon with the light and shade in the church adding to the magical sound of children's voices so that, there and then, I decided to put the work on at Cornell.

Stateside again and now a full Professor, Keith was narrator for *Peter and the Wolf* on 1 November. A student recital followed on the 9th, while on the 16th students performed Purcell's *St Cecilia's Day*, followed by performances of *Patience* on 4, 5 and 6 December, with another student recital on the 16th. The Christmas recess was welcome.

1959 began with a visit to Myra Hess and to see, as guest of the Barbirolli's, a performance of *Gerontius*, Sir John conducting the New York Philharmonic. On the 27th, accompanied by Bill Austin, Keith sang the Somervell cycle *Maud* for The Friends of Music.

- Ever since RVW had given me *Menelaus* in 1954, I had been haunted by Ursula's words: 'Homesick wanderer, you will come home to a home more ancient, waiting your return'. I had heard that on his return home RVW had said 'We must get Falkner back!' Now, early in 1959, came a mystifying letter from Adrian (Boult), saying he was delighted and when was I arriving? A week later, as Christabel and I shared a cup of tea, I opened an official invitation from the Honourable Secretary of the Council of the Royal College of Music to succeed Sir Ernest Bullock as Director. With tears in our eyes at the surprise and joy of this opportunity, we pondered the enormity of it. When I thought of Sir George Grove, Sir Hubert Parry, Sir Hugh Allen, Sir George Dyson and Sir Ernest Bullock, I began to feel very humble. How could I, as a performing musician, possibly follow in their footsteps? Chris and I talked at length, deciding that since we had been so honoured, we would do our best to make the College the happiest place we could for students, professors and all concerned. No longer would our music-making be of importance, rather our lives would be devoted to others.

There were still commitments to fill, however: in April there were student performances of Clement's *A Game of Chance* and RVW's *Riders to the Sea*, and on 3 May, Keith was in a performance of RVW's *Mass*. The spring also held plenty of cricket before Keith sailed for England on 5 June. On the 18th he was to be found at Lord's, but most time was spent with David McKenna and Sir Ernest Bullock going over details and dates for his takeover as the new Director of the Royal College of Music. In August he joined Francis Toye and his wife for a brief holiday in Portofino before sailing back to the States.

To mark the Housman centenary on 27 September, Keith presented a solo recital, with William Austin, of works by Butterworth, Ireland, Peel and C W Orr. After the recital, Morris Bishop spoke about and read Housman poems.

On 19 November, Keith was in Ohio for a Handel lecture and Purcell concert with Jack Carruth, formerly organist at Cornell, but now Director of Music at Wooster. Back home, he discovered the news was 'out', with letters of congratulation beginning to pour in, all expressing delight at the appointment. Alwyn Surplice wrote that 'music in England will be the better for your return to this country', while Edmund Rubbra expressed great pleasure saying 'I can think of no better choice ... ' 'I'm sure HPA must be pleased (Henry Ley), while Lady Jessie (Wood) wrote: 'Students of music and the art in general are indeed doubly blessed.'

From Benjamin Britten came this note:

> ... let me say how thrilled both of us are to read of the new appointment at RCM. It is wonderful to think that the old place will have civilised, enlightened, efficient and practical direction at last ... I congratulate them on their choice ...

The only sad note came from the Chairman of Arts and Sciences, Dean Francis Mineka, who expressed regret at the impending departure of Professor Falkner, yet congratulating him on 'a distinction richly deserved'.

A replacement had to be found at Cornell. A number of people were interviewed but in the end it was Keith who suggested his replacement:

- At a faculty meeting I recommended they offer the post to Isobel Baillie 'Who', they asked, 'is she?' I sent to the library for her recording of *I know that my redeemer liveth*. Not two phrases were heard before there was joint concurrence that she be invited, and at once. She did accept and was a fillip to students and audiences alike.

In her book, *Never Sing Louder than Lovely* (1982), Isobel Baillie wrote:

> I took over from Keith Falkner ... To this day I do not know why Keith put forward my name. We were not exceptionally close friends, though we had, of course, long been working colleagues. Perhaps he liked my work ...

Keith's parting gift to Cornell was to introduce Britten's *Noye's Fludde* to the United States. It was an undertaking for which the first order of business was to convince both the Ithaca Public Schools and the Board of Education of the value and viability of putting on such a work – not an easy task. But consent was given for eventual performance, after many rehearsals, on 16 January 1960, with Keith declaiming the 'Voice of God', senior students in principal roles, and Thomas Sokol conducting. It was an extremely moving production, and as fellow colleague Beatrice MacLeod recalled:

> ... the rights were secured by way of Keith's friendship with the composer ... the impetus for the undertaking was to honour Keith for the blessing of his years with us ... when the magnificent 'Voice of God' spoke the final words 'And now farewell, my darling dear' and the great arch of rainbow slid quietly back out of sight, there was a stillness, the whole chapel holding its breath, unwilling to emerge from the spell.

A final appearance in Montreal, at McGill on 8 February, had Keith again performing *Façade* and Alexander Brott's *Sept for Seven*. Also in February, Poulenc came to Cornell:

- I had the pleasure of turning over pages for him when he gave a recital with the marvellous singer Denise Duval. He often deviated from the score, while her performance of his *La Voix Humaine*, was dramatic.

Learning of Keith's interest in Poulenc's music, I tried to buy some songs for his 60th birthday. The local music shop had yet to discover this composer but agreed to check their stock. The clerk grabbed my shopping list and disappeared. Bemused and somewhat embarrassed, I waited. At last he was back, expostulating as he came, 'I have nothing with titles "Butter", "Bread", "Juice", "Toothbrush", "Tissues", "Etc"!' I left the shop in a hurry ...

Winding up this final semester was a busy affair: at Columbia University, Keith sang in Bach's *Magnificat* on 10 April, also singing *Komm, süsses Kreuz* from the *St Matthew*. On the 11th he paid a futile visit to the Rockefeller and Ford Foundations to solicit funds for a new building for the Royal College of Music. He was back then to give a recital at Wells College with William Austin, followed by a performance of Kodaly's *Te Deum*. His farewell concert came on the 12th, at which he appropriately sang *Ich habe genug*, directed by Karel Husa, who subsequently wrote:

> ... his artistry was immediate in rehearsals and concert: absolute command of the music and text, perfect diction and beautiful voice ... his modesty disarming. In all, marks of a great artist ... I heard one of the best-ever performances of solo singing in the *German Requiem* with Keith and the American soprano Helen Boatwright. Keith (also) sang the part of Jesus in the *St Matthew*. Throughout the two-part work his performance was serene, illuminating and moving in its simplicity ... he was an extraordinary artist ... always absolutely in command of his part, always most positive and kind in rehearsals and always a perfectionist ... one of the great consummate artists I have had the privilege to meet in the world of music; he confirms to me that genius and humility can exist next to each other.

On 20 May, Keith's students presented a final programme for The Friends of Music. After the interval there were Strauss waltzes for dancing.

Farewell parties abounded, everyone wanting to wish the Falkners well. All Keith's students joined forces for one particular gathering, given in lavish style. At another, a few days later, The Friends of Music presented the Falkners with a silver salver:

- It was then that I realised how feeble I was as a public speaker, trying to thank so many Cornell friends with whom I had made music for ten years. It was now time for us to return home, home to the Royal College of Music, and I spent the next few days with assistance from my students, packing up my music. One charmer totally disarmed me: 'I'm sorry', she said, 'that I was born forty years too late!'

As Karel Husa wrote in 1994:

> [Keith] was loved at Cornell, especially by his students for he was a devoted teacher; they admired his intellect, artistry, kindness and simplicity in dealing with them ... when Keith left Cornell, we lost not only a great artist and teacher, but also a perfect gentleman and kind colleague.

From England, Keith wrote for the *Cornell Music Magazine* which he himself had established and edited for a number of years:

- ... It has been a privilege for me to know and work with my distinguished friends and colleagues and to live for ten years within the great Cornell tradition.

Chapter 8: 1960–1974

June 1960 had us parting again. The 8th was a warm day. Those left behind watched, behind shielded eyes, as the *Queen Mary* banked westwards towards the Jersey Palisades before heading south out to the Atlantic.

It was a sad parting, yet we were in good spirits, the voyage giving time to dwell on the public life ahead of us. While I was excited and thrilled about my new position, there were things that worried me, namely that instead of being a practical musician I would be an observer and advisor to professor, student and administrative staff alike, a public figure expected to state policies and preside over meetings. Further, I would have to deliver an address each term to the whole College. Remembering the epic ones at the RCM by Hubert Parry and Hugh Allen, so full of wisdom and common sense, I feared, in my inexperience, that I could say anything of consequence.

It was the busiest time of the academic year when we arrived and it was good that I was able to visit and watch the College before taking up the post. As we walked up the steps, we were greeted by Sir Ernest and I felt very much as I had when chosen to open the innings in 1921 for Cambridge, where I had had to face Michael Falcon, who had just helped skittle the Australians. It had not sunk in yet that I would also be expected to take on, because of my position, committee work for some thirty organisations related to the College and arts. On 20 June, Sir Ernest handed me his keys and wished me well. As he left, I watched him walk up the steps of the Albert Hall and thought how sad it must be for him now that it was all over. What would I feel like when I had to do the same?

Guy Warrack wrote in *The Royal College of Music: The First Eighty-five Years – and Beyond* (Vol 2):

... to many the appointment seemed a revolutionary one: the occasional eyebrow was raised at the idea of a singer as Director, but not for long. There was no reason why a singer should not be Director provided he was the right singer with the right experience behind him, and this was never in doubt ... Adrian Boult justly described him as 'one of the most respected figures in British Music' and who was to lead the College through a programme of huge and imaginative expansion comparable only with the great days of Sir Hugh Allen forty-odd years before.

Ivor Newton, in *At the Piano – The World of an Accompanist*, wrote:

... Keith Falkner has broken down what has been called the 'tyranny of the organ loft' ... he seemed in no time to win not only the confidence but the hearts of every student and every Professor at the Royal College. His achievement is all the more remarkable for few singers are efficient administrators and capable of dealing sympathetically with the problems of large numbers of other people, young and old, whose often conflicting interests require skilful and just dealings from those in authority. There must be many musicians and students of all sorts who would happily quote the words of Gustav Holst which Sir Adrian Boult showed me one day; Holst had written a letter to him which began flamboyantly, 'Let us now praise Keith Falkner!'

Keith commented:

- Eyebrows were certainly raised in some quarters and for two reasons: one being, of course, that I was not an organist, and two, when I stipulated, on arrival at the College, that no engagements were ever to be arranged during the Lord's Test Match. On the third week of June of this year, and all successive ones, I made the yearly pilgrimage to sit on the roof of the pavilion with old friends Alec Waugh, A D Peters, Eric Gillett, Norman Allin and George Baker, all, alas, no more. To the last, Roy Henderson and I shared reminiscences as we watched.

Diplomatic and academic experience behind him, Keith assumed the directorship, 'which by an unavowed tradition is recognised as the unofficial head of the musical profession' (Frank Howes in a 1970 tribute to Keith). During the summer the new Director was learning the ropes, with his own performance on 11 July of *Ich habe genug* with Boult and the LPO in Southwark Cathedral.

- Two memorial services for old friends made it a sad homecoming. Horace Clive of Erlangers, an ardent lover of music and cricket, and Armstrong Gibbs, who loved music, cricket, golf and tennis, a composer of some very fine songs: *Silver*, *Five Eyes*, *Nod*, and *Semmerwater* to name a few.

The Junior Department adjudication, held in July, proved a real eye-opener. I had not realised the vast improvement in technical and artistic standards that had taken place, largely due to the ABRSM examinations and wider scope for music in schools. The excellence of teenagers staggered me. Halfway through this adjudication, I had more or less decided on the winner. However, with the last candidate, I had to change my mind, for here was a pianist who played the Beethoven *Variations* with brilliance, strength and insight. I asked him what else he knew of Beethoven's music, to his reply, 'Well, Sir, I can play you the nine symphonies from memory'. This same young man, after graduating as a Senior Student, was placed on the staff before going off to Moscow to win the Tchaikovsky Prize. On his return, as he came through Customs, he waved and hurried to me, saying: 'I shan't give up my teaching at College'. The time of course came when he had to, for the world became his oyster: he was John Lill.

Late in July, before truly settling to the job, we had a short holiday in Vitznau. Here I began to put pen to paper for my first Address to the College. As I said to Roy Plomley, some fourteen years later in reference to my appointment to the RCM, this was the one thing I longed to do, never thinking I would get the opportunity. I wanted to make the College the happiest place in London and give everybody an opportunity to develop their full capacity. This was the gist of my opening Address in 1960.

How lucky I was to have so many old friends and colleagues to help me. There was the Registrar, John Stainer, my number 2 and Director of Studies. Captain Shrimpton, Bursar, was just the man to keep us within our budget; the heads of General and Finance Offices and my PA had all been young office boys when I was a student. I found Percy Showan, 'Jumbo' Reid and Tom Manning in responsible positions. Tom had been PA to Sir Hugh, Sir George and Sir Ernest and ably shepherded me through the initial formalities. Still better were the large number of old friends on the teaching staff: Herbert Howells, Arthur Alexander, Angus Morrison, Kendall Taylor, Cyril Smith, Veronica Mansfield, Harry and Margaret Stubbs, Topliss Green, Mark Raphael, Sir John Dykes-Bower, George Thalben-Ball, Sydney Watson, H K Andrews, Richard Latham, Ruth Packer, Oda Slobodskaya. All were a wonderful cushion.

There were hints and suggestions about change but Keith had his own ideas. He did not wish to impose them until the right time, for he had seen, elsewhere, what havoc and unhappiness was caused when a new broom sweeps away much that is good, along with the bad.

Keith's final singing appearance took place on 27 November in the Sheldonian Theatre, Oxford, in a performance of RVW's *Sancta Civitas* with Sydney Watson conducting the OUMS. At the first performance of this work, which took place in 1926, conducted by Sir Hugh Allen, Keith was to have sung but laryngitis intervened, so that Arthur Cranmer sang instead. Following this later performance Dr Watson wrote:

> I don't know how to thank you for the splendid contribution that you made to our goings-on today, and of the interest that you showed in all activities ... after more than twenty years, it was a great delight to hear again that lovely voice and that magnificent diction ... All people who I have met, old and young, saw and heard you today with the greatest pleasure ...

There would be no further public appearances as Keith settled down to running the College. Registrar John Stainer wrote:

> ... the College was ripe for an infusion of new blood and in appointing Keith as Director the Council made an inspired choice. It is difficult to imagine two people less like each other than Ernest [Bullock] and Keith. The appointment of a singer instead of the usual organist must have seemed quite daring at the time, and Keith's outgoing personality, informal dress and friendly chats with all and sundry in the corridors soon created an entirely new atmosphere. His love of cricket and outdoor sports was also a great asset in a new Director, normally thought of as a rather sombre figurehead ...

David McKenna wrote in the College Magazine, Spring Term, 1995:

> ... Keith's advent was described by students and professors alike as an opening of the windows. A breath of fresh air swept through the corridors of an institution which, for all its merits, appeared to many to have become stuffy and old-fashioned. He lost no time, in his first address to the assembled students, in summarising his philosophy with these words: 'We want you to know that we think of you not as a body of students but as individuals'. Note his use of the first person plural. The most modest of men, he regarded his own contribution as but one component in a combined effort on the part of professors and staff, and of the students themselves to make the life of every individual student as rewarding as possible.

Keith tells of a Royal visit:

- Quite soon, the Queen Mother, President of the College, came for her annual visit. Naturally, I was apprehensive, not having experience of Royal visits or the responsibility of acting as host to them. As the royal car slid into view, the policeman on duty told me how they all loved working for the Queen Mum. The car stopped as Gentleman-in-waiting Captain Alistair Aird jumped out to assist her Majesty. 'I think this is the thirteenth time I have come to the College', she said as we met. I began to relax as I got through the introductions, concert and tea. Escorting Her Majesty to her car, I ventured to say that we had all been so pleased to hear she had had three winners at Haydock Park. 'Oh', she replied, 'I felt like standing on my head in the paddock!' After that, her visits were always a delight. On another occasion, she was guest of honour in the Albert Hall for a joint concert with the Royal Academy of Music, Guildhall School of Music, Trinity and the RCM of the Verdi *Requiem* conducted by Sir John Barbirolli. The soloists had been chosen from the four schools. As the performance began, Her Majesty turned to whisper: 'Which are ours?'.

In 1960 it was the turn of the Director of the Royal College of Music to take up Chairmanship of the Associated Board, shared in alternate years with the Principal of the Royal Academy of Music, Sir Thomas Armstrong.

- I was fortunate to have his help and guidance for it was a strange feeling to preside over the Board, but at least I was well aware of the pleasures and irritations of a travelling examiner, after so many years as an adjudicator.

Relations with other Colleges of Music were friendly but, in some cases, rather distant. The RCM, RAM, Royal Manchester College and the Scottish Academy of Music and Drama were allied through the ABRSM Examinations Board, but the Trinity and London Colleges, the Guildhall and Birmingham Schools were less so:

- Experience in Italy and America had convinced me that this rather insular policy must be vitalised by a broader and more open relationship with all colleges of music in Great Britain and Europe. The friendly rivalry between the Ivy League universities contributed a great deal to the exchange of ideas and standards. Tom Armstrong was the only British representative on the Association of European Colleges of Music or the Association Européenne des Conservatoires, Académies de Musique et Musikhochschulen. He asked me to take his place and I did so with alacrity, for I saw the chance to knit not only the British colleges of music together but also those of Europe, thus to kindle a similar Ivy League of joint ideas and aspirations. In due course I called a meeting of heads of the British schools, which became a yearly get-together, free of jealousies and subtleties, persuading all, eventually, to join the European Association.

The International Music Society held its congress in New York during 1961, with twenty-six countries represented by some one thousand delegates, of whom the RCM Director was one:

- The Symposium on Performance Practice was vitally interesting, for historians say that performers are ignorant and narrow-minded while performers say that historians are impractical, have no sense of performance, their writings bearing no relation to modern conditions or historical accuracy versus personal expression. However, there were several performing historians in attendance, none more practical in both fields than Cornell's Donald J Grout, who chaired many meetings. A discussion on 'Revolutionary Trends in Music from the Ars Nova in 1324 to the Present Day' was also of interest. The American composer Milton Babbitt said that he was not interested in new or old, only interested in 'individuality' in music. I quite agreed and returned convinced we must be aware of the findings of music historians; facts, not expression of opinions, and must develop critical appreciation of fact versus fiction in performance. As Edwin Roxburgh said: 'To listen is the only way of coming to terms with an idiom which may be unfamiliar ... the only true criterion is the effect and impression it produces on the individual. If we talked less analytically and listened more artistically, *performances* might well improve as well as opinions.'

Some four hundred aspiring musicians were enrolled during Keith's first year, and it was inevitable that those who stood out in one way or another should be noticed. A few years later came the mezzo Oriel Sutherland. She was an extrovert, who used her magnificent voice well but chose, at the age of thirty-five, to abandon singing as a career.

One of a party from the RCM giving a series of concerts in Germany and Switzerland, Oriel recalled:

> The Director came with us and on the morning of the first performance in Cologne he and I went for a walk together. As we passed a florist's shop he suddenly asked me to wait and disappeared inside. Moments later be emerged with a corsage for me to wear. Realising how nervous I was, he had hit upon the perfect solution. That imaginative gesture made me feel more like a real soloist than a thousand words of encouragement could ever have done. This was typical of Sir Keith's dealings with students, to which he brought a distinctive flair. He understood their difficulties, and out of that sensitivity came swift, apposite and effective action.

With the increasing influx of students, College buildings and facilities required expansion. Plans had already been initiated by Sir Ernest, though not as yet approved, and a certain amount of fund-raising started. The government grant of £13,000 was negligible and it would take years of lobbying and arguing before the Treasury granted £50,000 towards financing the necessary £250,000. John Stainer recalled:

> ... Keith lost no time in modernising the place. His own office was quickly changed for the better with a new carpet ... the appalling acoustics of the Concert Hall were vastly improved by carpeting and new curtains. The cricket net gave pleasure to a number of students and obviously to Keith himself, and the greenhouse, provided largely for the benefit of the newly appointed caretaker, who was a keen gardener. This is a good example of Keith's concern for, and interest in, all those who worked at the RCM. Of course these things and many other improvements cost money ... but Keith was so much admired and liked that there were generous benefactions. The Professors' Common Room ... which came into being when the Library was

transferred to the new building, added tremendously to the comfort of the professors and senior members of the administrative staff.

Keith adds:

- It was a godsend to have Peter Morrison, Member of the Council, as friend and benefactor. He would stroll into my office about 10am, asking how he could help our latest project. He refurbished the Concert Hall and Senior Common Rooms, and commissioned portraits of our President and Herbert Howells. It was his generosity to students and staff alike that made him 'universal Uncle' of the College.

Another project was the long disused East Courtyard to be converted into a recreation ground for students. An old friend offered financial aid for a non-musical present, and so the enclosed cricket net and badminton court came into being. Keith said he believed that for a sound mind one must have a sound body, and that exercise was a necessity. So the enclosed wire-netting pitch outside the Concert Hall became extremely popular.

Thomas Allen remembers:

It hardly seemed possible that somewhere amongst the Victorian redbrick of the RCM and harsher concrete of the neighbouring science buildings, nestled for years a cage where at regular intervals sounds of leather on willow joined those of lips on brass, horsehair on gut. How we weren't killed or severely maimed in the close confines of those nets I'll never know. We survived, and the cricket team was an important, though not very successful, alternative to the musical routine of life.

- The lack of practice rooms was another concern. I managed to obtain permission from the Royal College of Organists – the original home of the RCM – and the Commissioners of the Royal Exhibition of 1851, the landlords, to convert the unused basement into fourteen such rooms.

Keith set out to create an atmosphere of well-being among students, Professors and Administration, all free to develop individual skills. John Stainer recalled:

... At regular intervals there were Board of Professors and Faculty meetings. For these, Keith always arranged that there should be a copious supply of wine and saw to it that glasses were charged right at the start, ensuring smooth proceedings and a happy atmosphere! Of these meetings the Singers' Faculty Meeting was the most exciting, as strong views were often expressed and it was predictable to us that an opinion expressed by one person would be flatly contradicted by another. On these occasions Keith and I sometimes exchanged knowing glances, enjoying the fun. A capable chairman at these meetings, Keith kept everybody in good temper by his genial manner.

In his January 1961 address, Keith spoke of the 'Parable of the Talents' as vital to the students' future, emphasising that discipline, no matter how unpopular that word had become, was essential to all artisans. He also drew attention to the unique contribution England had made in the world. of music, from the Reformation in the 16th century to the present day:

- I urged them to go to St Paul's, The Abbey, Temple Church, and Southwark Cathedral, to widen their knowledge of music history and to experience a sense of depth and serenity whilst listening to this unique music in beautiful surroundings. As Sir George Grove said in 1886, 'I wish I could communicate to you some part of my enthusiasm for the great English School (Cathedral Music), a school not matched by any of the most famous nations abroad'.

Great student unrest on university and college campi had spread quickly across America in the late 1950s; at Cornell, Keith had naturally been aware of this and found in the 1960s that it had reached Europe. As the Registrar noted:

Keith did an excellent job in putting the Student Association on a sound footing and in advising on a proper constitution for it. He wisely had a weekly meeting with the President of the Association, and thus kept himself informed on student opinion and needs. It is largely thanks to him that we were able to avoid the wave of student unrest which beset many colleges and universities during the '60s ... Auditions were also held in Keith's room for soloists in choral works which were coming up for performance and many singing students went to him for advice ... Keith and Christabel attended most of the College concerts ... wisely refraining from extravagant praise .. but when something had been really rather good, he was often heard to say, with a look of satisfaction. 'Not bad!' 'Not bad' became a password for all the best performances ... he was the perfect boss, never interfering in a tiresome way in my activities, but was someone to shield me when things became too hot ...

In accepting the position as Director, Keith had elected to give up his own singing career to concentrate on nurturing the College. He did, however, sing at a Professors' Concert in 1962, singing English songs accompanied by 'Christabel Fullard'.

- In order to be a full musician, an aspiring young person should be versed in other arts beside his own. Thus I inaugurated a series of lectures on 'Music and the Allied Arts': English literature, painting, opera production, etc, with Eric Gillett, Basil Taylor and Sir David Webster.

Each term, outside celebrities met and talked with students as an antidote to technical discipline: Neville Cardus, Colin Cowdray, Yehudi Menuhin, Vlado Perlemuter, The Archbishop of Canterbury, Daniel Barenboim, Antony Hopkins, Nadia Boulanger and Leopold Stokowski were among those invited. Master-classes were held by Flor Peeters, Yehudi Menuhin, Vlado Perlemuter and Andre Navarra, with, among other visitors, Prince Michael of Kent, Eugene Goossens, David and Igor Oistrakh, Malcolm Sargent, Benjamin Britten, Sir John Barbirolli, Aaron Copland and Andrés Segovia. In all, visitors from some twenty countries.

- All were memorable. The Archbishop stayed for lunch and I invited students of different faiths to join us. As we sat down, the Roman Catholic student rushed up to ask: 'Sir! Am I representing the Pope?' The *Emperor Concerto* was dissected by Barenboim and Hopkins, after which Barenboim was asked whether his recent recording was the 'definitive' performance. He replied: 'Every time I play the *Emperor* it is the definitive performance. Next morning I know it was not'. Boulanger came on the first of many visits, to hear a string quartet by Haydn. There was an unrhythmic start. She stopped them and asked the cellist to play the first violinist's melody. 'How can I? I don't have the music', came the reply. She retorted: 'You mean to tell me you don't know the tune he is playing?' It was frightening, which often had a student in tears, but such discipline is essential. Her encouragement and goals were unique.

Adrian Boult returned to the College to take over the First Orchestra as Keith felt it essential that the pedestrian, term-after-term routine conductors should be changed. They were good, yes, but only at a scholastic level and he felt it necessary to have someone like Boult to open the minds of students to imagination in performance.

Many gaps existed in the singers' curriculum, particularly the knowledge of language. Keith was quick to remedy this with Italian and German classes taught to build up repertoire. Vocal ensemble with Reginald Jacques became essential, listening to quality and balance.

- During one of his trips to England, Stokowski, a student at the RCM in Parry's time, rang me about a proposed visit to the College. He asked whether I was talking from the Director's Room, standing by the same desk that Sir Hubert had used. I answered 'yes', and he said, 'I must tell you that when I was a student, Parry spoke to me at that desk for an hour on music and life. It had a profound influence on my future, and way of life, which I have never forgotten.'

The Appeal continued with Lord Astor as Chairman. Past students rallied to the call, a press conference was given by Sir Malcolm Sargent; Benjamin Britten and Peter Pears gave a recital; orchestral players from six orchestras gave their services for a concert, sitting side-by-side with College Junior students. The Student Association put on a performance of *Elijah* and continued to organise concerts in 1963, '64 and '65. The money had come from wealthy friends and charities such as Peter Morrison, Ralph Vaughan Williams, the Gulbenkian and Wolfson Trusts, Chase Charity, EMI, and alumni fund-raisers. Leopold Stokowski gave a concert in the Albert Hall. There was Lady Boult's Mile of Half Crowns: she estimated one mile would yield £6,336 in old coinage and in the end realised £7,138. When the new building was opened by the Queen Mother in 1965, the target of a quarter of a million pounds had not only been reached but stood at £252,774/15/1d.

- Apart from the new building, providing proper library space, recital hall, teaching and practice rooms, there were many other things to consider. One of my first actions was to request the return of the famous RCM Collection of four thousand manuscripts which had been sent to the British Museum for safe-keeping during the war. I was determined to have the collection where it belonged, where it could be consulted by staff, students and research scholars alike. At last, the RCM Collection came home, giving me great satisfaction.

The original Parry Room was reopened by Parry's grandson, Lord Ponsonby of Shulebrede, in part laid out for student study and reading. Oliver Davies was appointed Librarian.

In 1963, Keith addressed 'noise' versus 'sound' in daily life, talking of the way scientific inventions and commercial enterprise were beginning to swamp lives with mechanically produced or canned music of all types:

- Even musicians are becoming confused as to what is 'sound' and what is 'noise'. Once upon a time, 'noise' was described as an agreeable or melodious sound; today we describe it as a din or disturbance. It is high time we should say, as God said to Job, 'Hitherto shalt thou come but no further'. Music is something you make or listen to with your whole heart and mind; any sounds forced on you when your heart and mind are engaged elsewhere is background noise and, as such, a confounded nuisance. But we are all different. On a warm morning, I walked up the Albert Hall steps to a combination of sound and noise: a young coloratura soprano, in a top room with the window open, was producing mellifluous notes 'in alt'. Down below a builder was unloading heavy steel rods, dropping them one by one on the pavement. As I passed he dropped another 'clanger' and looking upwards, shouted: 'Lady! Will you shut up!' I also spoke about charity, described in the 15th century as 'a disposition to judge hopefully of men and their actions and to make allowances for their shortcomings'. Sir Charles Santley, the famous bass-baritone, said charitably: 'It is not the absence of faults that makes an artist but the presence of noble qualities'. Charity has not changed through the ages: it has always been the prime virtue within which all other virtues are contained. Let us eschew noise and practise charity.

Keith had been under the impression that the College was a place where anyone with talent could enter and develop. He was brought up short as pressure came from outside to reduce numbers, the argument being that the College had no right to admit students unless they could be promised a living in the profession:

- I was accused, during a BBC broadcast, of having thirty clarinet students: 'There aren't thirty clarinet jobs in the country!' Who can tell what is the requisite to guarantee a living, I replied. Sir Colin Davis, for example, was a clarinet student but he became one of the world's conductors. 'But Colin Davis didn't enter the College as a conductor!' That is just the point, I said, for no one can tell how a young musician is going to develop as his technique and personality evolve. Musicians cannot be kept in a straight-jacket for music is an art, not a trade. As I said in my Address in 1963: '... The Arts have always been hazardous and always will be. People become painters, actors and musicians because they are determined to do so – not because of the plums waiting to be picked. No college or university that I know of ensures a good job for its students after graduation ... ultimately it is the individual who by his diligence, personality and ability determines his future ... it matters more that we help you to develop the art of music in its highest sense so that you leave here artists and musicians and not just qualified wage-earners ... the practical point is that all of us, performers and teachers alike, are entertainers. If we cannot interest our listeners we are not doing our job properly. Music through the ages has always been emotional: madrigals, jazz, Bach, the Romantics and the contemplation of twelve tones all mean something emotional to different people. You must stimulate this emotional response in your listeners if you are to be a success.'

It was also Keith's belief that all types of music should be given audience at the College, whether it dismayed him or not. In 1964 he invited the Beatles, who had been raising money for a number of worthy causes, to give a performance which, alas, they were unable to accept. As Keith stated in an article for the Rochester, New York *Democrat & Chronicle* (6 October 1964): 'The Beatles can teach all of us something ... I do not despise them, by any means. On the contrary, I think they are doing something for music that may bring home the meaning of rhythm to what our younger composers are turning out. After all, we who are in music seek to entertain, and that is what the Beatles do ... '

Back in 1942, Keith's technical officer had told him mechanical production of music was advancing at such a pace in the world of commercial music that there would be little hope for singers in the future. He had dismissed this as fantasy:

● Now, I began to realise this might be true for the BBC, and young composers were experimenting with electronic music. Heinz Schroter, Head of the Hochschule für Musik in Köln, had established an electronic studio and invited me to take students for an exchange concert and to inspect this new facility. Impressed, if somewhat dismayed, I persuaded the College Council that the RCM must be the first music college in England to establish such a studio. With the BBC's advice, two small rooms were allocated, its first student flourished under the direction of Tristram Cary, then outstanding in the field. Much of what we listen to today is manipulated by electronic adjustments, often a ghastly noise. I fear my technical officer of 1942 is proving his point, yet I know nothing can approach the sound of fine singing, live and without manipulation.

The Queen, in her capacity as Patron of the College, visited twice: the first time to thank alumni for their work on behalf of the Building Fund; the second, to confer the Honorary Degree of Doctor of Music upon the Queen Mother:

● Both occasions were memorable. When I became Chairman of the annual November Royal Concert, which was part of the Musicians Benevolent Fund Santa Cecilia Celebrations, it was my duty to invite members of the Royal Family as Guest of Honour. I had heard Prince Charles sing with the Haddo House Choral Society, but perhaps Princess Anne is not so musical, for I once saw her pull quite a face over a twelve-tone composition in the Festival Hall. The culmination of these affairs was an invitation to lunch at Buckingham Palace, where I was able to ask the Princess, during pre-lunch drinks, if she was not fond of music. 'Oh, I like music, but it's too long!' When I discovered, with trepidation, that I was to sit on the Queen's right at lunch, I wondered what I could possibly talk about. 'How are Ben and Peter?' she asked; after this, it was easy.

Throughout his hectic schedule, Keith always made time for sport, finding these activities vital for his physical well-being, a way to unwind from the pressures of his position and to renew energies. The yearly holidays and adjudications also helped.

Eventually Keith became joint President, with Heinz Schroter, of the Association Européenne des Académies, Conservatoires et Musikhochschulen. In retirement he would be appointed Membre d'Honneur. The result, for the College, were exchange concerts, including the opera schools, the RCM providing *The Beggar's Opera* and *Figaro*; and the Chamber Orchestra on tours to Holland, Belgium, Luxembourg and France.

- One of the off-shoots of the European connection was that I was often invited to judge at international competitions such as the Bach Wettbewerb in Leipzig, the Schumann Competition in Vienna, the Radio Contest in Munich and the Hertzogenbosch in Holland. In Munich one day an American soprano came up to sing. After no more than four bars, I thought, 'My God! This is someone else! No one to touch her!' And how right I was, for she was Jessye Norman.

Keith was also involved in competitions such as the BBC Choir of the Year, Blackpool and other festivals, and the BBC North Singer of the Year, where Thomas Allen first showed his great talent.

- One of the most enjoyable appointments was to the Board of the Royal Opera House. It gave us the opportunity to occasionally have the Royal Box and to take students. It was impossible for us to be at Covent Garden as much as we would have liked, as the RAM and the RCM each had some fifty student concerts each year. Tom Armstrong and I were often admonished for not attending all performances.

A bolt-hole was needed for quiet weekends and in 1965 the Falkners settled on a derelict building, originally four 1840 cottages. Transformed, this Suffolk refuge became their retirement home, where Keith maintained lawns for croquet, bowls and putting. They often took separate holidays, daily letters of love flowing between them. Keith was recovering from jaundice in February 1966 when he wrote from the Isle of Wight:

- ... I sometimes deplore the phlegmatic way I take you for granted. You are the last person I should do this to – for I love you so much I cannot conceive life without you. Of late, when I hear people on TV say 'I'm sixty-five and an old man', I realise we cannot live together indefinitely and I am appalled that in five, ten, fifteen or twenty years we must part. Yet here we are, like thirty-year-olds, getting excited with Low Cottages as though we had thirty years to plan and live for. Maybe we have. It would be lovely to become a nonagenarian with you ...

They would in fact share another thirty-four years.

John Stainer, in daily communication with Keith, by 8 March was able to write:

... very glad we shall see you again soon ... I have not found the extra responsibility very onerous. You have always made your policy so clear that it has not been difficult to decide on action you yourself would have wished. We have missed your cheery presence very much, however.

A request from Dr Thomas Fielden, FRCM, came in May 1967, asking if Keith could help in getting his songs performed as 'publishers will only look at songs that are sung in public'. He added that he was tired of retirement. Keith's response is typical of his interest and sympathetic concern for all musicians:

● ... I do sympathise with you ... A composer today can only hope that a performer will suddenly take an interest ... the emphasis everywhere is on youth and many of you older composers are being neglected. (When we have passed on – who knows what age or future Ph.D will not discover your songs.) Here, the emphasis must rightly be on the students ... I suggest that you let us have a complete set of your songs ... we will put them in the circulation library and hope for the best. I sympathise with you, too, over retirement. Again I notice, in the present temperature, that little interest is being taken in the older artists unless, like Adrian Boult, they have been in the public eye all their life. I'm afraid this is something we all have to bear. I must count the terms until my retirement and I am sure, if I am not invited to do work after it comes, I certainly shall not lobby for it. I have a private regret that no one ever asks me to sing nowadays or to play cricket ... With happy nostalgia of the good old days and learning *Papillons* with you in 1922 ...

The big news for 1967 was Keith's knighthood. Announced in the Queen's Birthday Honours for 10 June, the ceremony was held on 11 July. Keith wrote to his former Italian secretary, Hilda Colucci: '... we are naturally a bit bewildered at the moment about it all.' Neither daughter could share this great occasion, although Keith, hoping for the impossible, carried our tickets in his pocket to the ceremony. It was not to be.

The year also brought NBC's *Today Show* to London. States-side, the family was delighted, one morning, to see Keith being interviewed by Hugh Downs on the steps of the Albert Hall, the College in the background. In November, Keith was in Vienna for a week's judging at the Konservatorium. From his diary:

- ... So many sing the broad, slow songs too fast and so avoid the long phrasing which would win high marks with me, if they could do it ... Great tendency nowadays for too much nasal resonance and not enough warmth. The winners were chosen for overall averages on their three auditions ... I can see the jury as a whole decided precision-intensity of tone in the big songs in the final rounds must win ... all very interesting and an object lesson not to be swayed – perhaps too much – by personal taste ...

Walter Hendl was also in attendance and it was here that he and Keith discussed the possibility of establishing a Francis Toye Scholarship for exchange of graduate scholars between the Eastman School of Music and the RCM. The first exchange took place in September 1968.

Keith performed once more, at the Director's Concert this same year. The programme contained Stravinsky's *The Soldier's Tale*, narrated by Neil Jenkins, and *Façade*, narrated by Natalie Wheen and Keith.

Aside from his administrative duties and outside adjudicating, Keith made frequent journeys abroad to promote international exchange concerts. In 1960, concerts had been organised between the RCM and the Royal Danish Academy of Music. Later travels to America and music schools throughout Europe brought further exchanges. Some were unreciprocated visits, such as the visit in 1966 of the Cornell Glee Club directed by Tom Sokol.

By now the RCM Opera School had been expanded. In 1968, thanks to a number of trusts, came the announcement that a new Exhibition Hall was to be built for the collection of historical instruments, providing proper conditions for display of the precious instruments which, hitherto, had been stored all over the College. Keith described the collection as one of the five most valuable in the country. The curator, Elizabeth Wells, stated recently that since its opening the museum has become a valued resource for researchers worldwide and has made a special contribution to the education of music students within the College. The opening of the Museum of Instruments, on 23 April 1970, was held in the presence of Her Majesty the Queen Mother, with a concert and exhibition. The story is told that on that occasion HRH, the Queen Mother, made the delightful remark, 'This is the nicest concert I've been to!' To which Keith replied: 'I think, Ma'am, you must mean the shortest!' A concert on the 25th anniversary of the opening was, in part, a tribute to Keith.

Overall, the Royal College of Music during the 1960s became vibrant, due to growth and expansion in student numbers, staff, syllabus, premises, salaries and grants. ' It was clear', wrote Guy Warrick in his history of the College, ' that Sir Keith had a comprehensive grasp of the many problems in providing as efficient a musical education as possible. He was well equipped to rebut criticisms and anticipate well-meant suggestions.'

Keith noted that some students found it difficult to settle to the discipline of college life. Therefore, he announced the establishment of a tutorial system, appointing six professors to advise first-year students. A men's hostel would also be established.

On the occasion of Keith being made Honorary Doctor of Music at Oxford on 25 June 1969, Sir Thomas Armstrong wrote to his old friend:

> ... How glad I am that Oxford has conferred upon you the Honorary Degree that you so fully deserve: it's intended, I know, to be a mark of their great admiration for you and your great work in music; and there was never a gesture that would gain a more wide-spread and general applause throughout the music profession. So it's a case of joy and felicitations to all concerned: and if HPA (Sir Hugh Allen) had lived to see it he would have been the happiest of us all ... I'm sure you found many friends; and it must have recalled to your mind the performances in which you took part in the Sheldonian and elsewhere in Oxford – such unforgettable experiences, many of them were.

Before leaving for a tour to America in mid-October, Keith sent a letter to his friend Herbert Howells on the 17th:

- ... it was resolved at the Executive Meeting of the Council that from now on you should be known officially as Emeritus Senior Professor. I do not know if you will consider this gives you added dignity but we certainly do. Yours ever. KF.

When a professor is irreplaceable, as in the case of Herbert Howells, I, as Director, always insisted that a professor remain as long as he cared to. An amusing corollary occurred when Norman Allin was 'retired' from the RAM at 76. I immediately called him to come and teach at the RCM for as long as he wished.

In New York, the Falkners were with the Royal Choral Society, before Keith went on for a series of lectures and visits to family. He had hoped to renew acquaintance with Rudolph Bing, General Manager of the Metropolitan Opera, who replied to Keith's letter of inquiry: '... Whether or not I can invite you to the opera, I can, unfortunately, not yet say – because we have no opera right now! We are involved in the most serious labour dispute in the Metropolitan's history ... and I cannot foresee whether or not it will be open in October or November ... '

As part of the tour, the Falkners were at Cornell in November for a 'Concert of English Music with Sir Keith Falkner and the Cornell Chamber Orchestra', conducted by Karel Husa. Composers represented included Tippett, Dowland, Fricker and Blow. After the interval, Gaynor Jones and Keith were reciters of *Façade*. From Keith's diary:

- *Façade* went very well. Karel a most sympathetic conductor and so efficient in tempi. The players were very smooth and accomplished, especially the trumpet ... Gaynor Jones really came up to scratch and got better and better. Very well received and very good applause at the end.

The *Ithaca Journal* reported:

The work ... is a rather brilliant parody of sentimental genre pieces. The irreverent humor of the poetry is in every case thoroughly complimented by the irrepressible humor of Walton's music ... The musicians played wonderfully throughout but the success of the performance must be attributed to the charming and enthusiastic readers, Sir Keith and Miss Gaynor Jones ... The spontaneity of their reading imbued the entire afternoon with a particular enjoyment that perhaps only British humor of any century can afford.

Back in College, Keith announced, in his report of March 1970, that Peter Morrison had offered to commission Leonard Boden to paint a portrait of Queen Elizabeth the Queen Mother. On a lighter note, he added that the Professors' and Administrative Staff Party, held in January, had been approved as an annual event.

During 1970 a prostate operation became necessary and, while in hospital, Keith suffered a momentary late mid-life crisis. This would have gone totally unnoticed had he not confessed to a dear friend that he was 'in love with the most wonderful woman', a nurse in hospital. Years younger than Keith, and unnamed to this day, she would often meet him when he was in London. Christabel never knew, though throughout the years she had been concerned over the flock of ladies professing to be in love with her handsome husband.

The time had come for Keith's own portrait to be painted, entrusted to the artistic hands of Sonia Mervyn. When viewed by the Executive Committee of the Council, it decided that, while it liked the portrait as a picture (with its Free Forester tie), it was not prepared to accept it as the portrait of a Director of the College. Sonia Mervyn wrote to Keith on 29 October 1971:

> ... But the whole point of your portrait is your kindliness, humanity and understanding and this is it – why you have made the college what it is – greater than it has ever been, anyhow in my lifetime. One only had to go to a Union party to get the feeling of happiness and well-being. But I fear your Council had no inner eye to see and understand. Never mind, it will look very well in your drawing room!

A second portrait was commissioned from Leonard Boden and this now hangs in the Concert Hall with past directors. It is a typical board-room photographic portrait with, in the opinion of the family, little of the essence of the sitter.

Throughout the years there had been much talk of the amalgamation of the Royal Schools of Music in London, ie, Royal College, Royal Academy and Trinity. In reference to the Gulbenkian Report, aired on BBC 2 TV in January 1968, all Principals had agreed to it, except for Article 3, that of amalgamation. As John Stainer commented, '... (it would) put the clock back 83 years. When the RCM was founded, it was intended that it should combine with the RAM to form one national school of music. The RAM would not agree and who can blame them?'

What did evolve was closer cooperation of the College with the RAM. As Keith reported in 1972: 'Our financial applications for 1972/73 have been submitted and we intend to submit a joint letter shortly, setting out our future policy of cooperation to avoid overlapping.'

The subject recurs from time to time, Keith again concerned in the 1990s.

In his Report for January 1972, Keith mentioned an amusing and splendid address given by Robert Morley; that Szymon Goldberg would begin his series of master classes on 'The Ten Beethoven Sonatas for Violin and Piano' in February; that remedial or relaxation classes for muscular tension be given daily by Dr Lefever; and that he would be travelling to the Eastman School of Music to read a paper, 'Training the Professional Singer Yesterday and Today'.

During the summer the Falkners were invaded by family. A visit Keith much looked forward to was that of Donald Grout, expected in

September, though he wrote: 'By the time of their (daughters) departure we may, of course, be in a nursing home.' As it was, he retired to Osborne House for a much needed rest. Christabel wrote daily about goings on in the growing garden at Bungay. One began: 'How lucky I am to belong to YOU! It is a marvellous happening. I lie in bed and often think about your devotion to me; and wonder if it is really possible that I should be so blessed! Aye me. When a loved one is far away, it strikes one so forcibly ...

Keith was invited to write an article for the first issue of a major music annual from the publisher of Grove's *Dictionary of Music and Musicians*, *The Music Yearbook 1972-3*. His subject: 'Preparing for a Career: The Solo Singer'. An editorial for *Music and Education* by Gordon Reynolds read:

One of the delights in *The Music Yearbook 1972-3* is an article by Sir Keith Falkner. It gives advice to those who would like to embark upon careers as solo singers. I'll begin by quoting a little of what Sir Keith has to say: 'It has been a standing joke in this century that singers are not "musicians". Instrumentalists begin training at an early age, singers often too late. It is a tragedy that many singers with fine voices only "discover" their voice at the age of 16-18, without previous musical training. Ear-training, sight-reading, expression, articulation – these are things which by the age of 18 should have become instinctive. At choir schools and specialist music schools this is possible. It is interesting not only that many of the successful male singers in Great Britain have been choirboys, but so also have a large proportion of eminent organists, composers and conductors. They have learned the alphabet of music early in life and do not have to start from scratch when they discover "another" voice later on. It is remarkable, too, that in solo classes at competitive festivals, trained boy and girl trebles will demonstrate good tone quality, rhythm, breath control and phrasing, putting many adult singers to shame. There are over thirty choir schools in England and other schools giving specialised musical training: if I had a son aged nine I would certainly wish him to benefit from this excellent early start. More schools on these lines would go a long way towards making us not a nation of music-lovers but a nation of performers. An interesting parallel is the modern Suzuki method of teaching the violin in Japan.'

During June, 1973 the Falkners were in Italy for the Concorso per Voci Verdiane in Busseto, where Keith was one of nine adjudicating 87 singers.

- In 1974, Sir Alistair Aird rang to say that the Queen Mother would like the College to provide a small choir at the funeral of a great friend. I asked Richard Latham to choose suitable voices from his choir-training class, and joined the choir myself. After the service we were driven to Her Majesty's house for drinks and luncheon, seated at tables of four. To our delight, Her Majesty joined us and, after thanking us, asked me to choose two to join her at her table. One of these was Philippa Thomson, the other, a young man who immediately raised his glass asking: 'May we drink your Majesty's good health?' And did so. The Queen Mother took me to another room after lunch, presenting me with a signed portrait, then stood in the garden to wave us off.

It had been normal procedure for directors and staff to retire at seventy. Keith reached this age in 1970 and the Council asked him to remain until 1974: that time was now fast approaching. The RCM Report of the Council for the year ended 31 December 1974, and presented to the 90th AGM of the Corporation on 16 December, stated: 'Mr David Willcocks CBE, MC, FRCM, has succeeded Sir Keith Falkner as Director of the College from April 1974.'

Many expressed the same feeling as Donald Sprink, who wrote on 25 March:

> ... I can't bear to think of it being your last term. The thought brings a very big lump in the throat, though I can't fully realise it yet ... And none of us, dear Keith, will ever fully realise *all* that you have been to the RCM, and all that you have done. I would dearly love to give you both a wee something.

Sir Keith's reply on the 26th:

- ... These years have been the happiest of our lives, and what more can one say. There is no need for gifts ... I should feel embarrassed. Indeed, it should be the other way around. Yours, ever, Keith Falkner.

Between 25 and 28 March the College presented a Bach Festival to honour Keith. It culminated in a performance of the *B Minor Mass* with the RCM Choral Class (Keith singing with the basses), the First Orchestra and soloists Caroline Friend, Margaret Cable, Neil Jenkins and Glyn Davenport, conducted by David Willcocks. It was the finest tribute to Keith and the happiest of introductions for his successor, Sir David.

Christabel would also be greatly missed. She had been of invaluable support to Keith, taking a keen interest in all College matters: concerts, meetings, and entertaining students, in whom she took concerned delight. A gracious influence and presence throughout her husband's tenure at the College, as she was throughout their lives together. No doubt in part recognition of her services, in his Report for 10 December 1974, under Honours, the new Director, having consulted the Board of Professors, recommended to the Council that the President be invited to confer the Degree of FRCM upon Arthur Rubenstein, Phyllis Sellick, Norman Del Mar, Harold Watkins Shaw – and Lady Falkner.

One of Keith's last duties was to write to Her Majesty The Queen. Her reply, via a secretary, in part reads:

> Her Majesty thanks you most sincerely for your message and is touched that your last official act as Director of the Royal College of Music should have been to send it to her.

Some saw the tears in his eyes as Sir Keith said adieu to the place he loved so well.

Chapter 9: 1974–1994

Keith's directorship of the RCM came to an end in 1974. He would greatly miss the daily involvement in College, but knew it was time to move on. Sir David Willcocks's 1974 Director's Address paid tribute to Sir Keith:

> When Sir Hubert Parry took over the Directorship of this College from Sir George Grove in 1894, he devoted the whole of his first address to an appreciation of the work of his predecessor. He began 'I cannot help being conscious that the strongest feeling which is present in our minds at this moment is the sense of the great loss we have sustained in the absence of our dear Director. It is a loss that we shall inevitably feel the results of for a long while. But the energy and ability of our professors and the goodwill and honourable conduct of all you scholars, exhibitioners and students may carry our College through the crisis; and is rather as the loss of a personal friend who made a part almost of our daily lives that we shall feel his absence most severely. There are few of you here present who have not felt the influence of his personality and realised the whole-hearted enthusiasm for whatever is really good, which was his most marked characteristic. And we unluckily older people, who could call him friend even in the days before many of you were born, can recall an even more lively phase of his (life) ... '
>
> How apt those words, spoken eighty years ago, seem today. There can be relatively few present in this hall who remember, as people of my age can, the apparently young Mr Keith Falkner at the height of his career as a singer. He became one of the great artists of his generation, partly because he possessed a voice of beautiful quality supported by superb technique; but more especially because his character and musicianship revealed themselves in every performance that he gave. Some older people here will remember especially his sympathetic singing of English songs, but for me as a hero-worshipping schoolboy it was his singing of Bach, and particularly the 'Christus' part in the *St Matthew Passion*, that was unrivalled. You who never knew the Mr Keith Falkner of whom I have spoken can at least be grateful that you have known the Sir Keith Falkner who did so much for the College ... If the College has, during the last 14 years, been a happy place in which to live and work, it is due in no small measure to the influence of Sir Keith and Lady Falkner ...

Keith escaped to South Africa in July to adjudicate for the ABRSM. Before leaving, he was a 'castaway' on *Desert Island Discs* hosted by

Roy Plomley, to be broadcast later in the month. Musical selections were: excerpts from an Evensong at New College, Oxford; Schubert's *Die Krähe* from *Winterreise*; Schubert's *C Major Symphony*; *The Ride to Rome* from Britten's *Rape of Lucretia*; the *Willow Song* from *Otello* (Verdi); the Brahms *Variations on a Theme of Paganini*; *For the End of Time* (Messaien); and an excerpt from the Bach *B Minor Mass*, this last being his choice if only one record could be taken. His one luxury? If he could not have the company of his wife, a Colin Cowdray batting machine would suffice. Of literature, a bound edition of Trollope.

The tour, lasting 105 days, took Keith all over South Africa. To relax from the long examinations and endless paperwork, there was golf and a visit with Colin Cowdray. Writing on 2 July to Christabel:

- ... It is 'fun' being busy and at full stretch musically for a change and meeting enthusiastic and interesting people ... At 11:30 I am being picked up by Harry Stone – he runs the Eisteddfod here and asked me to come last year ...

  [2/3 August:] We have finished our work here and jolly good it has been ... the Chairman of the Governors of the Rhodesian College of Music is coming to discuss the future of the College and asked if I would care to come next year for a week or two to advise further planning ... I am glad 'Desert Island Discs' had such a nice response ... were you pleased? ... 26 November is the Royal Concert. I'd very much like to do it provided we have adequate rehearsal ... I don't particularly want to get involved in such affairs until we have settled down together ...

  [From Bulawayo on the 7th:] ... In Julia's letter she said she'd a notion to write my biography – good child but I think it's better left unsaid – too many such which ...

  [15 August, Mount Nelson Hotel:] Yesterday David and Rachel Willcocks came to lunch, together with the music master of Bishop's School ... He is training the choir for the *War Requiem* next Tuesday ... Tomorrow evening rehearsal. Sat. eve., the Organists dinner at which David and I are guest speakers. Last night a Miss Deal of the SABC came to do an interview with me to be broadcast today at lunchtime ... (it) ended with *O let the Solid Ground* recorded in 1940 with Gerald Moore and it sounded dated but not too bad except for the top 'Es', which could not be recorded at that time properly. Monday evening an article appeared in the *Cape Argus* inspired by 'J.K.' (John Keith Sutton – nephew) about me – much hyperbole.

[19 August:] A nice visit last night – the first time I've been with David and Rachel without a host of other people around. We talked a lot about RCM. The *War Requiem* is tonight ...

Keith now received an issue of the *RCM Magazine* which included the article 'Sir Keith Falkner, Sixth Director of the RCM', a tribute by Herbert Howells:

- [23 August:] ... I stood in my room here and read the article Herbert wrote. I felt detached as though he were writing about a phantom spirit we know but are not closely in touch with. I was profoundly moved – as we were when we were invited to come to the RCM and by the magnificent gift from the RCM Union, I don't really understand it – or the nice words used by so many ... I just had to mention it tonight, for you and you alone are responsible for anything we have done together these 44 years. Don't leave me, my sweet.

[30 August:] I see Carlo Zecchi is to conduct here before I leave ... the last candidate (yesterday) 'put on an act' – school girl 13/14 burst into tears. The teacher could do nothing to assuage them. However, I had a little chat with her and had her smiling by the time I said I'd come all the way to hear her pieces. I managed to give her 101 – just passed.

[12 September:] It is exciting to think in four weeks I shall have been two days on my way back home to you: I feel exactly as I did at New College 65 years ago – counting the days and hours until the train home to Cambridge ... . Pierre Fournier is here – we had a chat – he is playing the Dvorak Concerto with Zecchi. Just off to Plumstead to put some flowers on my mother's grave – 14 May 1928. How *can* it be that it is over 46 years ago .. (Later) 'Boon' Wallace, friend of Colin Cowdray's, Head of Western Province cricket, collected me and took me to Newlands, the 'Lord's' of SA, to show me around and meet cricketers getting ready for the new season. Very pleasant including one 'Passmore', who remembered playing against The Wanderers with Stanley Colman in 1929!

[6 October:] And so I come to my final letter of the Tour, 'God be praised'. After posting my last to you, I had a quiet day and really felt I had retired for the first time ... The first ball of the season is being bowled here in 10 minutes so I am off to see it ... 'Home, James, and don't spare the horses!'

In October, Christabel joined Keith for a conference in Rotterdam, then he was at Sapphire Studios at the end of the month to make the RCM film. The year faded quietly, though there were innumerable meetings and luncheons. Mid-April 1975, Keith returned to the States to narrate a performance of Honneger's *King David* at Cornell, conducted by the

Keith Falkner, c 1936.

Keith Falkner at New
College, Oxford, 1912

Keith Falkner (right) in a RCM 1922 production of
'Qualis' by A Davis Adams (copyright RCM)

Christabel Fullard in 1918

Keith Falkner in the Royal Naval Air
Service in 1918

Above:
The Falkners in
concert mode.

Right:
Cartoon for the
Leeds Musical
Festival 1928.

Left:
Keith Falkner as Mephistophes in the film *The Singing Cop*, 1937.

Below:
Keith Falkner in the film *Mayfair Melody*.

Front cover of American concert management brochure 1938.

Left:
Flying Officer
Falkner and
Christabel with
daughters Julia and
Philippa in 1940.
Right (with the dog)
is Dr Emily Daymond.

Keith and Christabel, c 1930.

Above:
Music Officer's
Quartet in Sienna,
1950. Left to right:
James Eagleson,
Christabel Falkner,
Keith Falkner, Olga
Rudge (Secretary,
Accademia Chigiana),
Joy Hoodless, Vera
Terry, Count Chigi
Saracini.

Left:
The Falkners on
arrival in the USA,
1939.

KEITH FALKNER
Bass-Baritone
CHRISTABEL FALKNER *at the piano*

I

Das Kühhorn (Mondseer Handschrift) . . . . *Mönch von Salzburg*
(1370-1400)
De la crudel (a 13th Century Italian Lauda) . . . *arr. Fernando Liuzzi*
What if I seeke? (from "A Musicale Dreame" 1609) . . *Robert Jones*
The Self banished . . . . *John Blow (1648-1708)*
Sweet Kate (from "A Musicale Dreame" 1609) . . . . *Robert Jones*
How jovial is my laughter . . . . *J. S. Bach (1685-1750)*
  (Der zufriedengestellte Aeolus—Cantata 205)

II

Im wunderschönen Monat Mai
Aus meinen Tränen spriessen
Die Rose, die Lilie
Wenn ich in deine Augen seh' } from "Dichterliebe" Song Cycle
Ich will meine Seele tauchen   (Nos. 1-7) . *Schumann (1810-56)*
Im Rhein, im heiligen Strome
Ich grolle nicht

III

The Roadside Fire . . . . *Vaughan Williams (1872-   )*
The Chapel on the Hill
The Bold Unbiddable Child } . . . . *Stanford (1852-1924)*
Is my team ploughing?
Loveliest of Trees } . . . . *Butterworth (1885-1916)*
Love is a Bable . . . . *Parry (1848-1918)*

IV

Down by the Sally Gardens (Irish)
The Bonnie Earl O'Moray (Scottish) } *arr. Benjamin Britten (1913-   )*
Oliver Cromwell (English)
Mohacs Field (Hungarian)
Shepherd see thy horses' foaming mane (Hungarian) } . *arr. Korbay*

Programme of a recital given in Cornell University in 1952

Right:
Keith Falkner with students
at Capital University,
Columbus, Ohio, in the
1930s.

Below:
Keith Falkner (centre) with
pianist John Hunt (right), in
Bermuda, 1952.

Yale University in the early 1950s: Ralph Vaughan Williams receiving the Howland Prize. Left to right: The Dean of the School of Music, the President, RVW and Keith Falkner.

Keith Falkner with students at Cornell University.

Left:
Keith Falkner after the 'dubbing' ceremony for his Knighthood, 1967.

Below:
Cricket at Cornell in the 1950s.

Lunch for some of the 'vintage' singers of the day in 1974 to 'remember' Norman Allin. Left to right: Geraint Evans, Ivor Newton Robert Easton, Sir Thomas Armstrong, Richard Lewis, Redvers Llewellyn, Roy Henderson, Keith Falkner. Front row: Miss Cheseldon, Mary Jarred, Isobel Baillie, Dame Eva Turner, Muriel Brunskill, Carrie Tubb, Emmie Tillett.

Right:
The Queen with Keith
Falkner at the Royal
College of Music.

Below:
Keith Falkner and
Dame Janet Baker, the
new artistic directors
of the Kings Lynn
Festival, 1980. Left is
Nicholas Lane, the
festival committee's
chairman, with Simon
Ing, vice-chairman
(right).

The Queen Mother with Keith Falkner at the opening in 1970 of the Royal College of Music's Museum of Instruments. Next to him is Elisabeth Wells (curator), with (right) Philip Bate (copyright RCM).

Opening of the RCM Museum of Instruments in 1970. John Wilson (right) plays the barrel organ. (copyright RCM)

Keith Falkner, aged 93, in his Suffolk garden.

composer and Karel Husa, who had worked with Honegger in the mid-1940s. From the *Cornell Daily Sun*, 18 April:

> ... Sir Keith Falkner's noble, authoritative and often highly emotive narration wove together the many accounts sung of joy, sorrow, faith, human suffering and divine intervention ...

In a letter of thanks, Karel Husa wrote:

> ... thank you again for your most valuable contribution to our concert on 17 April. Your narration was beautifully spoken, warm and dignified and kept the performance on that high level of excellence. Many thanks from all of us for giving us this great pleasure ...

Lectures at Stephens College and the University of Missouri in Columbia followed. The diary for 24 April noted:

> - ... Such a responsive audience. Quite overcome with compliments from elderly academics and graduate students. Went on to a party ... so many interesting people and characters ... Really a boost to the ego to be flattered in warm American fashion once again ... 'When are you going to write a book?' they asked. Told Andrew Minor [Chairman] I hoped to stage a course on the revival of English language song. He said 'We must try and get you back here very soon' ... [later] regret that there has been so little time to be 'at home' with Julia. Why is it that the things that really matter in life one seldom talks or writes about ...

Keith was back in time for the match at Lord's on the 30th. In early May he was at Haddo to sing with the basses in a performance of Elgar's *The Kingdom* and *The Apostles*. An appearance on *Face the Music* in July, hosted by Joseph Cooper, had panel members Joyce Grenfell, Richard Baker and David Attenborough. Christabel thought it thrilling: 'You looked so nice and were so gracious and so modest.' There were two trips to Italy before the ABRSM sent Keith to Gibraltar in April 1976. In May, Keith was in Leipzig for a musical congress, serving as a member of the jury. Mid-June brought a visit to Busseto but he was in his seat at Lord's for the Test Match. *Intimations of Immortality* (Finzi) was presented at Haddo in the autumn with Keith joining the basses. In November he attended the Congress of Association of Music Schools, in Warsaw, where he resigned the presidency, paying tribute to the progress the Association had made during the past fifteen years:

> - ... Our discussions over the years have necessarily pursued the same subject, namely how to pool ideas for the development and improvement of music

education in our separate countries ... One of the greatest benefits of our Congressional meetings has been the friendly gatherings and informal discussions outside our official programme. I am sure many of us have thereby been stimulated and helped to make improvements within our own institutions ... I beg you to remember that music is not only the joy of our lives but of thousands of young musicians eager to follow in our footsteps. That talking about music is one thing, but that making music is all that matters.

Keith and Christabel's greatest complaint, as they aged, was the loss of relatives and friends. On St David's day 1977, his own birthday, Keith wrote to his beloved wife:

- My dearest in all the world ... When I think that you have kissed me or written to me on the first of March for 50 years I just cannot believe it. I keep on telling myself how blest and lucky I've been all this time ... and it is only when I wave and disappear down the railway line that a sense of void comes over me and I ask myself 'Why? What for?' When one is living in clover, why should one go scavenging about on other pursuits? ... A nice day yesterday with some very good players and singers ... Student told of a 45-minute rehearsal with Adrian (Boult) who let them play, got what he wanted without talking ... One remark he made to the tympanist in one of the *Enigma Variations*, where it is apparently usual to use a coin to tap the drums: AB asked 'What are you using, a half-crown?' 'No, Sir Adrian, 50p.' A smile and on they went, then as he slowly left the pit through the celli and past the tympanist he said dryly: 'A half-crown is much better ... '

Keith was in Hong Kong for the ABRSM in September, Christabel soon joined him there but they were back in time for the Royal Concert in November, later attending the *War Requiem* (Britten) at the RCM.

1978 was less busy. Locally, the Falkners presented speeches and awards to schools in Suffolk; were entrants and openers of shows, tickled to take first prize for onions and maidenhair fern. Low Cottages, nestling in the Ilketshall Saints, had become a permanent home, though both regretted being so far from London. Visitors to the area often stopped for directions to one Saint or another. One such occasion was recorded in Christabel's diary:

I was in the kitchen when there was a knock at the door, a man asking the way to St Peters. He looked friendly and nice, so I asked him in, to give him directions in the warm. As I began to do so, Keith entered the kitchen and turning to him I said, 'My dear, St Peter ... ' Keith, thinking this must be the new vicar, came forward with his smile and shook hands saying 'St Peter!

How nice!' To which our visitor replied, 'No, not exactly, but it's a nice thought!' Hardly able to contain ourselves, we gave direction and off he went ...

In 1978, Sir Yehudi Menuhin invited Keith to collect and edit a number of texts from eminent singers for the Yehudi Menuhin Music Guides. *The Voice* was published in 1983 and re-issued in paperback in 1994. It was neither a history of song nor a text-book on the physiology of the voice, least of all a singing 'method'. Rather,

- It is a symposium, an anthology compiled by artists I have long admired. I chose my contributors from those I knew from personal experience to be outstanding in their own branch of vocal music. Some of their articles are instructional, all are practical and all reflect professional experience and advice; the empirical knowledge of a score of world-famous singers and musicians. They don't always agree. How dull life would be if they did. This book is designed to interest both those who sing for fun and those who wish to make singing their profession. (They may still find it fun.) The voice is the finest instrument of music in existence. Each one is unique in sound and quality. To sing alone or with others can give emotional and physical satisfaction and it is the healthiest of occupations or hobbies.

In a letter dated 16 November (1982), Keith wrote to me with typical modesty:

- ... A nice letter this morning from Yehudi Menuhin thanking and congratulating me on *Voice*. He had just read it. The book is of course patchy but he seems to think my part is satisfactory ...

On Keith's 80th birthday, in 1980, the Royal College of Music presented an all-Bach concert in his honour. Included was the aria from Cantata No 82: *Schlummert ein*. Later in the month Keith was busy for the ABRSM, then the clan gathered to celebrate the Falkner's 50th wedding anniversary in June. Keith was appointed Artistic Director for the King's Lynn Festival in July, and in October he set off for Malta for the ABRSM, writing to Christabel:

- My dearest, here I go again. Leaving you and I never can realise why I do it ... It has been a wonderful summer with you – a glorious golden glow ever since May – a wonderful re-union of the clans, and such beautiful daughters you produced ... We have much to look forward to together: Malta, Abano, Canada/USA ... Take care. 'Good folks is scarce'. K. X

Home again, there were many visits to London. On one, Keith repaired to the RAC for drinks and dinner with friends. Afterwards, full of bonhomie, he walked the short distance to the Athenaeum. At the top of the steps he opened the door to find two nuns floating towards him, a Monsignor and second gentleman behind. Without batting an eye, Keith exclaimed 'Good evening! I'd rather be a doorkeeper in the house of the Lord than dwell among the tents of the ungodly!' 'Oh! Good evening', replied the Monsignor, 'DO meet the Papal Nuncio!'

In late November, with Keith away in Malta, Christabel sent him a poignant note: 'Dearest One, I like to think that this may be there to greet you, so that we may feel in touch at once ... I am missing you greatly. There does not seem to be the same point in doing things ... Thine forever.'

There was a gradual slowing down during the 1980s but it was hard to detect as garden and lawns continued to demand Keith's attention. He continued to travel to London, with visits abroad for pleasure and the ABRSM.

In 1982 the King's Lynn Festival celebrated its thirty-second year. Founded by Ruth, Lady Fermoy, its artistic directors then were Dame Janet Baker and Keith, who was instrumental in arranging the appearance of the Cornell University Glee Club under the direction of Professor Thomas Sokol. From the *Eastern Daily Press*, 27 July:

> ... Fine singing from Cornell ... last evening it was the turn of a choir of voices to fill the St Nicholas Chapel with some thrilling sounds from America as the King's Lynn Festival continued. Such was the significance of their visit that the BBC recorded it. Dame Janet Baker, who with Sir Keith is an artistic director of the festival, also sang with the Glee Club.

Elected a Vice President of the RCM in August, Keith wrote on the 6th:

> I am delighted and honoured. To feel that I am perhaps taking the place of Adrian Boult (my best man) or Herbert Howells (one of my oldest friends) gives me such pleasure. I pray and trust that the College will go through the next century with as much distinction as in the first ... As RVW used to say, 'Thank you for All'.

After all this there was a visit to Llangollen and of course cricket, watched with his old friend Roy Henderson. In mid-September the Falkners visited the States again. Home, Keith chose to resign from the King's Lynn Festival, writing:

- ... I must send a farewell message to wish the Festival a long and happy future. It has been the greatest pleasure for me, with Dame Janet, to plan and to experience three years of the unique quality of the Festival: so special and so individual. Your gift of the lovely Dartington goblets will keep us constantly in touch. Two are in A flat and one in G. So one wonders what Purcell might have done with a 'Fantasy of Viols' since he was so magical with a single note ... thank you for all.

In reply, Lady Fermoy wrote:

Thank you very much indeed for your very kind letter, but the thanks should all come from me ... you and Janet have most certainly brought new quality to our Festival and greatly enhanced its reputation. Each year has been excellent, but this year was the finest and also, I think, the happiest for all concerned. I can never thank you enough for having agreed to give us the benefit of your knowledge and experience for three years. I wish they hadn't ended! But we must try and keep up the standards and find programmes to match yours – a hard task ...

Dame Janet to Keith:

... thank you for your help, support and guidance over these last three years. I am deeply grateful to you for agreeing to take on King's Lynn and it is particularly satisfying to know that financially and morale-wise we leave them in a good position ... I have learned a great deal about the other side of the fence ... I can only say once again, a heartfelt 'thank you'.

Keith would, with Dame Janet, continue to be associated with the Festival, for as Sir Harry Tuzo, Chairman, wrote on 14 February 1984:

At their recent meeting the Board of St. George's Guildhall ... decided to ask you and Dame Janet Baker to become Vice-Presidents. Sir Geoffrey Agnew is, at present, the only holder of such office and we thought that it would be appropriate in the highest degree that your unfailing help and generosity should be similarly recognised ... More importantly, and more selfishly, we will perhaps be able to consult you on our affairs from time to time ...

Keith's response was immediate:

- I shall be honoured and delighted to accept your invitation ... My association with the Festival has been nothing but happiness: to join with enthusiasts in planning and making music is a tonic in itself. It will give me great pleasure to take a 'vice-presiding' interest in 'today' and 'tomorrow' in the remarkable vitality of the Festival ...

Highlights for 1984 were trips to Haddo to join the basses for *Five Tudor Portraits*, *The Music Makers* and *Songs of the Fleet*; Leipzig in late May, at Lord's in June, with a stay at Osborne in September. He was at the Royal Concert in November and at the RCM Council Dinner in December.

Concert No 3572 was given by the RCM on 1 March 1985 to celebrate Keith's 85th birthday, with *Ich habe genug* sung by Gerald Finley. April brought cricket; the 47th Norwich Triennial; Haddo in May with, later in the month, the Memorial Concert for Sir Adrian Boult at Westminster School. In June he was at St Paul's for the *B Minor Mass*, followed by the Lord's Test Match, and in July, at the RCM Council lunch and meeting. The composer Michael Ball came to visit, recalling in a letter dated some ten years later:

> ... Quite apart from my actual years as a student at the RCM, when Sir Keith was wonderfully supportive of my work as an emerging composer, it was immediately evident, even if I had not guessed this before, that for him all musicians were a common fraternity and he continued to take a lively interest in my doings as in those of all Collegians, throughout the coming years ...

In 1986, Keith spoke at the Norwich Opera and Eastbourne Gramophone clubs, and attended a press conference for the King's Lynn Festival in London. He was at Haddo again for *Elijah* in May, in London again for various functions before the imperative Test at Lord's. After the King's Lynn Festival there was the St Cecilia Service in November, and so the year came to a quiet end.

In April 1987, Keith flew to the States for the funeral of his friend and one-time colleague of Cornell days, Donald Grout. The year also saw a round of visits from family and friends, adjudications, cricket and festivals. David Fanshawe came to stay in September. 1988 brought trips to Haddo, this time for the Mozart *Requiem*; Lord's, of course, and so on until November, when Keith attended the Music Congress in Basle. Cherished memories: the occasional evenings he would sing, with Christabel at the piano.

Thus the years passed and 1990 dawned: a year of happiness, sadness and tragedy. It was not only the Falkners' 60th wedding anniversary but Keith's 90th birthday as well. David Imlay, a former RCM Bursar, sent 'A Tribute to Sir Keith Falkner on his 90th Birthday, St. David's Day 1990', a piece written for choir: *Be Strong and of a Good Courage* (Joshua I, 1.9.). In July, David Fanshawe wrote from Australia:

... It is with very great pleasure that I now send you my latest work, dedicated to you and Lady Falkner: 'Romanza Burlesque' ... I really hope you will like it, and we are now working towards finding a soloist who will première it ... we send you our continued Love and Admiration.

To further celebrate this occasion the *RCM Magazine*, in its autumn issue, paid tribute to 'Sir Keith Falkner'. Tom Allen's reminiscence:

In 1964, when asked, I volunteered the information that my golf handicap was a very respectable 3 and the silver-haired gentleman who asked me the question in the first place seemed to have no further hesitation in offering me a place as a first-year singing student at the Royal College of Music ... of course it wasn't as simple as that. I had had to prove myself musically too, by singing ... The next glimpse of the man came in the autumn of that same year when the student body assembled in the Concert Hall for the first day of term, when it was customary for him to address us all, old and new alike, after which we were treated to a lengthy 'postcard' of his summer activities. It was all very poetic and created quite an impression on the new boy. And I watched this man, tall and handsome, with that slight stoop common to people of such height and modesty, with his athletic gait – am I imagining it or did he really always wear tweed suits and leave a footprint of heavy walking-shoe soles along the college corridors? At least that was the impression ... The time came when I had an opportunity to watch him on the golf course. It was no surprise to find he always preferred carrying his bag. Not for him the awkward tugging of golfcarts up and down the fairways of the RAC at Epsom. But these were my own private experiences, and many more of us felt the benefit of his greatest sporting passion – CRICKET ... For the rest, we know his singing only from records. Fine singing in the manly, clean English tradition that so encapsulates the spirit of those interwar years. His help and encouragement to us all, whether performer or teacher, was of equal interest and concern ...

Sixtieth wedding festivities in June came to an end with the death of a granddaughter, preceding by five months that of Keith's Christabel on her 88th birthday, November 18. Sylvia Latham wrote in the *RCM Magazine*:

Past and present Collegians will have been greatly saddened by the news of the death of Lady Falkner ... As Christabel Fullard she was a student between 1922/26, during which time she won the Clementi Exhibition, Hopkinson Silver Medal and Charles Holmes and Ellen Shaw-Williams prizes. She was a piano student of Marmaduke Barton and also studied the violin ... During Sir Keith's term as Director of the RCM she served on the Council and on the House Committee of Queen Alexandra's House and was particularly helpful in the formation of the Friends of Queen Alexandra's House in 1973. She was an outstandingly pretty woman and her elegance and charm graced many social and musical occasions at the RCM ...

We consoled each other over these devastating blows, the pain and sorrow gradually easing so that Keith could write on his Christmas card to me in 1991: 'Thank you for making life worth living again'. With Christabel gone, the thing we missed most was the lack of music.

In May 1991, Richard Baker interviewed Keith and Roy Henderson for a BBC Radio 4 programme illustrated with several recordings. In December, Keith was interviewed again, this time by Radio Suffolk's 'Preview' show in which he talked about his career, a recording of which was replayed after his death. Keith was, of course, still greatly admired and respected, recognised by musicians around the world who wrote or came to visit, seeking counsel, or a chat with the – now – Grand Old Man.

1991 saw visits to London, though Keith was giving up directorships of a number of organisations, slowly letting go as the body, if not the mind, declined. He was at Osborne in March; at Lord's with Roy Henderson in April; Haddo in May; at the RCM Museum, Lord's Test and St Paul's in June; Oxford in July for the Haydn *Creation* and, later in the month, at King's Lynn.

Then there was the Aberdeen Festival, followed by the Test Match. Family came and went before, in November, we went to Venice, taking pleasure in each other's company. Looking at the dates now, it is easy to see why Keith wanted to be away, for it was exactly a year since Christabel's death. Early in 1992, Keith was again in London at the Abbey; at Osborne in February, in London in March and again in April for the *St Matthew Passion*. 1992 continued much the same. In August he was, of course, at Lord's, but disappointed not to go on to attend the Three Choirs Festival. We were at the Abbey on October 17 for Herbert Howells's Memorial Service, and he was at Osborne again in October; what remained of the year was fairly quiet with a welcome visit from his old friend Rosa Micallef Judge, organiser for the Associated Board adjudications in Malta.

Keith had always taken a keen interest in Neil Mackie's progress and put him 'up' for Athenaeum membership. The respect was mutual. As Neil wrote in the *RCM Magazine* (Spring Term 1995):

Listening to Sir Keith Falkner's recording from EMI's Golden Voice Series was, for me, a revelation – not only of a superb artistry but of the sincere, open and lovable person that he was throughout the time I knew him. I first met him in 1969 at my scholarship audition at the RCM ... After I had sung, with his customary generosity he complimented me on my singing, then asked me as a Scotsman, 'Do you play golf?' On learning that I didn't, he asked somewhat forlornly 'What about cricket?' Again I had to say no. In spite of these personal failings it was the beginning of a long and valued friendship ... Throughout my student days he took an acute interest in all that I did – helping and encouraging me with his wealth of singing experience .. He was truly concerned for the welfare of every student and for every member of staff, however lowly. In those balmy days, when College life was not as frenetic as today, it was everyone's experience – especially singers – to hear the studio door open and for DKF to slip in quietly for a few moments, then to offer a word of advice and encouragement as he left ... Keith Falkner's personal integrity and sincerity showed in his singing. The technical mastery of his voice, the clarity of diction and the perfection of the legato line were all subsumed in a naturalness of performance that contained the expression of every emotion and nuance. He was a great singer, loved by all with whom he came in contact. He was the father of an enormous family of College students and musicians whom be influenced by his generous spirit and professional excellence, perhaps no one more than myself, to whom he was an inspiration beyond adequate words ...

Neil not only instigated the birthday performance at Haddo in Keith's honour, but in 1992 initiated the 'Keith Falkner Prize' at the RCM.

On 9 February 1993 came the inaugural visit to the RCM of HRH The Prince of Wales as its eighth President, with Her Majesty Queen Elizabeth, the Queen Mother, retiring from the position. At tea, following speeches and concert, the Queen Mother particularly requested that Keith sit next to her. It was touching to observe these two nonagenarians together.

Honoured guest at a concert and supper party given at the Athenaeum by Neil to celebrate Keith's fifty years' membership, was great fun, though perhaps a touch embarrassing for Keith. He sat between two of the many ladies who professed to have been in love with him over the years. Another sat opposite. It was amusing to watch them vie for our Knight's attention while he, occasionally glancing my way, would lower an eyelid in a prolonged wink.

May saw a return visit to Haddo. Since 1960, and well into retirement, one of the most enjoyable events for Keith was his close association with

Haddo House Choral and Operatic Society, and friendship with David and June Gordon, the 4th Marquess and Marchioness of Aberdeen and Temair:

- June invited me to stay and sing with the Haddo House Choral Society for the annual May Music Festival, begun in 1945 by June and her husband (then Major David Gordon), deciding to use Haddo House Hall as a home for the performing arts. As she has said, 'It was a challenge I could not resist' ... Certainly, it is a great joy each year to go to stay at Haddo House with soloists, professional and amateur musicians both young and old, and to join with the Choir in rehearsals and performances, standing in the back row ... with fine bass voices. It is a benison to enjoy the friendly welcome the choir give to those of us musicians who are allowed to come and join in. Lady Aberdeen's recent direction of the Bach *B Minor Mass* (May 1992) was in classic style: the tempi so well balanced, the slow movements long and broad in phrasing and the quicker movements full of vitality ... For Lady Aberdeen to plan, rehearse and conduct these performances over nearly fifty years has been a great achievement. I know of no other woman musician in my experience capable of carrying out such a programme with so much charm, integrity and excellence. Amazing, considering her civic and official duties.

In a letter (November 1990) the Marchioness recalled:

I first heard Sir Keith when I was in my teens – in a performance of *Acis and Galatea* – with his splendid good looks and gorgeous red hair, I fell instantly in love with him, and have been ever since! Subsequent yearly *Matthew Passions*, his total integrity and beautiful singing is what I remember. When he became Director of the Royal College of Music, the help was instant, and the change from the dour atmosphere of the Dyson era wonderful ... He came regularly to sing with The Haddo House Choral Society and the sight of this great singer in the back row of the basses was very uplifting, and this support was tremendous. His courtly manner and friendliness made everyone love him ... This year (1990), at Neil Mackie's instigation, the Haddo House Choral Society performed the *St Matthew Passion* to celebrate Keith's 90th birthday, and we asked him to stand at the end, and he had a tremendous ovation from the choir, orchestra and audience, for all he has done for music ...

In May 1993, not guessing this would be his last visit, we were both at Haddo for a performance of *Samson* (Handel). This time, Keith was a member of the audience while I joined the choir. Keith spent a day with Roy Henderson at Lord's in the summer, another last visit as he was finding London increasingly difficult. Rocky on his feet now, he resorted to the telephone, while endless letters continued to arrive from musicians and friends. He found the Radio Three Evensong broadcasts both nostalgic and satisfying, often wondering whether the New College choir still sang with gusto and relish 'He smote his enemies in the hinder parts, putting them to a perpetual shame'. In July we drove to King's Lynn for the day and in August he spent three weeks at Osborne. From then on, most engagements in his diary are crossed off. The winter passed quietly and 1994 dawned, bringing several bouts in hospital.

Keith died at home the evening of 17 May 1994. Immediately I filled the house with music – the *St Matthew Passion* recorded in March 1937, with Jeanette Vreelane, Kathryn Meisle, John Priebe, Keith Falkner and Fritz Lechner, the Harvard Glee Club and Radcliffe Choral Society under Serge Koussevitzky. On the 23rd, cremation followed a service conducted by Reverend Lyndon van der Pump with the Royal College of Music Chamber Choir directed by Dr John Birch. And so it was that Sir Keith Falkner came to be buried in Sawston with his beloved Christabel and father, John Charles. Keith's epitaph: 'Ich habe genug'.

Epilogue

A Memorial Service was held on 11 March 1995, in New College, Oxford, with music by Howells, Vaughan Williams, Parry, Bach and Elgar. The reading and address were given by Keith's nephew, Alexander Falkner, and David McKenna. Gerald Finley sang *Schlummert ein* from Cantata No 82, *Ich habe genug*.

The Royal College of Music paid tribute the following day to its sixth Director, presenting a moving performance of the *St Matthew Passion* conducted by Sir David Willcocks, with the RCM Chorus and Sinfonia. Every seat was taken. The programme notes in part read:

> The legacy of Sir Keith Falkner is still to be found in many strands of College life more than two decades after his retirement . . . students from Sir Keith's time remember above all the man: a dignified, gracious and gentle person whose natural humility coloured every action and word; a musician of sensitivity and stature; a teacher unfailingly interested in each individual, a constant source of wisdom. In the words of the late Sir Thomas Armstrong, writing in *The Guardian* on 23 May 1994: 'All who worked with Keith during his long career, whether as artist or administrator, knew they were dealing with a man of complete integrity, great intelligence, warm-hearted generosity of spirit and absolute loyalty. He was not only respected and admired. There was more to it than that. He was loved.' . . . The beautiful quality of his voice and dignified yet imaginative delivery of Christ's words (*St Matthew Passion*) will always be remembered by those who were privileged to hear him perform.

On Sunday 8 October, 1995, during the Haddo House Choral and Operatic Society's 50th season, a performance of *Messiah* was dedicated to Keith's memory. My daughter and I joined the choir for the occasion. The conducting and dedication was by June Gordon:

> Sir Keith Falkner was one of the most outstanding musicians of his generation and very much beloved. I first encountered him in my teens when he was singing, absolutely marvellously, in *Acis and Galatea, O Ruddier than the Cherry* . . . I fell in love with him there and then and remained so all his life! Our friendship developed when be became Director of my old college, The Royal College of Music, and he invariably came to sing in the chorus with us for all the works that he loved, and even some he was not so fond of! The sight of this great singer in the back row of the chorus was a

great stimulation to us all. He kept saying to me in his latter years, 'When will you do the *Messiah*' and I said, 'On our 50th anniversary, as it was the first oratorio we started with', but alas, it was too late for his participation but I am sure he is with us today and we salute his memory with joy and happiness.

Two quotes, the first from the *RCM Magazine* 1990 by Ralph Nicholson, former Professor of Violin:

The name of Keith Falkner came into my musical consciousness in the early 1930s . . . One was immediately struck by singing of a purity of tone, aided by a minimum of vibrato and clarity of diction, which reflected a musical mind of a high order. One felt at the time that here was an example of musicianship of a quality which lesser aspirants might ignore at their peril! . . . John Hare (Head of the General Office RCM in the 1920s) once said to me: 'Do you know the finest student who's ever been at the College? Keith Falkner!'

The other, in a letter (1994) from Geraint Jones:

I remember the first time I heard Keith sing – in the *B Minor Mass* at Queen's Hall about 1933, when I was still at boarding school . . . You can imagine my excitement when in 1942 I shared a recital with him at one of the National Gallery concerts. My daughter was then only a few months old and he looked after her while I was occupied on the platform! He was director of the Kirckman Concert Society, which gives young artists opportunities to perform at the Wigmore Hall and on the South Bank. In a tribute to your father, which I made from the stage at our most recent concert in the Purcell Room, I was very glad publicly to be able to describe him as the finest British baritone of the century, a fact of which I and a host of my professional contemporaries have never been in any doubt . . . He was a wonderful man as well as singer.

Chapter 10: The Sportsman

Throughout there have been numerous references to Sir Keith's keen interest and participation in sports. In fact, before singing took precedence, he had expected to become a music and sports master at a public school. He was introduced to cricket at an early age, after which the game became an obsession.

- My father and brother were responsible for my love of cricket and I was terribly excited at the age of seven to be given a small cricket bat by none other than Thomas Hayward, the famous batsman of the 1860s. I enjoyed other games as well and played soccer, badminton and hockey at New College, often using a walking stick on an asphalt playground – splendid training for eye and stickwork. I was introduced to rugby when I went on to the Perse. In my first game I asked what I was supposed to do and told that if I got the ball, I was to run like hell for the line! This I did and was soon flat on my nose in the mud. Later I came to enjoy being a No 8 in the scrum, while as a left-hander at cricket I soon got into the XI and was most impressed to have DLA Jephson bowl lobs to us in the nets.

  After I joined Barclay's Bank, I played regularly for my father's mid-week side. At one wartime charity match he persuaded Tom Hayward to play. After we 'teenagers' had failed, Hayward and my father, whose ages added up to a hundred, got sixty apiece while I was concerned about their running between the wickets. Jephson, who with Tom Richardson often opened the bowling for Surrey at the Oval, also played regularly in these matches and it was exciting to field his bowling at short cover point, the only man 'on the off'[1] waiting for an 'outside edge'. An early contact with some of cricket's greats.

The Royal College of Music in the 1920s encouraged inter-college games and Keith found himself playing soccer, cricket and golf, with chief matches against the Royal Academy of Music, known as 'the other place', for the Farjeon Cup.

- In these games I met my life-long friend and colleague Roy Henderson, who was always a thorn in our side, helping the Academy to win. He was an excellent goalkeeper, a crafty slow spinner and a batsman very hard to shift. We often recalled these games on the Concourse at Lord's in later years with Roy reminding me of one we played on the Nursery Ground in which I was

---

[1] 'On the off': Eight men on the 'on' (leg) side of the pitch, four out and four in.

well set. The RAM captain handed Roy the ball, saying sotto voce, 'See if you can get the bugger out!'

While at the RCM, Keith played regularly for Sawston at weekends in early rounds of the Cambridgeshire Cup in 1921. Sawston, which had not won the cup since 1901, won it that year, curiously the same two years Tottenham won the FA Cup. In 1901, Jack Hobbs was on the losing side.

- Treviss Teversham (local Sawston historian), who played in both years with my father as captain, told me: 'Your father said "We shall be all right if we can get young Jack (Hobbs) out".' In 1950 Sir Jack recalled the match with Teversham, saying: 'Do you remember that catch of Falkner's that got me out in the second innings?'

    In 1921 Sawston played Pampisford, 'Pahnser' in local jargon, in an early round for the Cup. My partner was given out, caught behind. The ball had touched nothing en route to the wicket keeper. I objected to the umpire. 'I ain't umpirin' for Sawston', was the reply, 'I'm umpirin' for Pahnser!'

In a later round, Keith scored a hundred and because of this received a telegram inviting him to play for the County against Norfolk. He was thrilled and, on arriving at Fenner's, awestruck to be told that he was to open the innings.

- I was doubly awestruck for Michael Falcon, the Norfolk skipper, had just helped to skittle the Australians for A C Maclaren's XI in their only defeat of the tour. It was a perfect Fenner's wicket, and I played with trepidation yet managed 29 runs, hitting Falcon for two fours over his head. It was one of the best innings of my life. During lunch, Falcon encouragingly asked me what I was going to do about my cricket.

During the 1921/22 season, Keith played rugby for the Saracens, enjoying the rough and tumble of a wing forward. This came to a halt, as previously mentioned, when Garcia refused to teach him unless he gave it up. He was then persuaded to join the Southgate Hockey Club.

- I turned out for a trial game and asked where I played: left back it was. The game was one of the hardest examinations I can remember for I was repeatedly diddled by the stick work of the right inside forward. At the end of the game I asked who he was and told that he was Jimmy Savile, captain of England. At that moment Savile came up to me and said 'You are playing for the first eleven next Saturday'. It was a wonderful year of first-class hockey and I was actually picked for a county match, that of Middlesex versus Essex at High Beech. We lost 3 to 2.

This Saturday hockey also had to cease, so instead, in 1922, Keith joined the HAC (No 4 Company), playing 'Army' hockey for the mid-week side at Armoury House in the City. Here, body obstruction was not illegal, and he gradually got used to body-contact hockey:

- My first experience of it was against Cambridge University, when GEC Wood used his body to frustrate my stickwork. I certainly gained disapproval from Dr Charles McPherson when I turned up one day for full choir rehearsal at St Paul's with hockey stick and kit straight from a match. Looking at the game today, one is aware how far it has developed, causing penalties which, to my mind, are spoiling the game.

For the 1922/23 season, Keith played for the Chiswick Park Cricket Club and, as he lived a mile away in Turnham Green, had to walk a mile each way, lugging his heavy cricket bag. He also joined the Wanderers, captained by Stanley Colman of Surrey fame – he with his ancient limousine and gigantic 'Methusalah' scorebook to hand:

- It was at a match against Surrey Club and Ground at the Oval that I first met EW (Jim) Swanton, where he got some runs, I a few wickets. At weekends I played matches for Major Mallison's XI at Hackbridge and was soon invited to join the Grasshoppers and eventually the Free Foresters. One vital match increased my ambition to join the MCC. I was playing at East Grinstead for Colonel Munn's side and put in to bowl against a fellow batting 60 not out. After exploratory length on the off stump, I bowled him a slower ball which he hit for six. I again bowled him the same ball but this time from a yard short of the crease. It bowled him. Colonel Munn rushed up to ask if I was down for the MCC and, if not, could he propose me; Desmond Roberts seconded me while I sat down to wait.

The prospects were of course thrilling but by 1928 Keith was too busy with concerts to play regularly for Cambridgeshire; he could in fact only manage two matches. Then in July, versus Oxfordshire at Fenner's, 'batting suddenly became the easiest thing in the world' for him. He got 143 and a mention in *Wisden*.[2]

- I travelled back to London with the umpires, Beet was one of them, and there was much talk about the various bowlers they had 'stood for' during the season. Walking on air after my hundred, I arrived home to be informed that Colonel Miller Mundy of Red Rice, Andover, had invited me to play for his

---

[2] 'Keith Falkner, a newcomer, who registered the only one hundred for the county, unfortunately could play only four innings.' Batting averages: innings: 4; runs: 188; highest innings: 143; not outs: 0; average: 47.00.

side in the Andover Cricket Week, and you may imagine my elation. I immediately accepted and told I would be replacing HDG (Shrimp) Levenson-Gower, who had cried off as he was needed at Old Trafford, being one of the Test selectors. Our team was captained by C D McIver, who won the toss and asked me whether I had got any runs lately. Informing him that indeed I had, he said, 'Good! Come in first with me and let's have a look at you'. I got a hundred before lunch, to have Collin say: 'We must get you on to the MCC players list.'

I soon found myself playing out-matches for the MCC but batting never came as easily as it had done earlier. With my cricket bag at Lord's, I got regular net practice with the Ground staff, Walter Brearley ever eager to bowl. It was a great day when Gubby Allen asked if he could come and loosen up by bowling to me; several whistled past my eyebrow but I kept my wicket intact and then managed to bowl him out instead.

In 1930, Colin invited me to play two matches with the MCC against the Gentlemen of Ireland in Cork and Dublin. It was the apogee of my cricketing career, for I was on the same team with the likes of the Nawab of Pataudi, Claude Taylor, Denis Morkel and Garland Wells! We arrived at Cork by the night boat and, having kissed the Blarney stone, were taken to our hostesses. Claude and I were billeted in a house with two very attractive daughters, who soon discovered we were both newly married. It amused us to watch the speed with which these girls moved on to other houses to entertain the team's bachelors.

In the Dublin game, the catch I held to dismiss EL Kidd in full flow is vivid: he hit a cannonball at me at deep mid-off, chest high, which I managed to catch side-handed; had I missed it, I would have been in hospital. Gradually though I came to realise that I had, after all, chosen the right profession, that of singing.

The most enjoyable cricket of my life occurred each year during the 1930s; certainly it was the most hilarious when I played for Clifford Bax's side, The Old Broughtonians. Based at the Fernley hotel in Bath, it was a ten-day tour of Somerset and Wiltshire, the side consisting of characters and eccentrics – musicians, writers, journalists, literary agents, politicians and school masters – very similar in fact to the *England, their England* team. Each match was written up by a member of the side and became part of the *Old Broughtonian Cricket Weeks*. Eric Gillett wrote about my first match on 2 August 1933[3]:

... Keith followed ... In the years to come the Grittleton match of 1933 will be remembered for the first appearance in our ranks of the most eminent Queen's Hall and MCC batsman, who has long delighted in equal measure Lord Hawke and Sir Henry Wood. The very first ball he received Keith hit

---

[3] Volume VI, Favil Press, 1938.

to top E or some such surprising altitude and went on to make 19 in a few bars.

The following year, Patrick Knox Shaw wrote on 9 August:

> ... Keith's arrival at the wicket widened the field of interest. His first six went soaring like a great night-bomber over the expanse of the local tennis courts, and a moment later, as I stood trembling at the other wicket, I saw a sprawling group of spectators spring to sudden activity and take cover beneath their deck chairs ...

In 1938, Maurice Foster invited Keith to tour Northern Ireland with the Free Foresters. The side included Ian Akers Douglas, J T H Comber, Denis Morkel, Charles Fiddian-Green and J W Greenstock, all guests of the Cecil Lindsays at Lisburn. It was a delightful tour with matches interspersed with golf at Newcastle, County Down, one of the great courses.

The impending war, in 1939, brought an end to much that Keith had enjoyed in the way of sport, though it continued to play an important part in his life. Early in 1940, and back in the Royal Air Force, he was posted to Orkney, to find no cricket. Reposted to Middle Wallop in 1941, he managed some enjoyable games with Wing Commander Richard Rickett, an old friend. At his next reposting, the Scilly Isles, again he found no cricket, but by 1942/43, when posted to Northern Ireland, he found lots of 'keen' cricket being played.

- On one weekend visit to Dublin the British High Commissioner invited a Combined Forces XI to play against his team on Trinity College ground which turned out to be two days of first-class (club standard) cricket, two days of generous hospitality, of peacetime-quality enjoyment, with no lighting restrictions or rationing. It was almost like a Buckingham Palace garden party, with ladies in colourful summer hats and dresses, a band playing, flags flying.

  I moved on to Patrington near Hull in 1943/44 and, considering the small number of personnel, with my Number 2, George Richmond, we had a very good side and beat several of the larger RAF stations in Yorkshire. In 1944, following D-Day, the Patrington Station began to relax with a great deal more time spent on athletic and social affairs. We had a mixed hockey side which was very good, with Richmond as centre half and myself at left back; we lost only one match, to Sector HQ by the odd goal. The standard of cricket was even better and we had close matches against Hull and Pocklington RAF stations. My diary for 19 June 1945 reminds me that we played against Leconfield, winning 127, 130 for 6 (67 not out). On our side we had a very fast bowler and I suggested he try and get his line and length before he 'let one go'. Time after time he got a couple of early wickets this way while I, at a game at Withernsea, was able to repeat the century I had made there twenty-five years earlier.

1946 saw the family move to Italy and it was here that Keith found some amusing cricket played on dusty wickets for the Embassy and English and Scottish Theological Colleges. There was always squash, tennis and golf to fall back on, including many foursomes with the Ambassador, Sir Victor Mallett, Brigadier Geoffrey McNab, the first secretary to the Swedish Embassy, Targa Grunwald, and Major Clive Robinson. During the winter there were cold swims in the Mediterranean.

Arriving at Cornell in 1950, Keith discovered that cricket had been played here many years before[4] but had long given way to baseball, due primarily to the climate and the American temperament, which is better suited to the faster game of baseball. From 1950, however, cricket saw a revival, largely due to the entry of Commonwealth students to American universities and in no small part to Keith, who felt that young men brought up in the cricket tradition were the richer for it.

- In re-founding the cricket club at Cornell in 1952, I was shown a cupboard full of moth-eaten bats and pads which had been lying fallow for decades. I had to ask the Athletics Director for permission to play on Cornell's Hoy Field, and he showed me one corner of the ground, roughly the size of a baseball diamond. In explaining that I needed the whole field, he thought for a few moments and then said I could have it so long as I canvassed for funds for the Episcopal Church. I readily agreed and coerced my wife to do the canvassing. From then on she and the girls provided endless gallons of strong tea and cucumber sandwiches at the home matches.

'Import from England ... Cricket Returns After Long Absence' reported the *Cornell Daily Sun* on 22 April 1952:

The English game of cricket, which was the first competitive sport to be played at Cornell, has returned to the campus. Under the direction of Professor Keith Falkner and Handel Devies, both Englishmen, a Cornell

---

[4] Cricket, dating back to the thirteenth century, when it was played by English monks, was outlawed in 1477 by Edward IV because it interfered with his favourite sport, archery. In 1748 the law decided cricket to be a manly sport and no longer illegal, and it has been played in America for well over 200 years, the first recorded match between New York and a London XI being in 1751. In about 1880 it was superseded by baseball as a summer sport and reached its lowest ebb between 1920 and 1950.

Cricket Club has been formed with thirty charter members ... Cricket is in some ways comparable to baseball, though an avid cricket fan would never admit its connection ... Cricket, like baseball, is learned slowly and most good players have been brought up on the sport ...

The Ithaca Journal, 4 June 1952:

'Cornell Lists Cricket Match on Hoy' – Ithaca sports fans who would like to see something a little different will have the opportunity this Saturday when the Cornell Cricket Club meets the Rochester club in a return match ...

It seemed that the humour of the well-worn picture of the puzzled and bewildered American watching cricket was slowly going out of date, though most were speechless when told matches could last for five days.

- My first team was an interesting assortment: a Welshman, two Englishmen, a Pakistani, a Portuguese Goan, a South African, two men from Australia and New Zealand, a Nigerian and a Highland Scot. The few Americans initially interested were very keen and good bowlers, though their batting was weak and the umpiring, well, inexperienced. At one of the first games the Cornell baseball captain came to watch, only to exclaim dumbfounded as he stood in the slips: 'He don't even try to hit the b....... thing!' It was unlike baseball, where you 'slog' at every pitch.

  Each season we played 'away' matches at Harvard, Princeton, Haverford College, Rochester and others. No one seemed to mind the travelling as we often left at 4 am to drive 400 miles and get home at 2 the following morning. One American undergraduate who played with us for about three years had just returned from a year at Oxford, where he had enjoyed watching the game. His fielding was energetic and accurate, his batting just energetic, while his great ambition was to be a good bowler. I coached him week after week, year after year at the nets, but he could not master the action. Eventually, so as not to break his heart and as we were doing well in a match against the United Nations XI, they were 50 for 7, I allowed him to bowl. They plastered him all over the place and he was getting dispirited when, at last, a long hop, then a wide, then a full pitch throwing down a full toss. The batsman took a mighty swipe, missed and saw his wickets spreadeagled. Beside himself, the young American turned to me ecstatically, waving his arms in the air, and with face pale, eyes shining, he ran down the pitch towards me shouting: 'I got an out! I GOT AN OUT!!'

Cricket, of course, was not the only non-musical pastime in which Keith showed great interest. He put the Cornell Golf Club to good use and attended most inter-mural meets, football and basketball games, and enjoyed walking holidays in the Adirondacks.

When he returned to England In 1960, there was less time for participatory sport except for golf, squash and swimming. In retirement, and to his dying day, cricket continued to hold his avid interest. In 1981, and again in 1983, he gave parties at Lord's, inviting old friends Roy Henderson, Bernard Shore, Robert Easton, Jim Swanton and Colin Cowdray, among others. Both Richard Rickett and Bernard Shore wrote after the gathering in 1981:

> I cannot wait a minute longer to write and thank you for your superb hospitality this afternoon. It was the most civilised gathering I have been privileged to attend for a great many years. 'A great many years' is also applicable to the sum total of the ages of those present, and that too was good because elderly people talk more sense than striplings. I was particularly glad to meet Bernard Shore again ... I think Lord's is a sort of oasis in the whole of London, the only place where a gathering such as today's could possibly have taken place. It was like an afternoon in the 1930s ...

And,

> That was a day and a half that was, you gave us at Lord's. It was a bumper of all the good things of life. Renewal of old friendships, good talk, lovely, civilised food and service and cricket to tie all the threads together ...

Keith was particularly proud to have been a member since 1931 of the MCC, which in 1991 granted him life membership. Other clubs included the Grasshoppers (1930) and Free Foresters (1916). He was made an honorary member of the Southgate Hockey Club in 1978.

The retirement home in Suffolk had lawns maintained to perfection for an 18-hole putting course and croquet lawn which, over many years, saw family and friends enjoying endless games. The crack of persimmon mallet on croquet ball seems to reverberate still ...

PART TWO

Keith Falkner
on aspects of music

Training a singer or, what is good singing?

There seems to be a general belief that singing is a natural gift which needs little or no training. It has been said that 'Anyone can stand up and sing and it's either pleasant or unpleasant – but to play the violin you must practise steadily for ages before you can create sounds worth listening to.' Of course there is some truth in this – but let me assure you that no singer gets very far in the development of his or her natural talent without similar, though somewhat different, application to steady work as the violinist. I deliberately make the comparison between voice and violin for in both cases you have to create your tones and listen to them carefully for quality and pitch.

So often, singers are spoken of disparagingly by other musicians. Why? Because singers rarely take the trouble to learn their job properly, missing out all the musical training that is essential to any performance of decent standard. Even when I was a student at the Royal College of Music, the football and cricket teams were made up of Musicians versus Singers. I remember on one occasion the Singers needed four runs with the last ball of the game for victory. A Singer hit it hard, straight back at the 'Musicianly' bowler, who promptly jumped out of the way and let the ball go to the boundary. As his fellow musicians remonstrated with him on his unsporting behaviour he exclaimed, 'What about my hands? I'm an organist.'

It is an interesting fact, in England at any rate, that you will find many of the successful male singers have been choirboys in their youth. They have thus learned the ABC of singing early in life and do not have to start from scratch when they discover, later on, that they have a good tenor or baritone voice. It is remarkable that, often, in solo-voice competitions a whole group of boys' unbroken voices will demonstrate good tone quality, rhythm and phrasing that put many of the grown-up singers to shame. Incidentally, the musical side of many of our choir schools is being curtailed in the interest of general education. This is a tendency which should be strongly resisted. To my mind these schools, if developed to include *all* young musicians of talent, could provide us with the nursery about which Russia and other countries crow with satisfaction.

What is good singing? What *is* good singing? You and I think we know what good singing is, but it doesn't follow that either of us is right. Having performed, worked and lived in various countries during my career, I have observed with interest the different standards of singing demanded by the concert-going public. In England, for example, the public demand intelligence above everything else. A singer may not have a remarkable voice or a flawless technique, but if he interprets well, he can often be successful. In Italy a singer must first of all possess a remarkable voice plus good technique; not until then will he be given a hearing. Many times I have been aware of the tension in the hall when an Italian audience realises that it is listening to a singer with fine voice and technique, one can sense the audience thinking with excitement, 'We know you can sing well but are you also a good artist and interpreter?' In the United States a singer must not only be well equipped vocally: he or she must also possess great confidence in his or her own ability to impress an audience. This tends at times to eliminate the depth or sensitivity of the performance and put too much emphasis on its extrovert qualities.

Now which type of singing do you prefer? I can only tell you which I like and try to explain why l think the Italian assessment of good singing to be the best.

Since the great school of Italian singing in the 17th century – when, incidentally, nearly all the famous composers were singers, and when the schools in Naples, Rome, Florence, Milan and Venice all taught the same method, ie, the open throat – the Italians have required that to be a good singer you must first of all possess a natural voice of pleasing quality and intensity, and further that you must develop it to its full capacity over a number of years. Finally, that your own mind, intelligence and emotions should be at one with your voice. In other words, it is no use being a good driver if your car isn't running well, and it's no use having a perfect engine if you are a bad driver. How do you set about tuning your engine and learning to drive well? What are the first steps?

Like a child taking its first walk, the steps must be slow and careful. Each note must be listened to carefully, not only by your teacher but by you yourself, for one of the first things to learn in singing is the ability to judge the quality of sound you are producing. Later this faculty becomes instinctive and the mere fact that your mind and ear anticipate the sound you wish to make will help you find it.

Of course it is not only beginners who have to watch each note slowly and carefully. I remember an example of infinite patience and care taken by one of the finest pianists of the century, Rachmaninoff. Shortly before he died, he was to give a recital in Syracuse, New York. He asked the Steinway agent for a studio and piano for the afternoon of his concert. Most of the staff and a few lucky customers spent the afternoon sitting outside the door, spellbound, as he rehearsed his whole programme at half speed, examining each phrase for the slightest flaw. If a great artist finds it necessary to go to such pains, how much more important it is for the beginner.

Your teacher will instruct you first in sound breathing: control of breath in inhalation, holding it and in steady emission, and, secondly, like the Italians, with an open throat. You will learn to sing single notes on your best vowel sound, in the easiest part of your voice. From this you will develop a similar quality for all your vowels, for it is this basic singing quality, or fundamental tone, which is often lacking in young singers. When you can maintain this quality over an octave or so you have solved, partly at any rate, the problem of singing with an open throat. This is what I mean: so many singers are able, for example, to sing a good 'ah' vowel but when they attempt other vowels, like 'ay', 'ee' or 'o', the quality becomes shallow, pinched or 'hooty'. If they attempt to sing songs before all the vowels are well-matched, they are trying to run before they can walk.

Let us assume that you have acquired your open throat through a range of ten notes and that you are able to sustain them steadily up and down. Now your teacher may select a simple song like *Verdant Meadows* by Handel, which is legato in style and ideal for a young voice to attempt. The words present no great interpretative problems beyond a general feeling of reflective beauty. How are we to make it effective? We must breathe it well, sustain each phrase easily and sing them smoothly, to be accurate in values and intonation, and to keep a steady tempo. Finally, we must remember to sing with an open throat, our fundamental tone with similar quality for all vowels. Having got these technical details right, the song may still be without expression.

It was Plunket Greene who said 'There is an implied crescendo in the rising of a phrase and an implied diminuendo in the descending note or phrase. This is the first elementary rule on which phrasing is based and like most other rules it often pays to break it.'

This question of expression in a song is not as difficult as one might imagine. It always pays to look a song over both musically and verbally before attempting to sing it, to find the climax and the opportunities for expressive treatment. A lot of students make heavy weather over their consonants and let them interfere with the fundamental singing tone. We must remember that consonants are made only with the tip of the tongue, the teeth and the lips and have nothing whatever to do with the singing tone. It is a great help to remember that the shorter the consonants and the longer the vowels, the more intelligible and beautiful will the song become.

Let us suppose that our second song is to be *Since first I saw your face* by Thomas Ford, one of the finest of the Elizabethan Lutenists. It is similar to the Handel song only in its simple melodic line. Now we have to consider the words much more carefully. It is a beautiful love song and the poetry must be allowed full expression. The inflections we use in reading the poem should be just as evident in our singing if we are to make the song fully effective. We must remember too that a singer's first and last duty is to recreate the song the poet and composer have written, so that the audience can experience its full meaning.

What are the next steps to be taken? At this stage singers are often criticised for faulty attack, such as scooping up to a note, or for lack of rhythmic vitality in their singing. Have you ever watched a big choir when it is really letting itself go during, say, the singing of the 'Hallelujah' chorus? If you have, you have been amused, as I have been, to notice that there are always a few singers who take in a great gasp of breath, lifting their shoulders, just as the conductor's stick brings them in. That sort of thing doesn't matter of course in a large choir, where so many mixed qualities blend to produce a good choral tone. But put any one of those violent breathers or 'blockbusters' out in front to sing by themselves and the result would be rough, uncontrolled and shortwinded. Why? Because to ensure proper control, and therefore proper clean attack that can be sustained, it is necessary to take breath and hold it before starting to sing. If you don't hold it, your breathing is like a tidal river without lock gates, as the air pours in and out in bulk without any resistance at all. It is this resistance or holding the breath that is so important. You can get the right sensation in a variety of ways: just hold your breath, as you do unconsciously when you run upstairs or, when you lean down to pick up a parcel. You feel a resistance of the breathing control muscle called the diaphragm, which is acting like a lockgate and preventing the air from being pumped out as you climb or bend down. It is this resistance which is so important to singers, because it means you can use as little or as much breath as you need when you start to sing. To be a bit more practical I suggest four short exercises to illustrate what I mean:

1. Take in a breath slowly and fully through the nose and mouth together, for this ensures an open throat, and hold it for a few seconds before releasing it. This holding gives you a feeling as though you are leaning on your breath.

2. Inhale as before, hold it for 2 seconds, then release it as though whispering the word 'who' on the palm of your hand, sustaining it gently and steadily for 10 seconds. During the 10 seconds you will be aware that your diaphragm is in control.

3. Inhale, hold and intone a note steadily for 10 seconds.

4. Put you hand on your diaphragm or breathing muscle, inhale, hold and then give a series of short attacks on 'ah' sounds. You will notice the reaction the muscle makes to control the release and holding of breath.

The great Manuel Garcia described the 'attack' as being like a gentle cough, but to my mind this can become too harsh a sound unless well understood. Madame Arnhold in her admirable *Treatise on Singing* describes the attack as 'mentally preparing a note and starting with a light short movement, as though one caressed the vocal chords in a downward back-to-front movement. This creates a sensation of space at the back of the tongue, in other words an open throat.' Another way to ensure the lightness of an attack is to hum several preliminary sounds. I think you will find among these various descriptions a way to ensure a clean, light start, straight into the middle of a note and without any scooping or slurring. When you can control these 'attacks' gently and warmly, you can then attempt louder attacks, for louder attacks mean greater resistance and pressure. You will find that when your inhalation, holding and attacks are well controlled it is a physical impossibility to force or strain your voice.

Lack of rhythmic vitality is also a question of faulty breathing. How often one hears an accompanist wait for a singer at the end of a phrase? The whole problem is easily solved if you will remember to take time out from the final note of a phrase and on no account be late for the first note of the next. I have never understood why vocal music is not printed as we sing it, ie, with final notes in a phrase slightly shortened where we must breathe. It would make it so much easier for us all and especially for students. In a Bach aria you sometimes find a florid passage lasting for several lines of the score without a visible breathing space. As a result we have to take what we call 'snatch' breaths. This is not an attempt to fill the lungs but to get just enough air to get us to the next breathing place, rather like running across a stream on stepping stones. Snatch breaths can become very noticeable and noisy. It is important that the mouth and throat are kept open so that there are no obstructions for the air to whistle round. Also, one must not attempt to take a full breath or the result will be a terrific gasp which will be irritating to the throat as well as your audience.

Posture, facial expression and concentration whilst singing are, of course, very important. Is it necessary to express every emotion with a suitable facial expression? What do you do with the hands while singing? How do you walk on to the platform, and where to stand? These questions are all very important for the young singer and indeed for all public performers. The first thing to remember is that everything a performer does, from the moment he steps on to the platform, has some reaction from the audience, the slightest gesture or look meaning something. I remember Dame Myra Hess saying that it is necessary for an artist to be in sympathetic contact with his audience *before* he begins to play or sing. In other words, it is vitally important that you should walk on to the platform in a courteous manner, showing an awareness that your audience have come to hear you, and that you have a job to do that needs all your concentration. Don't, for example, walk on to the platform talking to your pianist, adjusting your dress or putting your tie straight for it will give the impression that you are ill-prepared or unaware of the attention you owe to your audience. Also, it makes you look more like a comedian than a serious artist.

During the Second World War I met Joyce Grenfell in Northern Ireland, where she was touring for ENSA giving a series of character sketches at each camp. Joyce became concerned about the order of her programme. Her performance began as an old woman staggering on to the stage with stick and shawl, followed by younger impersonations. She knew the troops were so certain she *was* an old woman that her more youthful acts were falling flat. I mention this as an example of the importance of first impressions.

Many of my colleagues have told me that it helps them to take up a singing position with open throat as they walk on to the stage. In effect this means walking upright but naturally with ribs expanded, aware of your diaphragm, and with your stomach slightly drawn in. By so doing, your carriage will look dignified and purposeful.

You may be feeling very nervous but you mustn't let it show. The mere fact that you put on a 'façade' of repose will help you to control your feelings and enable you to concentrate on your singing. Incidentally, one of the soundest remedies for extreme nervousness is deep breathing. You need more oxygen. Some steady breathing will often help a great deal. Athletes often adopt this remedy just before a race. I read recently in a book by a Tibetan Llama that it is possible by correct control of one's breath 'to sit naked on ice at 17,000 feet above sea level and keep so hot that the ice is melted and the adept freely perspires'. Whether or not we are prepared to try this, it should certainly encourage us to develop our own breath control.

What to do with the hands worries a lot of singers. It is best to let them hang loosely or hold them together, with perhaps a programme in hand at waist level. I say loosely because muscular tension can easily be set up if you clasp your hands together. On no account sway from side to side with your hands extended in front of you. This will look as though you are imploring help or begging for applause.

The question of facial expression is contained in the word concentration. If you have done your preparatory work well, the fact that you are living the song will naturally produce the right expression. Nothing is more sickening to my mind than to watch a singer being arch with the audience. Of course there are songs in which you have to take your audience into your confidence. Even so, a singer should still be concentrating on the story he has to feel. Concentration reminds me of Elena Gerhardt. Years ago I went with a young soprano to hear Gerhardt sing Schubert's *Winterreise* at Queens Hall. Her pianist was a very attractive girl called Paula Hegner. After the first song, *Gute Nacht*, Gerhardt walked round to Paula, smiled and spoke to her before going on with the programme. We were very inquisitive as to what the joke was. My soprano friend, who was studying with Gerhardt at the time, asked, at her next lesson: 'What was the joke you had with Paula Hegner at your recital?' 'Oh,' replied Gerhardt, 'that Paula! She is so vain, she think all the time of her new shoes. I said to her, much smiling, "Paula, for God's sake concentrate!" That was the joke.' You will find that, like the greatest singers, if you concentrate and forget about your new shoes, all the other things will take care of themselves, and you will be in direct contact with your audience.

How much should a singer practise and how careful should he be of his voice? I wonder how many of you have read Sir Henry Wood's stupendous work in four volumes called *The Gentle Art of Singing*. I don't suppose any English musician ever worked harder or did more for music in our time than did Sir Henry. In his book he sketched out a timetable for a voice student which left no time to be wasted between 7 am on Monday morning and lunchtime on Sunday. It involved early rising, breathing and physical exercises, vocal exercises, piano practice, theory work, frequent walks in the park, transposing songs, reading poetry, languages, memorising, listening to concerts morning, noon and night until Sunday afternoon. On Sunday afternoon he wrote with his own whimsical humour: 'Visit friends, if any'. I don't say it is possible today to carry out such a full timetable, but it does point out the importance of a general musical background combined with healthy living.

I consider it vital that a singer should be healthy inside and out, with plenty of fresh air and gentle exercise for, as the early Italians said, 'It clears the tubes'. I have often heard people complain and question the value of steady practise at technical exercises. I can only tell you that no professional singer would willingly forego his daily practise.

Was it Patti or Jenny Lind who said, 'If I don't practise for one day I know it. If I don't practise for two days, my friends know it, and if I don't practise for three days the public know it.' In a general way I would recommend that beginners limit their practise to fifteen minutes at a time and not more than three times a day. Later, practise for longer periods as the voice and technique develop. In any case, practise should stop at the slightest sign of vocal fatigue, otherwise it will lead to strain. In the early stages your exercises will be slow, and you should concentrate on beauty and purity of sound. Later it is desirable to make the voice more mobile and elastic. Technical exercises, like the scales and arpeggios of the pianists, gradually prepare the voice for the technical difficulties in songs and arias.

I am often asked: 'Is smoking bad for singers?' It is like so many things in life that, taken in moderation, can do you no harm. But in excess, can vitiate your whole character. I seldom smoke myself as I don't enjoy it, but I wouldn't like to say it is harmful to a voice. If it dries your throat or makes you sneeze, give it up. I seem to remember that Caruso was very fond of a cigar, and Plunket Greene said he would rather give up singing than smoking. There is one aspect of smoking which is extremely irritating to a singer's nose and throat: a room full of stale smoke. Foul air should always be avoided.

The early Italians used to say that spirits are bad for singers; sweet wine good for young voices, with dry wines for the older ones.

With some singers the question of colds and sore throats is a constant problem, as some people are much more susceptible than others. There are a few rules with which most singers will agree. Don't stand in cold or draughty places after singing. It is a known fact that a singer's vocal chords turn slightly pink after a good sing, instead of the usual white. This is a healthy sign and only means that your voice and vocal apparatus have been taking exercise. Take special care at such times and, like an athlete, keep warm until you are back to normal. It is wise to keep your feet warm and dry at all times, as many singers' colds develop from cold and damp feet. Otherwise, be rational and sensible about your health.

Now I would like to say something about the various styles a singer is expected to understand in his work. There is no doubt that if a student will take the trouble to understand the different types of recitative, it will never be said of him: 'He sings well but I can't understand a word he says.' For recitative is speech in song – without it you might just as well sing vowels and songs without words. There are, roughly speaking, three types of recitative: dry, accompanied and dramatic. To sing *Dry Recitative* (Recitativo Secco), you must be able to get rid of unimportant words quickly and clearly, exactly like speech, whilst you reserve a singing tone and vocal accent for the important syllables of a phrase. Innumerable examples are found in Mozart's operas and Stanford's 'patter' song *The bold unbiddable child*, which can be described as Dry Recitative or 'speech in song'.

Accompanied Recitative (Recitativo Accompagnato) must be sung smoothly and steadily, so that a good ensemble can be obtained with the accompaniment of orchestra or other instrument. The consonants will be short and crisp but the vowels as long as possible. Bach's *Was in the cool of eventide* is a fine example of accompanied recitative, or 'Arioso', in its most eloquent form, a beauty in which Bach particularly excelled.

Dramatic Recitative (Recitativo Drammatico) is, of course, much more emotional and exaggerated in colour and emphasis. It can be a mixture of both dry and accompanied recitative. *I rage, I melt, I burn,* from Handel's *Acis and Galatea,* is a fine example of this style.

Apart from recitative, the three recognised styles of singing today are *Plain Style,* or *Canto Spianato*; *Florid Style* or *Canto Fiorito,* and *Declamatory Style,* or *Canto Declamato.*

Plain Style requires perfect intonation, steadiness and beauty of tone, clear and expressive articulation, atmosphere, swelled sounds, embellishments when necessary, portamento and rubato.

Florid Style requires the ability to sing rapid passages, ornaments, roulades, arpeggi with a light tone whilst sparing the voice.

Declamatory Style needs dramatic expression, strength of rhythm, incisive articulation and dramatic illustration. It can be comic or serious and demands no great facility of vocalisation.

The *Plain Style* is used for about three quarters of all singing today. The *Florid Style* is mostly used by light or coloratura sopranos in arias by such composers as Bellini, Donizetti, Bishop and Rossini. The *Declamatory Style* is used in narrative songs, ballads, quick 'diction' songs, characterisation songs and many Wagner roles such as Beckmesser in *Die Meistersinger.*

To obtain proficiency in these styles, a singer must have command not only of legato, agility, pure intonation, but of marcato, portamento, staccato and aspirato. And he must be able to express feelings of, shall we say, regret, prayer, menace, mockery, anger or joy.

One often hears that so-and-so is a good oratorio or good opera singer. Is there really much difference in style? One is static and the other mobile. One relies entirely on vocal effects and the other on visual as well as vocal effects. One is sung with control and subtlety, the other in a theatrical manner.

What do oratorio and opera have in common? Both demand singing in the grand manner – in other words, the singer is using plenty of tone and colour with very little opportunity to use a light voice, as in songs with piano. In opera and oratorio a singer usually has to contend with large orchestral forces and therefore is likely to be using nearly full voice throughout. Take the bass solo in *Messiah.* There is little chance for delicate colour and all the solos must be sung with plenty of depth and resonance. I had a personal experience which taught me a very good lesson early in my career. It was my first engagement with one of the famous Yorkshire choirs, the conductor world famous as a choral conductor. My first entry was a dry recitative marked 'piano' in the score, so I sang it quietly. After a few bars the conductor shouted 'Nay lad, we're payin' thee £10.10 to coom up 'ere to sing. Never mind what it says in't music, sing out and let public 'ear yer.' Humiliating, but a fine lesson.

It must be remembered that oratorio and opera first appeared at the turn of the 16th century in Rome and Florence respectively. They were both performed in costume with hidden orchestra. They should therefore be very similar in vocal treatment. But the 19th century, with its vast choirs and ponderous treatment, set a tradition for oratorio performance which until recent years threatened to divide oratorio and opera for ever. Fifty years ago it was rare to find an oratorio singer who was also an operatic artist, though there were one or two well-known exceptions. Oratorio demanded a stiff, white-gloved, flat-footed approach which was supposed to be the proper frame of mind for singing Handel. Hence, so many of the edited editions of the time, which pay little regard to the dramatic qualities in the music but everything to a pious stolidity. Thank goodness Beecham came along with the courage and wit to debunk a lot of the so-called traditional ideas and to bring back vitality and vivacity into the oratorios. Apart from the visible addition in operatic singing, there should be no difference at all in oratorio and opera style. In fact, the test of a fine oratorio singer is that he can portray all the dramatic elements by pure singing, while the test of a fine operatic singer is that he can portray his role vocally as well as theatrically.

In oratorio the singer should try to invest his part with the utmost vitality to make up for the lack of visual help; in opera the singer should not rely on the visual but should also be able to *sing* his role dramatically. There are many instances in oratorio where dramatic vocal colour is essential. The most obvious instance that comes to mind is Bach's *St Matthew Passion*. The parts for Judas, Peter, the High Priest and Pilate are often sung by one voice: it calls for a very high degree of vocal characterisation to make each part convincing. Similarly in opera, when the singer is static, the emotion must be apparent in the vocal colour. A classic example is 'O du mein holdern Abendstern' in *Tannhäuser*, where the singer is motionless and the aria pure legato singing. Another example is the father in *Simone Boccanegra*, when he sings the famous aria 'Il lacerato spirito', overcome with grief at his daughter's betrayal.

It is the use of appropriate vocal colour that is so important. How seldom do we hear *I know that my Redeemer liveth* sung as it should be, with joyful exaltation, and how often we hear it sung like a funeral dirge. How often we hear *On with the motley* sung with grunts, shocks of the glottis and other tricks of the trade substituted for the anguished colour the aria demands.

Each singer has a natural timbre, a quality determined by the shape of his throat and resonators. But each singer during his years of study learns to manipulate his breathing apparatus and resonators (pharynx, mouth, nasal cavities) to correspond to the emotions he is feeling, and the tone and colour instinctively adjusts itself to the mood.

A song recital is without doubt the highest test of a singer's art, for in its preparation and performance the singer's mind and vocal equipment are laid bare for all to see. A student's first recital is perhaps the end of the beginning of his career. Previously his teacher has been his mentor, advisor and critic. Now his own personality becomes much more important. It is this stage of a singer's career that often influences the range of future success. To begin with, the teacher must be supreme. He must slowly build the voice and the aural and mental judgment which is of such vital importance to a student. Slowly the 'parental' care becomes less important and at the recital stage, shall we say after five years' work, the student is judged as a potential competitor in the professional field and no longer as so-and-so's promising pupil.

The song recital is the highest test for a young singer on two counts. First, the whole of the world's song literature is at his disposal and he is tested in his choice and management. Second, he must show that he understands the different periods and styles and be able to sing them in an authentic manner. This means that not only must he be able to vocalise a programme with technical assurance, but he must invest it with all the wit, intelligence and imagination he can command.

Preparing a recital is not unlike the preparation of a banquet. The choice of dishes must be appetising and satisfying; each course must complement the others and be varied in texture, colour and flavour, be well blended without any strong jarring note.

In choosing a programme it is advisable to build it from the styles you are happy with. Don't choose too many different styles and languages, for your audience will be bewildered and feel they have had a meal of too many tit-bits and not enough substance. On the other hand, don't choose a whole programme of German Lieder, for then your audience will complain of indigestion and go home at the interval.

Let us suppose you wish to make up a programme of four groups of songs. First of all decide on the period and style you will put into each group. Make a list of all the songs you know which will fit into each category. If you have a plan, you will find it so much easier. Your *imagination* will provide a framework for an interesting plan. The most usual is to divide the group into chronological order, for example:

> Elizabethan Songs and early Italian and French Masters
> Purcell – Bach – Handel
> Mozart – Beethoven
> Schubert – Brahms – Schumann – Wolf – Strauss
> French Songs – Debussy – Duparc – Ravel
> Modern English Songs and perhaps folk songs of
> various countries

Enlist all the songs you know under the various headings. You will probably find that four of the groups are larger than the others, which might indicate that you should build your recital on these four groups. The next move is to put down the title of each song, its classification, reflective, atmospheric, ballad or patter song, its basic rhythm – double, triple or compound time – and its key. With each list try to build a group of five or six songs that are well contrasted in character and tempo yet related in key. It is important that contrasts in mood should not be too violent – that would be like putting ice cream with your vegetables – and that the key-relations should be neither monotonous nor unrelated. For example, D, C, D, D, C would be very dull; F, B, E flat, A, E would be too abrupt; whereas C, G, F, B flat, D might fit very well. Having assembled your group, try it as a whole and decide if it is a good one, one that you feel capable of 'putting over' and one that will be interesting to your audience. There are bound to be one or two gaps in your groups, of songs that you are doubtful about. Then, and not until then, should you consider new songs for your programme. It is a great mistake to include too many first performances until you are very experienced, for it is exceedingly difficult to make a 'first performance' really convincing.

Having drawn up your programme, begin to think of it as a whole – let your last thoughts before sleep dwell on it. Make sure that each song has been thoroughly studied. To quote Plunket Greene again, 'Find out what the song is about, find the fundamental rhythm and absorb it, learn the song in rough, memorise it, polish it musically, before going into details of varying treatment of the words, reconcile the phrasing to the text, absorb the accompaniment.' There is always more work to be done and it will be most unlikely that you have done all these things to all your songs. Remember that until your mind understands the composer's and poet's intentions, you cannot possibly give a trustworthy performance. The result, otherwise, may be similar to the examiner's report which read: 'A lot of notes but no music'.

Let us imagine your recital is now well prepared. A few last-minute words of advice. Remember that the recital is an expression of your own personality through word and melody. Be absorbed and you will not have time to be nervous. If you have worked well you will be confident – if you are confident, you will be anxious to get started. Remember that your audience is hoping for beautiful tone and phrasing; vitality of rhythm; emotional expression; that details should be apparent and yet part of the whole, meaning that over-attention to details will ruin a song as a whole, or that lack of attention to detail may make it dull. Speaking of dull singing, I once knew a student who had no imagination at all. Yes, he vocalised well but there it ended. He was working at Rachmaninoff's song *The Island*, making it sound like a technical exercise. His teacher advised him to go down to the beach that evening – there was a full moon – and look out to sea and conjure up in his mind the island pictured in the song. At his next lesson, he sang the song again and it was still dull and lifeless. His teacher asked, 'Did you look for your island as I told you?' 'Yes', came the reply. 'What did you see?' asked the teacher. 'Just scenery', replied the student. Such a singer should never give a recital.

Finally a word about German Lieder. So many people still speak of Lieder in hushed tones as though too precious to touch. Some of the greatest songs are to be found there, but it doesn't mean that they should be approached with an inferiority complex. Approach them open-heartedly and study them as you would any other song. You will find them a great source of inspiration and satisfaction. Sing them in the original language if you can, for the poetry, as Alan Detweiler says, 'the breathless beauty, the purity ... of a poem ... comes from the magical power over the word.' Translate a poem and substitute a colloquial text and the magic has gone. Not all the poetry of Schubert's songs is great, but the colour of the words, the German vowels and consonants, having everything to do with the songs' magic. It is desirable, though not necessary, that you should speak a language fluently before singing it. A phonetic accuracy, plus a keen knowledge of the meaning of every word, and of the character and mood, is sufficient. *The Times* music critic Frank Howes once said that it was a remarkable thing that singers often took greater pains over singing a foreign language than over their native tongue. There is, therefore, hope for us all.

The practical side of the music profession

Speech given at St Olave's, Hart Street, 28 October 1976

Not long ago my wife and I were passing though Berlin on our way home from the Bach Festival in Leipzig. I had two heavy suitcases to carry through 'Checkpoint Charlie' from East to West Berlin. A small boy rushed up to me and insisted on carrying one of my cases to the West Terminal. When I tried to tip him he drew himself up, clicked his heels and said 'Sir, I am member of club to assist the ancient.' I hope therefore that what I have to say will not be ancient history to your ears.

Many changes have taken place in the profession since 1945 throughout the world; thought, word and deed have changed beyond measure. Scientific discoveries have altered our whole way of life. These changes have affected the music profession greatly. Broadly speaking the professional musician has existed for several centuries. His success has depended largely on his ability to please the public. For what Dr Johnson said 200 years ago at the opening of the Drury Lane Theatre is true today: 'We that live to please must please to live'. It is therefore public taste which has dictated the training of successful musicians through the centuries – still very true today.

Fifty years ago a young performer put his faith in a teacher for several years, relying on his judgement and so slowly developing technique and style until he was considered ready for public performance. Later one picked the brains of different masters to help one become a finished artist. Thus we had performers of fine technique and skill trained on traditional methods. At that time no one in his right mind would think of becoming a professional musician unless his talent was so remarkable that friends and advisors urged him to do so. Nor would he attempt a public début until he had completed some years of basic training with a first-rate teacher.

Today this has changed. The car, aircraft, gramophone, radio, television, cassettes and other mechanical devices have revolutionised our way of life. Modern microphone equipment, for example, has made it possible for instrumentalists and singers of little stature to become famous and rich. No longer do youngsters wait for advice and encouragement from experts, with thousands trying to become professionals on their own initiative simply because they love music. This urge, today, to choose a career which gives pleasure is understandable as many young people hate the idea of dull mechanical labour with no outlet for creative ability.

Perhaps it is not entirely a new trend and I hope your illustrious parishioner Samuel Pepys, who lies under 'Ye communion table' near to us, will recall the entry in his diary for 1 May 1663. He wrote: 'Went to hear Mrs Turner's daughter play on the harpsichord; but Lord! It was enough to make any man sick to hear her; yet was I forced to commend her highly.'

One does not know whether to deplore or praise this development. For though we must provide the best possible training for real musical talent, we must remember that the profession is a pyramid of many facets and levels. It has surprised me that many young musicians of moderate talent do find good appointments and, at their own level, do good work.

Music education and appreciation has expanded at great speed and it is essential that we nurture talent at all levels. Administrators in music education throughout Europe have urged colleges of music to reduce numbers so that better training may be given to the best talent and to prevent the profession being flooded with unsuccessful musicians. In practice, however, such theories do not work out for it is rarely possible to pick the winners in the early stages. The profession is very much like a marathon where stamina and excellence emerge only late in the race. Also, in recent years there has been a vast upsurge in numbers of children taking music as an extra subject. Last year, for example, nearly 230,000 candidates took music exams with the Royal Schools of Music in Great Britain and nearly 70,000 overseas, to say nothing of the thousands of amateurs who, perhaps best of all, perform and enjoy their music without being dependent on it for a living. Yet we must ask, is it right to accept at the colleges all music students who wish to become professionals?

I said earlier that, 50 years ago, no one in their right mind attempted to enter the profession unless encouraged to do so by practising musicians. Today the student, like the world at large, asks for bigger and quicker results. Few are prepared to make haste slowly. This is sad, for young talent, if forced into precocious maturity, will lack stability and stamina. Unfortunately precociousness has been encouraged by television and radio, which often present only extravert and photogenic aspects of a performer. I think it is still true that an artist *must* be heard *live* and in the flesh without microphones and cameras. Only then can one judge the calibre and integrity of his work.

There can only be a limited number of outstanding musicians in each decade. Yet we still hear the parrot-cry that today there are few good teachers and very few first-rate soloists. These parrot cries come, I am afraid, from middle-aged and elderly musicians and music-lovers who remember vividly the performers who captivated them in their youth and are inclined to be critical of new talent. For example, many who can remember Rachmaninoff, Solomon, Flagstad, Chaliapin, Koussevitsky, Toscanini, Heifetz, are reluctant to admit that today there are young artists just as fine in our midst.

Fifty years ago, training in professional work was stereotyped and well-ordered. Instrumentalists and singers had small repertoires, confined to a few concertos and recital programmes; the singer to a few operatic roles, oratorios and a bagful of songs and ballads. Today, the range is much wider and young musicians more versatile and knowledgeable. This course means that training must be more comprehensive to ensure that a performer is also a first-rate musician.

It is vital today to acquire the ability for quick study, ie, to have the technical and mental discipline to absorb a new work overnight and perform it next day. My own singing career was much helped in this way when I had to stand in for Norman Allin in the title role of Bunyan in the first performance of *The Pilgrim's Progress* by Granville Bantock. It was to be broadcast by the BBC the next day. With my accompanist we worked on it for several hours during the night and again the next morning. Rehearsal was at 10 am and I sang the role that same evening. These sort of chances come but once or twice in a career and if taken they can establish a young artist overnight. *The Times*, commenting favourably, said 'Mr Falkner's "Bunyan" was remarkable.'

Requirements for various types of musicians: All have technical problems to be mastered before the interpretative and emotional sides can be considered.

String-players must begin in childhood to master their instrument. A discipline which cannot be avoided. Today the Western world kicks against discipline, though the Eastern world accepts it. Thus we find some of the finest string-players today are Japanese, Chinese, Malaysian or Indonesian. Most young string-players in England wish to avoid playing in a symphony orchestra and yearn to become soloists or to freelance in small ensembles, for they consider playing back-desk for 40 hours a week to be a drudgery. However, all find their level through necessity.

English orchestras have a fine reputation for sight-reading and quick study. Recently there have been complaints from the orchestras that budding violinists today are poor sight-readers and have stated that good sight-reading is the first requirement of an aspiring fiddler. However, when Solti was asked his opinion he replied, 'All I want to know is "Can they play the violin?"'

The Woodwinds need not start training as early as string-players, but it is more difficult for them to reach the top. More young people play the clarinet or flute than the oboe or bassoon, and must be outstanding to find their way into a professional orchestra. In Europe, most do so by sitting alongside their professor, who often has a permanent place in such an orchestra. Today our best young orchestral talent is fostered in school and youth orchestras. The NYO has of course the cream of young players and in my time at the Royal College of Music, many of the best students came from the NYO or junior music colleges.

Brass players seem to be a race to themselves and, *provided* they are good enough, do manage to earn a good living in wind bands and orchestras. There is a story in the profession that on one occasion, in Paris, there was such a demand for trombonists there were not enough to go round. One player was offered at short notice a TV appearance at double his normal fee and could not find a deputy to take his place in his orchestral concert. In desperation he told the concierge at his hotel he would pay him 100 Francs to go and sit in his place, saying 'I'll loan you an instrument, you will find three trombonists next to you. You hold up the trombone when they do, move the slide up and down, but don't blow. The conductor won't know the difference. There's just one place where the trombones play by themselves and the conductor will look at you. Give him all you've got: puff out your cheeks, move the slide up and down, but don't blow.' Next day the concierge reported that he had a wonderful evening with the other three players. But he said, 'When we came to that place you told me about, we were all working hard and the conductor waving his stick at us like mad but there wasn't a sound. We were all deputies.'

Pianists: More young pianists wish to become concert artists than any other faculty. Yet the chances of success are 1000 to 1 against. Many good pianists become teachers with occasional public performances as soloists or accompanists. A few of the best become repetiteurs and coaches in opera houses. I think it true to say, as was said recently at Wimbledon, 'It is character that wins matches, not technique.' John Ogden, John Lill and Van Cliburn achieved sudden fame by winning the Moscow Competition but I often feel sad for the competitors at these international affairs who have fine technique and go from contest to contest hoping for a break. Most of them lack the character or personality to be successful. When I warned students at the RCM each year of the hazards of the concert world, I would receive the same reply: 'We know the hazards but are determined to become soloists if we possibly can.' Many years ago one of my teachers, Harry Plunket Greene, stated publicly that the introduction of radio and gramophone would kill the music profession. Yet the profession is still as vital and exciting as ever. In any case I am convinced that the discipline of music training can never be lost. Some fail but they never think the time wasted; for music remains a joy however one makes a career.

Singers: Many of the successful male singers have been those who were lucky enough to have sound basic training in choir schools, for thus breath control, diction, intonation, tone quality and rhythm become instinctive. Singers who only discover they wish to become professional at the age of 17 or 18 have a difficult task to make up for lost time and many fall out because of poor musicianship. Musicianship is vital today to make a career for it is essential that a young professional singer can adapt to contemporary fashions and taste. Above all a singer must be eloquent in communications. Addison's comment in 1711 is still true today: 'All educated men and women are presumed to be capable of enunciating their native tongue with ease, fluency, clearness and correctness in song as in speech.' Of how many singers can this be said today?

The chief professional requirements include the ability to sing not only opera, oratorio and song, but to broadcast and be televised in many different styles, such as medieval, atonal, church music and improvisation, but above all must be the ability to read at sight. In fact perfect-pitch is today a god-send to a young singer. Many of today's top singers in England have passed through the John McCarthy group known as the Ambrosian Singers. They specialise in providing soloists, and support for choirs in small or large numbers at very short notice and, for radio and television. Dame Janet Baker is a shining example of this school of apprenticeship to the profession.

Composers traditionally were also talented keyboard performers and singers. Today a young composer may be successful without any or little textbook study provided he has character and originality. It is difficult to tell if this will continue. There is no doubt that new styles and sounds are emerging. Electronic music has also made its impact, for it is obvious that if any sound and quality can now be produced at any pitch, a great composer like J S Bach will one day emerge and consolidate all new ideas and methods into a masterpiece and in a style which is fully acceptable. It is my opinion that the live performer must continue in conjunction with electronic composition, for a manufactured piece with only the composer or mechanic sitting at the controls is as dead as mutton unless it is associated with a visual image, such as ballet or film.

Most of the successful young composers today have had traditional training but show a lively and emotional originality which commands attention. We should all avoid prejudice in judging new music. When we pass judgement on an avant garde, aleatoric or electronic work, we must beware we shall not be laughed at, for professional judgement must always be made from the standard of technique and creativity. Otherwise we may be like Dr Varley Roberts, the Yorkshire organist of Magdalene College, Oxford, who, when invited by Sir Hugh Allen to hear the first performance of Vaughan Williams's *Sea Symphony*, said, 'It's plain muck.' Yet he was a famous musician in his time and a fine choir-trainer.

Much of modern composition has been influenced by jazz, rhythmic and percussion. This has meant a demand by composers for percussion players of great versatility. Many young timpanists made a good living with freelance work, owning their own set of instruments. This is perhaps one of the biggest changes in the orchestral world, for sometimes a new work may need eight or ten percussion players, whereas only one or two are required in the classic repertoire.

Teachers: Because of the increasing demand for music teachers, financial support has been easy to get for young musicians prepared to take a teachers course at the colleges, whereas it has been much more difficult to obtain for those taking a performers course.

Most of those taking the teachers course will tell you, 'I'll teach if I must, but I really want to be a performer.' Seldom do you hear, 'I have always wanted to be a teacher and could never face the ordeal of public performance.' Yet from the thousands of would-be performers come some of our finest teachers. So many say later 'I had no idea teaching could be so rewarding. I find it very helpful to my own performance.'

Conductors: How does one become a conductor? Nearly all the great conductors have been orchestral musicians, but above all possessed of fantastic ear and memory. Academically one must insist that a would-be conductor play a keyboard or orchestral instrument well, is able to read an open or full score, and can easily detect errors of notes, pitch and balance. When Ralph Vaughan Williams was a Visiting Professor at Cornell University in 1954, a graduate student composer submitted a composition of his own. It was a complex score about three feet high, scored for a vast orchestra and battery of kitchen instruments. Saying that he couldn't possibly hear what had been written down, RVW said, 'Play me the principal ideas on the piano.' The graduate student replied, 'I can't, but I've written down what I want to hear.' As he left the room, RVW said, 'Goodbye and good luck. If a tune ever comes to your mind, don't hesitate to put it on paper.'

Speaking of conductors, I must mention Koussevitsky, for some of the most satisfying performances in my singing career were with him and the Boston Symphony Orchestra. One of my last recordings was a complete *St Matthew Passion* recorded live from Symphony Hall just before the last war. I am going to ask your indulgence to listen to the great aria *Come, blessed Cross* (*Komm süsses Kreuz*) with the viol da gamba obligato. I have only heard this once and it was recorded in peculiar circumstances. I was singing the 'Christus' role, but at the final rehearsal Koussevitsky took a dislike to the way the other bass was singing *Come, blessed Cross*. He turned to me and said, 'Tomorrow, you sing this aria.' And so I ask you for my own nostalgic reasons to listen to this aria, made without rehearsal in 1939.

I end by telling you what happened in a recent school music examination at the end of the Christmas Term. The final question was 'Who wrote *Messiah*?' One boy responded, 'God knows, I don't. Merry Christmas!' Next term he got his paper back marked 'God gets a hundred; you get nought. Happy New Year!' Merry Christmas.

Choir schools

Part of Cramb Lecture (1) Glasgow University, 1964

It is an interesting fact, in England at any rate, that you will find many of the successful male singers have been choirboys in their youth. They have learned the ABC of singing early in life and do not have to start from scratch when they discover, later on, that they have a good tenor or baritone voice. It is remarkable that, often, in solo voice competition festivals, a whole class of boy trebles will demonstrate good tone quality, rhythm, breath control and phrasing which far out-shines many grown-up singers. And it is not only true of singers, for a very large proportion of the eminent musicians in Great Britain have passed through choir schools in early life: organists, singers, composers and conductors.

It is worthwhile, perhaps, to trace a little of the history of choir schools and to acknowledge that they have always been the backbone of British music and continue to do so when not interfered with by changing patterns of educational policy.

There are thirty-five choir schools in England alone. The oldest, at York, was founded in 627 AD by St Paulinus. The choir, or Singing School, was founded in Rome by Pope Sylvester in the third century, and much good work on these lines was begun in England in the sixth and seventh centuries by Roman teachers. Until the Reformation (16th century) a song school was attached to all monasteries, many secular cathedrals and Chapels Royal kept by nobles and ecclesiastics in their Chantries. After the Reformation, most song schools were abolished and only those attached to the cathedrals and great colleges were retained. This inevitably led to a great decrease in the number of young musicians; there has never since been such a high proportion of practical musicians in the country.

In Scotland the 'Sang School' flourished from the 13th century. Teaching was mainly confined to 'Musick Meanners and vertu', and it is as well to recall that William of Wykeham's motto for Winchester and New College, Oxford, at this time was 'Manners makyth Man'. Looking round us today, perhaps a mixture of 'Music manners and virtue' might not go amiss. The Aberdeen School from 1370 was both lasting and famous. Both vocal and instrumental music were taught and Mace declared in the 17th century in *Music's Monument* that it was worthy of imitation south of the Border. Recently Lord Harewood paid tribute to the Choir School at St Michael's, Tenbury. In an appeal he said 'This is no routine appeal for funds, but a plea for survival ... (of what) ... can be regarded as part of our national heritage.' We hear on all sides the need for more facilities for training young musicians and I am astonished that what has been our national heritage has, in this context, been overlooked.

There is no doubt that if the choir schools were developed to include *all* young musicians of talent they would provide the country with the nursery that is needed. Norman Morris (*The Guardian*, 31 October 1963) said: 'It is nonsense to say that only the specially gifted should take music at school. Music is a discipline and cannot be taught any faster than any other language. Above all, it is a discipline of learning to sing and play that makes the musician. Unfortunately there are far too many so-called musicians today whose discipline has been in listening to music instead of making it.' There are, of course, other schools today where nearly every boy can read music and can sing or play an instrument. But this is still rare and only a very small percentage of our population can read a simple tune at sight.

Very few singers who begin training at 18 or 19 get beyond a very elementary standard of musicianship. Instrumentalists begin training at an early age and so do choristers in the choir schools. They learn slowly and naturally the ABC of singing. The singing alphabet is not large but it is made up of several important factors which become instinctive and form the stock in trade for any singer worthy of the name. It is a well-balanced physical and mental discipline. Begun at an early age, the muscles and mental processes grow and develop naturally and become instinctive. The most important factor is not the voice but the ear. During the whole of a singer's life it is his only measure of excellence. It is said that singing is so difficult because the singer cannot hear his own voice. But surely every aspect of singing, and especially tone quality, intonation and expression, are all controlled by the ear. It is instinctive in the singer who has begun his ABC of singing early in life.

I remember a strange practical example which happened years ago, to show you what I mean. Many of you will have heard of Jack Thurston, the brilliant clarinettist. We were students together at the RCM. He vilified some of us for mistakes in reading though Holst's *Hymn of Jesus* for the first time. We invited him to sing with us at the next rehearsal and he, a fine musician, confessed that it had never occurred to him that what to him was a matter of fingering on clarinet was a very much more complex matter with the voice.

Only a few days ago I listened to 'Evensong' in New College, Oxford. The singing was intimate and specialised in style, to suit the acoustics of the Chapel. What intrigued me most was the high technical standard of the boys in the chanting of the psalms. They showed all the clarity and eloquence of a fine speaker. In fact they enhanced and re-created the words so well that I went again the next day to hear the beauty of it once more. There were, of course, a few boys who led the singing, instinctively and simply with an exact knowledge of the right inflexions of tone and verbal accent. But it was the evidence before my eyes of younger boys, singing less confidently, but with ears alive to the music and absorbing slowly and naturally an instinctive sense of tone quality and expressive diction. Every day we listen to singers who obviously have not used their ears and who have neither a sense of tone quality nor expressive diction, yet here were boys of 10 and 11 years singing as intelligently, though immaturely, as a first-rate professional singer.

I am astonished that so little attention is paid in Great Britain to the unique quality of English cathedral music. Abroad, musicologists often speak of this British contribution to music history and are amazed that music-lovers in England seem to be unaware of its beauty and even of its existence. I would like to pay tribute to the choirmasters and organists who have done everything in the past and so much today for professional training of musicians in Great Britain. We often hear today disparaging remarks like 'the tyranny of the organ loft' made by critics who should know better. The same people are inclined to hail any new idea as a heaven-sent short cut to be adopted at once by all teachers and colleges. The truth of the matter is, of course, that you may have all the latest equipment, facilities and methods, but it is the teacher that counts.

What greater tribute can be paid to a professional musician than was said of Dr Osborne Peasgood, sub-organist of Westminster Abbey for over 40 years (*The Elizabethan*, January, 1962, JRCE p 127): 'It was not just that he was a virtuoso ... the real attraction was that any man could appear so utterly casual ... yet be so relentlessly efficient ... it meant that to do a thing well was not enough; it was worthwhile only if one could do it without effort and with unspeakable nonchalance.' For hundreds of years we have had such men at the hub of professional training in this country and there are many known to us today.

More music schools for young people on the lines of our traditional choir schools would go a long way towards making us not just a nation of music lovers, but once again a nation of performers.

Teachers and accompanists

Of the teachers Keith Falkner studied with, not all were singers themselves; indeed, many famous teachers, such as Victor Beigal, Herbert Caesari and Gillis Bratt, were not renowned as singers, but they were excellent observers and listeners who could pass on what they understood.

At various stages in a singer's vocal and musical development coaching is needed. Falkner chose his teachers well: Garcia for foundation; Harry Plunket Greene for rhythm, poetry in song, personality in interpretation; Ernst Grenzebach and Theodore Lierhammer for Lieder and the classical German oratorios; and Deane Dossert and Yves Tinayre for French Song. In addition there were Emily Daymond and Francis Toye.

- Sir Hugh Allen, of course, was a great influence in my years as a chorister at New College, where I learned breathing techniques, articulation, a sense of style while making music intelligible to the listener. He had an exhilarating sense of humour. One day, while Professor of Music at Oxford, he had an urge to play a street organ. Finding an organ grinder, he gave him money for a drink and took over. Soon, a benevolent passerby gave him sixpence. 'Thank you, Sir! I was once Director of the Royal College of Music but now have come to this,' said Sir Hugh. 'Oh, my man,' replied the benefactor, 'stick to the truth for it will serve you better.'

Later, as Director of the RCM he was the most influential and dynamic man in music performance in England. When he discovered a composer with a worthy new work, he would jump in a taxi and rush to Lord Reith to insist the work be performed immediately. Today this can no longer be done. He was also a great choral conductor with an instinctive sense of tempi and dynamics. His wisdom was also remarkable. It is said that Sir Edward Heath, while at Oxford, told Sir Hugh he would like to become a conductor. Instead he was advised to go into politics. Allen also helped Douglas Fox, a brilliant young pianist whose right arm had been shot off in France in 1917. For all of one day Allen did everything with his left hand and then took Fox to New College Chapel, where he played Evensong with pedals and left hand only. This done, he told Fox to get to work and so he did, becoming the most versatile one-armed pianist of his time. I discovered this at a song recital at Bradfield College when he played *Das Wandern* (Schubert) for me. How the devil he played it I shall never know, but it was magnificent.

The first woman to take an Oxford Doctorate of Music was Dr Emily Daymond and I doubt whether I should have become a professional singer without her warm friendship and guidance in the critical years following initial college training. I was, like so many other young singers, wasting my time between lessons until one day she bore down on us like a south-west wind, picked us up and bore us along with her unbounding drive and enthusiasm in her elemental approach to music. She was a great talker and later became an adopted family member. She requested we call her 'Schramm', reminiscent of a German character and the saying: 'Put Schramm's pipe in his mouth and stop him talking.' All through the years, I felt the sensation of being 'borne on the wind' in her presence and overwhelmed by her generosity. In 1926, following 17 concerts in 19 days and a second appearance at the Three Choirs, I developed a bad case of laryngitis. A sea voyage was prescribed with complete rest of my vocal cords. Within hours, Schramm had planned a six-week cruise in the Mediterranean at her expense. What impressed me most was that she enjoyed it as much as I did and brought home vividly that it is indeed more blessed to give than to receive.

One night, in 1926, after I had gone to bed, the telephone rang with the news that Norman Allin was ill and could not sing in the first performance (1926) of Bantock's *Pilgrim's Progress* at a BBC concert at Queen's Hall. Could I do it? I had no doubt that it was impossible for I did not have a score, had never seen one, and could not get one at this time of night, etcetera, etcetera. Schramm had other ideas, saying that yes, I would sing the work and was coming round to fetch the score. We sat up until 2 am breaking the back of the work; in fact, we soaked in it until the orchestral rehearsal and performance took place. *The Times* reported: 'Mr Keith Falkner's *Bunyan* was remarkable.' How we laughed and, while I got the credit, it was Schramm's *Bunyan* from start to finish.

During the icy winter of 1928-29 my father and I were homeless following the death of my mother. Schramm took us in for several months at her house in Clarendon Road, next door to Harold Samuel and Howard Ferguson, and made us feel her life was centred on our comfort and well-being despite an intensely busy life. She was an outstanding woman and teacher who gave me impetus, moulding me into a singer at the perfect time. She was a pedagogue or motivator, realising the essentials and knowing the right teachers, pushing me to get on for voice improvement. It was at Schramm's urging that I went to Harry Plunket Greene. While she generously remembered me in her will, she has left little that a new generation can appreciate. Like Sir Hugh Allen, it was her personal power which endeared her, having a profound influence on her multitude of pupils, acquaintances and friends.

Harry Plunket Greene influenced me most, and to this day I have never heard anyone give such a thrill as a Lieder singer or, indeed, as a song recitalist. By words, rhythm, interpretation and personality he carried the audience away with his great gift. So often you hear a singer who makes a beautiful sound; the articulation is good and the story told well but somehow something is missing. But with HPG, you were swept off your feet by the 'march' and 'climax' of a song ... the way in which it was built ... the whole piece as a unit ... it was so evident in his singing that it became vital. It did not seem to matter whether he sang in tune or not for here was a fine artist holding us in thrall, but as he continued to give recitals in later life, he has in more recent years been criticised for singing out of tune.

Schramm insisted I go to HPG, saying I was only half-baked and would never be a fine singer unless I did so. The first lesson was the most illuminating ninety minutes, for I had had no idea that you could take a piece of music to bits and interpret it as he did. He 'opened the book' for me and I realised that I would have years of very hard work. He was not a hard task-master, pointing things out gently while making one aware of the awful gaps in your own mind: one had never thought of this or that, never realised what words meant, the colour he would suggest for certain moods. His insistence was on breath control and above all rhythm, his theory being that if you sang a patter song, you should be able to sing each verse in one breath, that the breath should never impede the rhythm of the song. For practice I used to sit in a tube train and hold my breath between stations; I could do this between Marble Arch and Bond Street but not from Hampstead to Golders Green. The art of voice production, vocalising, interpretation and presentation were what I learned most from Albert Garcia and Plunket Greene: they trained me for the hurly-burly of the professional world. It is essential that a young singer, with the right material, should have such a slow and steady preparation; today's tendency for young un-ready voices to flit from teacher to teacher, master class to master class, is deplorable.

[173]

On the advice of Adrian Boult, I went to study with the famous Austrian baritone Theo Lierhammer. It was to him I owed the sense of style in Lieder similar to Plunket Greene in English repertoire. One day he asked me whether I had heard Battistini the previous evening in one of his last concerts. Lierhammer had gone to congratulate him and afterwards Battistini had replied: 'Yes, but now you hear that, at last. I have to aspirate my runs!' Ever since, I have had a horror of staccato runs. What would happen if obligato instruments did the same? Of course it is suitable on special occasions, but 'legato' runs should never be treated in such a 'Ha, Ha, Ha' manner. I did hear the famous Richard Mayr, then still a star with the Vienna Opera, able to observe the flat tongue and open throat as he sang the higher notes in *Fidelio*. Lierhammer arranged a meeting where I sang to Mayr, who was most encouraging, suggesting I join the Staatsoper, gradually moving upwards to principal parts. However, opera, despite its attractions, did not hold for me the chance to express beautiful words in song: I knew then that that was what I wanted to do more than anything else in singing. How strange it is that some things in life are decided by a spin of a coin. It made me a fatalist and I often wonder how different my career would have been had I taken Mayr's advice.

I met Francis Toye in 1929. He had written a critical notice of my singing, stating that, while my singing was good, it lacked great authority in projection, that I was too 'internal'. At Adrian Boult's advice I went to Toye for lessons. He was a down-to-earth coach and got me to open up more in public performance. He became a good friend, being equally generous, rude and eccentric.

In 1934, needing a critical 'refresher', Bruce Flegg and I went to Berlin to study with Grenzebach. He always spoke of 'sitting on the voice', opening the throat and flattening the tongue, talking of the 'Heissen Kartoffel' (hot potato). His dictum: make your breath support you in big passages by sitting on it and 'immer trinken'. Always to feel the tone in your head, never the throat. To place the tone in the head and then to play it like a cello, hearing the sound and supporting it entirely from below. He was a great help with my singing of the Hans Sachs's *Monologues* and Brahms's *Vier ernste Gesänge*. During one lesson Hitler passed by and he hurried to the window, saying we must give the 'Heil Hitler' salute but I, standing behind Grenzebach, did not. Bruce and I were in Vienna when Dollfuss was assassinated.

I went, in 1930, to Paris to study French repertoire with Deane Dossert to get the 'inside' of French Song. Her message was never to compete with bad acoustics, whether 'dead' or over-resonant, but to sing naturally. She also helped with her 'open throat as the origin of sound' and the identity of the manner of production of all tone, high or low, loud or soft.

I found that no two performances were ever alike. Each performance should seem spontaneous, a new creation, not simply a repeat. This is especially true with different accompanists for there will always be a new and vital response between the partners.

I found James Bell, a Scotsman and fellow student, down-to-earth. He was a brilliant reader and executant, working hard with me in the 1920s as I prepared oratorios, choral works and songs for performance. Michael Mullinar, accompanist for the CBSO when I first met him in the 1920s, played for me in recitals every year until 1939. He was marvellous to sing with, always managing to imply that I was singing better than I realised: a real fillip for a singer. When I met up with him again on becoming Director of the RCM, he often came to my room to play for me. And still he tried to persuade me I was singing better than ever! I began to wonder whether I had made a wrong decision in giving up my singing career. However, I soon had the sad duty to tell him he must retire as he was now 70.

From 1929 onwards it was arranged by HMV that Gerald Moore should play for most of my recordings. He became one of the most famous accompanists of this century, playing for all the great singers of his time; a fine musician with transposition at sight 'no problem'. He was a most generous person, one of the wittiest public speakers and a keen cricketer. He accompanied me for the French Colonial Exhibition in Paris, held at the Bois de Vincennes, where I represented England.

In 1932 the BBC asked me to prepare a half-hour of songs by Mili Balakirev and, needing a repetiteur, I invited Charles Groves, then about to graduate from the RCM, to help me. Several of the songs were not in the right key and he demonstrated his brilliance and musicianship by transposing them on the spot without blemish. He was so good that I asked him to do the broadcast with me and we followed this with a recital which included the Balakirev songs for the St John's Wood Music Club. In 1945 I was able to resume singing and broadcast some songs from Leeds Studio. Within the hour Charles, then conductor of BBC North, rang to thank me, recalling our broadcast and recital.

Another of the international accompanists in demand by all the best artists was the red-haired perfectionist George Reeves. We shared a recital at the Bedford Music Club where his variety of tone quality amazed me. The programme included French songs by Charles Loeffler with viola obligato played by Bernard Shore. It was a delightful experience, although my French left something to be desired. We last met in the 1950s when Reeves came to Cornell to accompany Elisabeth Schwarzkopf.

Ivor Newton was an accompanist always in demand. He had a cheerful personality, always a chuckle in his voice no matter how important the moment, making light of technical problems. He played for me in England and Scotland for a Max Mossel concert tour in which I sang the Bach secular solo cantata *Amore Traditore*. I marvelled at his dexterity and innate musicianship, for the last movement is remarkable for its cembalo part, fully written out by Bach.

The famous pianist Harold Samuel played all the Bach clavier works from memory and, as we found ourselves in New York at the same time, he offered to play *Dichterliebe* for my first recital there. While it was an exciting experience, it could hardly be called a team performance, due to his strong personality. For the Brahms *Liebeslieder*, both he and Myra Hess accompanied, but they became so excited in their interpretation that it was hardly an ideal ensemble. But the vitality! While Harold had played the *Dichterliebe* cycle for me, Edwin McArthur accompanied for the remainder of the recital and while he was young, he was efficient and helpful. He later went on to become Kirsten Flagstad's accompanist, also an orchestral and opera conductor and composer.

The senior accompanist for the BBC, Ernest Lush, also played for me, as did John Wills, much in demand at Broadcasting House. Lush could tackle anything at short notice with panache, and Wills's sensitive interpretation of a broadcast of *Die schöne Müllerin* left me full of gratitude.

Coenraad von Bos, who played for many of my concerts in New York, had great sensitivity for the singer, best shown in his manipulation of dynamics. He was also accompanist for Nelson Eddy and was greatly disappointed when I turned down the Hollywood offer.

John Hunt had studied under Schnabel in Berlin but his career had suffered during the war. In 1952 I suggested to Cornell that they engage him while professor of piano John Kirkpatrick was on sabbatical. So he came and it was a very beneficial year for we often performed together.

In 1953 we recorded *Dichterliebe* for the University radio station, one of the best recordings I made. There was some discussion of re-recording the work in England for commercial release but nothing came of it. John gave an unforgettable performance of the big Schubert B flat Sonata before leaving Cornell and in parting we agreed to give two recitals in the Wigmore Hall.

Howard Ferguson was a protégé of Harold Samuel, intending to become a concert pianist. We got to know each other well as we lived almost next door in Clarendon Road. Together we performed, while still in manuscript, Finzi's song-cycle *Earth, Air and Rain* for Leslie Boosey. Boosey & Hawkes immediately decided to publish the work. We worked together again on 4 April, 1940, giving a performance of *Die schöne Müllerin* at the National Gallery, and again at a recital in Belfast. Howard was a splendid pianist and a delight to work with.

Following the war, and before I left for Italy, Eric Gritton often played for me. A professor at the RCM, he was well known in the profession, a soothing and efficient accompanist making all lively and effective. He reminded me of Michael Mullinar for he always gave the impression that I was giving a good performance.

Conductors and 'vintage' singers

My first performance with a world-famous conductor was for Sir Henry Coward in a performance of a Handel oratorio in Derby. My first recitative was marked 'piano' so, at rehearsal, I sang 'piano', only to have Sir Henry's stick smash onto the desk as he shouted: 'Sing oop, lad! Let the public hear ye! We paid ten guineas for ye to come oop here!' It was the best bit of advice for it is important to make a first favourable impression. You must be heard and no nonsense about it.

Among professionals there are always jokes about conductors and, while not meant to be derogatory, show what can happen in performance I am indebted to my friend Roy Henderson for an anecdote about Sir Henry during a performance of Bantock's *Omar Khayyam* in March 1929 with the Sheffield Choral Union:

> At one point the old boy turned to me, seated as near his right side as consistent with safety, and whispered: 'Now, listen to this!' There followed a magnificent chorus. Sir Henry was so thrilled and so excited he forgot to turn the pages of his score. He began to fumble for his place, with thick stick stuck on the last beat of the bar. The orchestra petered out. He turned to the second fiddle leader beside me and whispered: 'Is there a coot (cut)?' The fiddler tucked his instrument under his chin, put his left hand behind his ear and whispered back in a broad Yorkshire accent: 'I beg your pardon, Doctor?' A little louder and with greater intensity Sir Henry demanded: 'Is there a coot?' 'No, Doctor,' came the reply, 'You beat three and you'll be alright!' By which time, the old boy had found his place and did as advised.

It was Sir Henry Wood who in 1925 gave Stuart Robertson, Frank Phillips and myself our first 'Promenade' Concert. He was immensely popular and it was his interest and encouragement which made him so splendid to work with. Prom programmes for 1895 and 1935 indicate that public taste had moved from 'lollipops' to serious music, due entirely to Sir Henry. In 1912 he introduced the Schoenberg *Five Orchestral Pieces* and is reputed to have told the recalcitrant orchestra: 'Stick to it, Gentlemen! This is nothing to what you will have to play in twenty-five years' time!' I sang with him every year until 1939: Bach and Handel, *Hans Sachs's Monologues*; RVW's *Songs of Travel*; Stanford's *Songs of the Sea*, etc. In a performance of 'Revenge, Timotheus Cries' (*Alexander's Feast*), he made the slow movement intensely dramatic for me. The following day I received a letter of congratulations in which he wrote of the performance in detail. It was this lifelong dedication to performance that made him unique. A Victorian Londoner, he was a man of homely tastes, honest feeling and regular habits, with painting and carpentry his hobbies. At seventeen he chose music as his career, becoming as busy teaching as with conducting. In one season he conducted 130 concerts and gave over 500 singing lessons! As a conductor Sir Henry believed in efficiency and accuracy, calling for singers at Prom rehearsals at 12.50 pm for run-throughs with no repeats. Details were sorted out later in the Artists' Room. With Sir Henry's vast repertoire of classics and new works, he had to play for security. As Neville Cardus wrote: 'Others may feel the masterpieces with more intensity; nobody knows them as intimately.'

I sailed home with him in the *Manhattan* in 1934 and we gave a recital one evening, Sir Henry seated at the piano looking just like Brahms in the famous portrait. Another evening there was a marvellous sunset and after gazing at it for some time, Sir Henry turned to me and said: 'I'd give all the music in my life to be able to put that on canvas!' As a parting present he gave me a copy of his magnum opus, *The Gentle Art of Singing*,[1] inscribed: 'To that fine singer – Keith Falkner; A souvenir of our delightful journey together in the *Manhattan* from New York to Plymouth, Jan 31-Feb 6, 1934. Always sincerely yours. Henry J Wood.'

I met Sir Edward Elgar at a Worcester Festival in the 1920s. In his late years, I found him rather immobile, seated heavily on his stool. But, when it came to a passage marked 'nobilmente', he would half rise to his feet, making all of us feel this was a tremendous moment, just as effective as the scarecrow antics on many platforms today. He was also passionate about horse-racing and, like Vaughan Williams, loved to have attractive women around him. I appeared with him in 1930 for *The Apostles* at the Three Choirs Festival with Elsie Suddaby, Astra Desmond, Heddle Nash, Roy Henderson and Norman Allin. At a rehearsal, all went normally until we came to the Judas solo of the betrayal. Judas begins his marvellous song of anguish in which, to quote Elgar, 'a proud sinner is swayed by all sorts of feelings', while he sings

---

[1] *The Gentle Art of Singing*, Sir Henry Wood. The book describes voice training and includes a suggested timetable for the student, resembling his own life of discipline and dedication.

to music that ranks among the most movingly intense that Elgar ever wrote. Norman was halfway through, singing it magnificently. Suddenly, Elgar burst into tears, saying, as he leaned on the piano, 'I can't go on!' I had never seen him in such an emotional state.

Sir Thomas Beecham was to conduct a massed performance of the *Messiah* in the old Crystal Palace in 1928 when I first met him. He wanted some new voices, so several of us were invited to sing for him. Instead of asking for all the solos or 'Why do the Nations ...' he asked me to sing 'The People that Walked in Darkness'. I had only sung two phrases when he said I should turn up for rehearsal the following Monday. So, I had the job. When at rehearsal we got to 'Why do the Nations ...', Sir Thomas turned and asked me if it was fast enough. Trying to please I said, 'Oh, Sir Thomas, as fast as you like.' 'Oooh?!' said he and at the performance it went like the wind, almost impossible to delineate the triplets. A bar before I came in he asked: 'Fast enough for you, Mr Falkner?' Afterwards his remark was: 'Not bad!'

On one occasion we performed the Brahms *Requiem* at a Sunday concert in the Queen's Hall. I won't say Sir Thomas loathed Brahms, it was just not his cup of tea. After about ten bars of 'Behold all Flesh' he announced in a loud voice: 'Melancholy piece, this!' When you sang with Beecham, you were on an altogether different channel from any other musician; wafted, it seemed, on to another element, half terrified at first, then carried confidently along with each phrase polished and points of daylight never overlooked.

I sang with him again at the Norwich Festival in 1936 in *Nocturne (Moeran)*, Schubert's A flat Mass, Bach's *Magnificat* and Handel's *Hercules*. In this last work there is nasty piece of recitative about nothing important. At rehearsal I made a 'Spoonerism' to Beecham's 'Oh? I'd like to hear that one again!' Naturally, I couldn't stop doing it, even at the performance, when his eyebrows shot up, making it a dramatic moment. Generally, I think audiences are unaware, getting an overall impression, with perhaps only five percent knowing the detail of the thing.

I joined Sir Thomas at several Leeds Festivals: a Verdi *Requiem* in 1934, a performance of Mozart's *Requiem* and Handel's *Israel in Egypt*, and in 1937 of Beethoven's *Missa Solemnis*. The only thing I had to sing in the Handel was a duet written for two basses, 'The Lord is a Man of War'. We had some fun with this for Dennis Noble, a high baritone, was down to sing the lower part and I, a bass, the top. The instruction from

Tommy was to sort it out ourselves. The performance of this work took place on the last day of the Festival, a day the local orchestra played by arrangement. Tommy was upset at rehearsal with the many mistakes going on in the string section. He finally exclaimed 'There must be something wrong with the parts!' and, pointing to the second violinist, demanded: 'Show me your part! There must be some mistake!' 'Aye, Sir Thomas', said the man standing up, 'if there are as many bulrushes in Egypt as there are demi-semiquavers in my copy, they'd never have found Moses!'

I auditioned for Koussevitsky, the greatest conductor I ever sang with, in Boston in 1931. He was as flamboyant and as egocentric a figure as the *New Grove* describes. While he never mastered idiomatic English, he never left any doubt as to his meaning in conversation or rehearsal. He was meticulous and, concluding the final rehearsal, pushed you behind him so that at performance you never thought about him again. Performances were marked by high emotional intensity, colourful phrasing and dramatic character. A wonderful experience. At my audition I sang the 'Quoniam' from the *B minor Mass* and the 'Et in Spiritum Sanctum', which is a third higher, and was presented with a pair of concerts for the following season. From then on I sang with Koussevitsky every year until war broke out, singing in either the *St Matthew Passion* or *St John Passion*, Handel oratorios or Beethoven's *Ninth*. Once, rehearsing a *St Matthew*, there was an amusing occasion when the tenor 'Evangelist' couldn't, or wouldn't, follow the beat between the 'Crucify Him' choruses and a short interjection from the Evangelist in which he says: 'But they cried out the more, saying:'. Finally Koussevitsky put his stick down and said to the chorus: 'Tomorrow, if some sing it arrive, you go wis me!' He always got what he wanted.

About 1933 I was engaged to sing the Mozart *Requiem* with the BBC Symphony Orchestra in the Queen's Hall, conducted by Bruno Walter. He conducted very much like Adrian Boult and was wonderful to sing with, though my low 'F' in the 'Tuba Mirum' was not as *basso profundo* as he would have liked.

Eugene Goossens conducted the orchestral version of *Four Serious Songs* (Brahms) at the 1939 Cincinnati May Festival. It was his versatility as a young conductor that made his career, evident in opera and Russian ballet, with Beecham relying on him to take over complicated works at short notice. I remember his opera *Don Juan de Manara* with Laurence Tibbett at Covent Garden and much enjoyed his incidental music to Margaret Kennedy's *The Constant Nymph*, while his fine setting of James Joyce were often in my repertoire. Gene was gentle and satisfying to sing with, always aware of a singer's problems, his comments always accompanied by 'Dear Boy'. In the 1960s at the RCM, he often came to sit with me at an orchestral concert and I was still 'Dear Boy'.

Then there was Adrian Boult, a life-long friend. I first became aware of him as a chorister, noting that this undergraduate was always on hand for Dr Allen when special concerts took place. Had I known his name I would have been thrilled to know he was stroking the Christ Church boat at Henley. Then, at the RCM in 1920, I met him, for here he was the young professor who took the conducting class. I got to know him better when asked to join a select madrigal group, and soon learned that he was not only a conductor and a strict disciplinarian, but a man with a warm and generous personality. He often joined the basses in choral class just for the 'heck-of-it' and, though modest, was always ready to listen and take an interest in other people. We became closer still when, in 1925, Boult conducted a rehearsal of Dohnanyi's *Variations on a Nursery Theme* with the emerging young pianist Christabel Margaret Fullard, my future wife. I was often invited to stay with his family at Landford, to sing with the choir and play cricket. Though from a strict family, Adrian had absorbed his mother's compassion and care for others, while he had his father's sense of honesty and decorum.

In 1927 my mother died while on a visit to South Africa and Adrian saved the letter I wrote at the time: '... I am truly thankful to you for your letter – it has helped me tremendously. I thought of you very soon after the first shock had gone (as) I knew that our loss had been similar, in that our mothers had played such a tremendous part in our lives and that their guidance and inspiration is irreplaceable. ...'

At the suggestion of 'Schramm', Adrian invited me to share his flat for a year at Chelsea Embankment, as both felt I needed discipline, my attitudes being too nonchalant to my profession. Certainly his well-organised way of life, his insistence on punctuality, the keeping of personal and household accounts, and his accuracy in performance all made a great impression. So did the cold shower up on the roof every morning of that year! While I lived with him, Adrian would walk the two miles to the Queen's Hall before a BBC concert in order, he said, to get into a proper frame of mind – performers and listeners need a quiet time before a performance. He lived a strict and rather puritan life, enjoying good food but preferring to drink only between meals. I have known him to sip champagne but he was, generally, a teetotaller; however, that did not stop him from encouraging others to enjoy themselves.

In the summer of 1929 I was to study with Lierhammer, and Adrian suggested a holiday together on my way to Salzburg. We made our way to Munich and heard a marvellous *Don Giovanni* under Knappertsbusch. That is, Adrian heard it for, desperately tired, I fell asleep. We went on to Lake Starnberg, Reutte and Neuschwanstein before ascending the Tegelberg. Then we made our way to 'Die Forelle Hotel' on the Plansee in the Tyrol to swim and scull and I was so enthralled with the place that I determined to bring Christabel there for our honeymoon. On our last day, we ascended the Zugspitz by cable car with one of the passengers, a beautiful blond portrait painter who had just 'done' Richard Strauss. On the way down, she clung to me with ardour, due, perhaps, to the cold raw air. I was so moved when we 'debussed' and parted I just had to say 'Ich weiss nicht was solles bedeuten das ich so traurig bin', which was received with acclamation, my remark taken either way. With an 'Auf Wiedersehen', I made my way to Salzburg, leaving Adrian to scull with the goddess on the lake. There was a sequel to this idyll. We had told our goddess that Adrian and I would be performing at a BBC Concert in the Queen's Hall in October. Following it, and much to our embarrassment, two large bouquets were presented to us on stage from 'our goddess' in Berlin!

Towards the end of the year, Adrian suggested I make my début in America and so we arrived to stay with the Vincent Masseys at the Canadian Legation in Washington. One evening, Adrian and I gave a recital following a large dinner party at which I was seated next to one of the Vanderbilt girls. She was so glamorous with her large green earrings and red nails that I felt tongue-tied as large Cape Cod oysters were placed before us. Knowing only the small Colchester or Whitstable oyster, I found courage to say: 'Bit large, these oysters ... difficult to swallow.' 'Sissy!' came her reply, which shut me up again for some time. At the recital Adrian's accompanying was amazing; not only did he play beautifully, he played orchestrally, so remarkable in Bach, Handel and operatic arias. With typical understatement, Adrian states in his book *My Own Trumpet* that I undertook the whole programme while he did what he could with the accompaniments. But he scoffed the day after when I went off to play golf with Raymond Massey: 'How can you waste your time hitting and following a little white ball all over the countryside!' But then, he was a wet-bob, not a ball player.

It has been said that Adrian was a cold conductor, whereas he was full of emotion. Unlike many conductors, he did not feel the need to show it but it was visible to performers, who sensed his innate concentration and feeling. He had no need to look like a mechanical scarecrow. As the *Daily Telegraph* noted in an article in 1983: 'The audience sees only the back of that tall, almost immobile figure, his baton mathematically directing the performance. But the orchestra sees the excitement in his eyes. Believe me, he's almost foaming at the mouth.'

Young artists performing with Adrian for the first time, could be apprehensive, for his beat was tentative. In fact, he was waiting to accept and accompany, not dictate tempi and reading, like so many others. Roy Henderson once told me: 'Adrian is the only conductor who encouraged me to give my own performance; all the others tried to put their rubber-stamp on it.' Casals and Solomon preferred Adrian to all other conductors, while Josef Krips once told me in Vienna: 'Of all English conductors, Boult gives me the greatest pleasure – even in Brahms.' He went on to say he had never been to a Boult concert without learning something new, which, coming from a Viennese, was highest praise. For me, his reading of the great Schubert C Major and of Bach's *B minor Mass* remain unsurpassed. His control and balance of tempi, line and dynamics were superb: a composer's conductor.

Three things irritated Boult: unpunctuality, inefficiency and dis-courtesy. Far too much reference has been made to his outbursts of temper which, though rare, were fully justified. There was the occasion when Ethel Smyth accosted him in the Artists' Room within thirty seconds of a performance of the *St Matthew*, a religious occasion for inner appreciation. Steuart Wilson, Mary Jarred and I, followed by Adrian, walked quietly off stage. Suddenly, with a clatter, the Green Room curtains parted as Dame Ethel marched in declaring: 'You must do my *Prison* with the BBC National Chorus!' Adrian turned his back and then, facing her abruptly, shouted: 'Get out! How dare you talk to me like that!' Dame Ethel retreated to Steuart's 'Thank God that woman has got it at last!'

I felt the brunt of Adrian's wrath on just two occasions. I was singing for him at the Kendal Festival in the 1930s which included *Ethiopia Saluting the Colours* (Charles Wood). With a bit of a sore throat, I had soothed it with a glass of port offered by our host. Just before the second

[184]

verse, I came in two bars too soon, to Adrian's fury: 'You're absolutely fuddle-headed with that drink you're always taking!' The second occurred when Adrian was to meet Christabel and me, between performances at the Colosseum, at a restaurant with two entrances. We waited and Adrian waited but, needless to say, at the wrong door. He was furious.

Adrian was 'Uncle' to many, his friendly advice and anonymous financial gifts to young musicians well known in the profession. My 'professional uncle', he was generous to me for over forty years professionally and personally, never patronising. In 1950 he was indirectly responsible for my appointment to Cornell, giving me £1,000 for the journey to America. Over the years, I sang with him many times but, regrettably, only once after the war, in Bach's solo Cantata *Ich habe genug* in Southwark Cathedral with the Royal Philharmonic.

When I think of Adrian I am reminded of *Cardus on Music*, in which he states that Richter called a famous diva to order at a rehearsal of *Fidelio* because she stayed on a high note too long. She justified herself by saying she always held it that way; it was one of her famous notes. Richter replied: 'If Beethoven 'ad wished pause he would have wrote. He 'as not wrote, so we do not make.' The prima donna has long since been deposed; in her place the conductor holds sway, and often enough he too 'makes' what Beethoven ' 'as not wrote'. Adrian was a great conductor and the last time I saw him conduct was a performance of the *Enigma Variations* for the ballet at Covent Garden. Before the first 'Variation' was over, several people around me had tears running down their faces. It was indeed moving to see him standing there; the tempi were slower than usual. He always maintained that if the performers were happy, then you got a 'performance'. At the end, it was very moving to see the whole company come forward to cheer and applaud his sensitivity and professional understanding. Though mentioned elsewhere, it is worth repeating the opinion of Josef Krips: 'I like Boult. Boult for me, even in Brahms!'

During the inter-war years I joined a select band of artists whose performances remain memorable and have taken on a somewhat legendary status: the 'Vintage Singers' as I call them. The sopranos: Elsie Suddaby, Eva Turner, Joan Coxon, Dorothy Silk, Lilian Stiles-Allen, Joan Hammond, Dora Labette and Isobel Baillie.

Sir Edward Bairstow helped Elsie early on for, as a choirmaster, he found her boy-like quality appealing, her pure tone almost entirely without vibrato. I never had the pleasure of singing with Eva Turner, who was one of the greatest sopranos; she had a glorious voice which carried to the back of any theatre, her *Turandot* justly famous. The delightful coloratura soprano Joan Coxon came to dinner in the early 1930s but she arrived late, having taken the wrong train, while another guest and I consumed a lot of sherry. Rather the worse for wear the following morning, and as I had a BBC broadcast in the afternoon, I went to my doctor, who prescribed sherry as a quick pick-me-up. It was just after 2 pm as I made my way to the nearest pub and informed the landlord of the good doctor's prescription. 'I've heard that one before,' he replied uncompromisingly, 'We're closed!'

Dorothy Silk and I often sang together, her light flexible voice ideally suited to Bach, her sense of style and power of suggestion such that she was capable of an unexpected but exquisite interpretation in Verdi's *Requiem*. Her ethereal singing of the 'Requiem Aeternam' and the impeccable high pianissimo B flat was followed immediately by a surprising resonance, soaring above the full orchestra and chorus in 'Libera me, Domine'. Lilian Stiles-Allen's voice was beautifully rich, expressive and of great power. Joan Hammond, though of a younger generation, had a splendid voice. Once, at Chirk Castle, there was a sumptuous party with Lord and Lady Howard de Walden, Jan Smeterlin and his wife, Ivor Newton, Piatigorsky, Joan and me. It was to be my first experience of the Amazonian qualities Joan displayed on 'course' and in 'court' for, as Joan wrote in her autobiography: 'The next day Keith and I played six holes of golf in the snow, using red balls. Our feet and hands were frozen. The snow was crisp and hard underfoot, and there were patches of green under the trees. The greens had been swept clear for us. The Welsh countryside was beautiful even in winter, but it was too cold to play golf, so Keith and I went back to the castle and played squash.'

I first sang with Dora Labette at a Goldsmiths' dinner. She was lovely to look at, probably the best-dressed soprano of her day and, while she had a pronounced London accent, it was never evident in her beautifully enunciated singing.

I wrote of Isobel in *The Dictionary of National Biographies*: 'Isobel Baillie's red-gold hair and lovely complexion were outstanding physical traits... She had a gift for silken legato and silvery tone. I first sang with her in Manchester. She was captivating with her serenity of voice and carriage. She was always right in the middle of the note with "none of this" as Toscanini, waving his hands, would say to indicate excessive vibrato. The clarity and vitality of "Rejoice Greatly" and the serenity of "I Know That My Redeemer Liveth" were acclaimed by all.'

Muriel Brunskill, Astra Desmond, Mary Jarred and Margaret Balfour were among the contraltos. Muriel had a beautiful voice and was once referred to as the finest heard in America, while Astra, the first of what was virtually a new wave, was a most intelligent artist and splendid interpreter with a fine personality. Mary had a voice of beauty, rare in that it was a true contralto. She was also great fun with her amusing anecdotes of experiences on the operatic stage in Hamburg.

Margaret, a rarity in that she too was a genuine contralto, had a superb voice. She was suffering from a cold on an occasion when we were singing together in one of the big oratorio weekends in South Wales. At rehearsal she only 'marked' her part, so that at a break a hastily called committee meeting discussed the situation, and a deputation sent to Margaret: 'Miss Balfour, we are very worried that you won't be heard at the concert and we have plenty of contraltos who can make much more noise than you!' Margaret's retort caused even greater consternation: 'Well, if that's what you think, I'll get the next train to London!' At the concert she sang as normal, the fine voice being delivered with all its customary volume and power. Margaret's voice is one of the four solo altos – Muriel, Astra, and Mary Jarred the others – heard in the famous recording of Vaughan Williams' *Serenade to Music*. RVW had asked me to be one of the sixteen singers but, as I was occupied in America at the time, Robert Easton sang instead.

Gladys Ripley, a mezzo really, began to make a name for herself just before the Second World War but her career was tragically cut short by illness which ended her life. I sang with her in a *Messiah* under Bairstow at Christmastide 1940. A lovely voice, she had with her quick wit and ready sense of fun an appealing personality. I had travelled by train to York in uniform and chose to sing in it, the gold initials on the collar proclaiming I was a 'Volunteer Reserve'. I sat down after singing 'But who may abide' as the chorus began to sing. 'What,' she discreetly asked, 'does VR stand for?' 'Volunteer Reserve,' I whispered. 'Oh!', she said,'I thought it meant "Virginal Research"!'

The tenors of the day were Parry Jones, Tudor Davies, Trefor Jones, Richard Crooks, Hubert Eisdell, Webster Booth and Heddle Nash.

Parry, a Welsh lyric tenor and former pupil of Vastity at the RCM, did not have a huge voice but one which was used with plenty of artistry and skill. Tudor, another Welshman, had a strong voice with baritonal qualities and for fun once sang a bass aria from *Messiah*. He was an amazing memoriser who, asked to sing the part of Rodolfo in *La Bohème* at short notice, knew it after we played through the score twice! A contemporary of mine at the College was the Welsh tenor Trefor Jones, who had great versatility, singing opera, operetta, musicals and oratorio at the Three Choirs. The American Richard Crooks, with a strong lyric voice, sang with me in a Cincinnati performance of the Verdi *Requiem*. I met up with him again in 1939 when we sang together in South Africa.

The matinée idol of the Ballad Concerts, promoted by the publishers Boosey or Chappells in the 1920s and 1930s, was Hubert Eisdell. An ideal interpreter of Roger Quilter's songs, audiences would almost swoon with delight when he sang *Now Sleeps the Crimson Petal*. Therefore, I was greatly impressed when he joined Steuart Wilson, Dorothy Silk, Margaret Balfour, Arthur Cranmer and myself in a performance of the *St Matthew* with the Bach Choir on 22 March 1931 under Adrian. His singing of the tenor arias, notably 'To Witness False' and the air 'Be Strong, Endure', which he sang with great vigour and intensity, with his dramatic delivery of words, were as fine and as moving as any I can recall.

It is a pity that the tenor Webster Booth is best remembered for light operetta for he could sing the more serious works almost as well as anybody else. He eventually settled in South Africa, becoming more famous there than in Britain.

Then, of course, there was Heddle Nash, following in the steps of Gervase Elwes, John Coates and Sir Steuart Wilson. I first met him in the 1920s at a concert presented at the Palladium on a Sunday evening; among conjurors and others, a soprano, tenor and bass were hired to sing songs. Before the performance he introduced himself, saying he had just come back after three years studying in Italy. 'I'm going to be the best tenor in England!', he said. What arrogance, I thought, but soon came to realise it wasn't; merely his buoyant and youthful belief in his future. He did in fact become the finest 'bel canto' tenor of his time, a confident colleague without malice. I sang with him for his first big *Messiah* with Malcolm Sargent for the Bradford Choral Union. At rehearsal, Heddle sang a few bars of 'Comfort Ye' and was stopped abruptly in his tracks. 'Mr Nash!' roared Sargent, 'It doesn't go like that at all!', and proceeded with his conductor's voice to demonstrate how he wished the passage phrased. 'But,' exclaimed Heddle, 'Dr Sargent. That's a revolution!'

'No,' came the response, 'It's a revelation!' On another occasion, he and I had been invited to lunch with Mrs Gwyn Holford, the Three Choirs hostess for Gloucester. Halfway through lunch and halfway down the table, Heddle exclaimed: 'It's all right! *Gerontius* is mine! Elgar has told me I'm the one!' With black hat a-tremble, Mrs Holford demanded: 'Mr Nash! What did I hear you say?' Heddle, without blinking, repeated himself. Mrs Holford: 'Mr Nash! You don't have the slightest idea what *Gerontius* is all about!' There was deathly silence as everyone wondered what would happen next but Heddle rose to the occasion, asking what was wrong, could he come to talk to her about it. Later we did the work together and I found him to be the best *Gerontius* of his time, certainly the best 'bel canto'. His death in 1961 was a grievous loss.

Walter Widdop was a 'Heldentenor', with full-blooded voice and delivery, always ready for a joke. During my solo 'Thus saith the Lord' and 'And I will shake ... ', during a performance of *Messiah* conducted by Sir Thomas Beecham at Covent Garden, Walter took hold of the wide cuffs of his trousers – it was the days of the 'Oxford Bags' – and shook them in time with my runs of semi-quavers. On another occasion he almost corpsed me during Beethoven's 9th. There are three orchestral passages sounding very much alike before the bass entry of 'O Freunde, nicht diese Tonen'. I heard the first one: no, not yet. A few bars on the passage was played again. Nudging me, Walter said, 'Go on! You're on NOW!' Edging forward on my seat, the orchestra played on. I glanced at Walter as I stood for the correct entry, to find him having a private chuckle at my expense. Some years later we were together again for Mahler's 8th and the conductor, Gene Goossens, said he had engaged two tenors because the higher baritone role was too high for me. After rehearsal, the other tenor remarked to Widdop that he'd nearly lost his voice trying to sing above the choir and orchestra. To which Walter replied: 'You haven't been singing the stuff, have you? I've been gold-fishing it! It's like trying to fart against a bloody thunderstorm!'

Basses and baritones are naturally rivals but many were good friends. A firm friend was Roy Henderson, a fine artist, his speciality singing long oratorio roles from memory. He deservedly made a big name for himself with *Sea Drift* and *Mass of Life* (Delius), going on to found and direct the Nottingham Oriana Choir and be teacher to Kathleen Ferrier. Most years we met at Lord's. Robert Radford was one of the finest, with an authentic and rich timbre of voice whom I first heard in *Messiah* in 1919. Soloists often sang this work without rehearsal, and Radford started *The Trumpet Shall Sound* in C while the strings came in on D, the trumpet in C. Chaos followed as the strings struggled to find their transposed copies. Robert Easton's deep bass was rich and characterful, used with much authority.

Norman Allin was the Grand Old Man of the singing profession in my time. I sang with him at the Three Choirs in 1925 and was awed by the depth of his rich voice and the curious habit he had of appearing to sing out of the side of his mouth. Later on, Norman, Roy and I would lunch on Saturdays at the RAC. On one occasion, Norman ordered a good vintage Burgundy and, putting the glass to his nose, his lips to glass, declared it undrinkable. Another bottle was brought, with Norman becoming benevolent again: the only time I saw him angry, or a bottle refused. After Norman died in 1973, I held a lunch to honour him at the RCM, inviting all his old colleagues and friends. These were the 'Vintage Singers'. *(See photo in the illustrations section.)*

PART THREE

Tributes to Sir Keith and a Falkner discography

Sir Keith – in person and on disc
ALAN BLYTH

I knew Keith personally only in his later years, when we adjudicated together at several vocal competitions. At these he was always a kind, considerate juror, both to his fellow judges and to the young aspirants (Keith was, of course, magnificent with the young). His predictably perceptive and acute comments consistently went to the heart of the matter. In addition his sly wit, the eyes still sparkling with fun and good nature, always managed to ease any moment of tension. Not to forget his huge fund of stories, fully chronicled in these pages by his daughter.

I knew him as well as my age allowed as a singer. I am reasonably certain he was the bass soloist at my first *Messiah*, heard at the Queen's Hall when I was about nine in the late 'thirties. I have a distinct memory of a tall, upright figure dispensing Handel with the utmost fluency. After the war I heard him in one of his Wigmore Hall recitals with John Hunt, and was pleased to have confirmed all the fine qualities I had heard in the meantime on disc. Later he was always a genial host at the RCM when critics visited the College for performances. He and Lady Falkner disclosed all the old British virtues of good manners, modest authority, inborn intelligence: features that were also attributes of his professional career.

The records, which are reviewed in detail by Wayne Turner (see later in this book) in his well-informed 1970 discography, speak for themselves as examples of British singing at its appreciable best during the interwar years. Among his discs, I have always cherished the Handel items – a manly *Arm, arm ye brave*, and eloquent account of *The people that walked in darkness*, a flow of smiling tone in *Droop not, young lover*. The Bach items disclose his dignity and authority in that composer's music. Just as rewarding are the deeply felt, surely articulated account of English song: B 9064 and B 9095 are templates of how to sing and interpret the genre. Then the Purcell items show a total mastery of Purcellian style before the composer had enjoyed the revival of interest evinced today.

At the time of writing there is just one Falkner entry in the *Gramophone* catalogue. That is as bass soloist on a previously unissued recording of Beethoven's *Missa Solemnis* made at the Leeds Festival in 1937. This is a most important issue, not least because it adds significantly to the very few complete recordings of any vocal work, operas apart, made in that era of 78 rpm discs. It is also a priceless addition to the Falkner discography, indeed to the discography of all the distinguished artists taking part – in addition to Falkner the solo quartet includes Isobel Baillie, Mary Jarred and Heddle Nash – and of course Beecham. All four soloists, in their prime, are in splendid form, sounding all the more spontaneous for being caught on the wing (Nash contributes some typically beseeching phrases).

What distinguishes their singing as a whole, besides its obvious sincerity, is the gift of *legato*, and nowhere is that more evident than in Falkner's singing on the bottom line. He places his refined, rounded tone on an immaculate line throughout and enunciates the Latin text with grave eloquence. He and his fellow-singers form a euphonious quartet in the many concerted passages, each as it were listening to the other's contribution, thus forming a cohesive whole.

One must earnestly hope that the rumoured re-discovery of a 1935 Three Choirs *Dream of Gerontius* with Falkner and Nash among the soloists doesn't prove a chimera. To have Falkner's account of the Priest's and Angel of the Agony's solos would be invaluable and, though we have a complete Nash Gerontius, made some ten years later, it would be good to hear him in the role earlier in his career, in fresher voice. I hope that even more of Falkner's work will be unearthed now that the BBC archives are becoming more generally available.

Yet what we have of him on disc is fairly representative, albeit in piecemeal form, of his repertory. It would be good if his account of *Dichterliebe* could at last be generally available, also his Christus on the 1937 *Matthew Passion*. Then his art could and surely would be more generally appreciated by a new generation, who could read, mark and learn from his distinction of style.

Sir Keith Falkner, Sixth Director of the RCM

HERBERT HOWELLS

Inevitably, in recent weeks, two names have been uppermost in our minds – Falkner and Willcocks; respectively sixth and seventh Directors of the College. To many of us, freely but with great respect, they are 'Keith and David'; the one just shedding responsibility of directorship, the other now accepting it.

It would be common sense, even gracious, if all who are associated with the College should give serious thought for the nature and scope of its leadership, and especially for the 'personal' factor in its history, as reflecting upon the distinguished men who, in a sixfold collective individualism, have already set their seal upon it.

That done, it is for all of us, in utmost confidence, and untroubled by any symbolic mark of interrogation, to look to the seventh directorship.

Meanwhile, this note essentially concerns Sir Keith. One writes in sheer gratitude and affectionate salutation, minus any hint of a spurious farewell that would be wholly misapplied if offered to a man still in the plenitude of his powers. But *any* note about him must suffer an initial difficulty. Simply stated, it is that there is no unitary Keith Falkner. He is, at the very least, a trinity. Not in the mere sense of progressive prefixes – Mr, Dr, Sir. These are no more than the social tabs of a wide-ranging career for which even trinitarian boundaries are too narrow. He cannot be summed up in any one of his main callings – singer, administrative and artistic ambassador for the British Council, in Rome; sixth Director of the Royal College of Music.

Soon, the inadequate three-in-one fiction breaks down, under American pressure. In 1950, and at the point of utmost maturity, the once-upon-a-time (1909) 'outsize red-haired choirboy' of New College, Oxford (Sir Adrian Boult's phrase for him), decided to submit to powerful influences in the USA. Cornell University's Department of Music decided they must have a Professor of Vocal Music. Dr Serge Koussevitzky and others of like influence supported the policy. They wanted the man of their choice, searched Rome, got him.

So came the Falkner of Fourth Dimension. He was 'translated' to Ithaca. The trinitarian idea was finished. Cornell had to face up – and *did*

– to a Professor of Singing who could say to his pupils *'This* is what I mean' as a usual preface to direct example. He *sang* his meaning in terms of (say) the Christus in Bach's *St Matthew Passion*, or Schumann's *Dichterliebe*. Cornell learned, what we in England had long known, that in singing Bach he had what kings would call 'Divine Right'. The University soon realised that he could, and did, go far beyond the normal task of voice-production. They found him organising and coaching operatic work. He brought England to Ithaca in *Riders to the Sea* (and Vaughan Williams with it); so, too, came Britten's *Noye's Fludde*, and Purcell's *Fairy Queen* and Locke's masque *Cupid and Death*. And – in his heart of hearts perhaps his own crowning satisfaction – he founded a Commonwealth Cricket Club with students and members of the Music Faculty: and risked loss of political decency by challenging and routing a United Nations eleven!

When, after ten years of tireless activity in the USA, the ruin of the Falkner-trinity myth, the retirement (here in London) of a greatly-loved fifth Director of the RCM, and heartache in Cornell, he came back to England, it was to what might be styled a Consortium of Royal Schools of Music: more precisely, to the Directorship of the RCM. Doubtless he knew the 'wind of change' had blown over the almond trees of Prince Consort Road, and changes there had not been confined to London Transport. There were other probabilities – that the RCM was not quite as he had known it in the hurricane days of the Third Directorate. These he knew. Most certainly and completely, he was aware that he would find more than a faint reflection of a new authority-and-student relationship. He knew that factor might be paramount. It often *was*. By great good fortune it was soon obvious that in his wise and sympathetic diplomacy he was rich in powers of guidance. And members of his professorial staff were quick to recognise those powers. Their attitude was never in doubt. Nor were their loyalties. For them, their expression of such was a familiar exercise; for Sir Keith himself unquestionably a major happiness.

To his tasks as he found them he brought internationalised experience. In himself he had rare gifts of sympathy and disciplined equanimity. But there would abide the unpredictable attitudes of the students-to-come; and the search for the least common denominator of their temperament would be ceaseless.

His own contemporary Victorians and Edwardians – even Georgians – have had the chance to know him in *all* his activities. Many of us may have wished recent students could more often have shared our wider knowledge of him, especially of the superb singer. And that, on purely human grounds, they could have seen as well as *heard* the disturbingly-attractive young man as he was in his own student and early professional days – in the years of compelling gifts alike on concert platform and cricket field, on golf links and (at the nth degree of charm and innocence) in forbidden practice-rooms, or on the out-of-bounds girls' staircase when the Bindonesque tyranny was still not yet overpast. By no other than Somerset House rules students of the 14 years' Falkner reign could not have shared phases of his career. Even so, he was faultlessly and uniquely *their* Director. So it remains. It puts the students beyond need of anybody's academic sympathy. I like to believe they were aware of Sir Keith's policies and understood his objectives and transforming power. They came to realise, more and more, that if they sometimes couldn't find him in or about the College precincts it was because he might be in Paris or the Netherlands, or Italy, Germany or Austria, in contact with the chief European centres of musical education in the context of vital policies of co-ordination and consultation.

It is good to think he took the RCM into Europe, widened its interests, thought of its mission and influence as reaching far beyond the Albert Memorial. Perceptive students shared knowledge of such acts and policies as being those of the Director of their own day. It was their great happiness – and ours.

This brief and thankful note has been mainly about one man's task and his brilliant but unostentatious service to it. But it must be clear to all of us that his own success was constantly subserved, in equal modesty and infinite grace, by another gifted Collegian. For some of us she is Christabel; for everybody Lady Falkner. But by whatever name or title we think of her, she has always been a gracious influence and presence in our midst.

Sir Keith Falkner, 1900–1994

An Appreciation by David McKenna
New College Chapel, 11 March 1995

I first heard Keith Falkner in a performance of Bach's *St Matthew Passion* in April 1930 in the old Queen's Hall. It was conducted by Sir Adrian Boult, and Keith was singing the Christus part, one which he had made very much his own. The first short arioso, 'Take, eat, this is my body', followed by the more extended 'Drink ye all of it', made an immediate impression, well remembered even to this day, by the beauty of the tone, the musical line, the sincerity, the sheer rightness of the interpretation. It was an experience, so much so that in measuring all subsequent interpretations against this one – and I am happy to say that I have heard a good number – none have quite come up to the magic of Keith's.

It could be said that it started in this very building. Described as 'an outsize red-headed nine-year-old', Keith waited here in 1909 for Dr Allen, who had a certain reputation for ferocity, to know whether he had been accepted as chorister in the New College choir and a pupil at its choir school. The young Keith, son of the headmaster of the primary school at Sawston, near Cambridge, had been brought up in a loving and cultivated, but a long way from luxurious, atmosphere. A lively and bright, but not so little, boy, he had won first prize in a summer garden fête singing competition with his rendering of *Robin Adair*, and his father decided he might have a shot at a scholarship at the New College choir school. Keith was successful, and there began a period of incomparable musical training at the hands of Dr Allen, later Sir Hugh, who became Professor of Music in the University and Director of the Royal College of Music, and was one of the most influential figures in British music in the first half of this century. Ferocious or not, Allen was at heart one of the kindest and most human men imaginable; and so, for some four years, two future Directors of the Royal College of Music made music together in their very different capacities to the glory of God in this chapel.

Keith moved on to continue his education at the Perse School in Cambridge, near his own home, where he had obtained a county scholarship. He was growing up a boy of considerable spirit, energy and enterprise, with a strong taste and aptitude for sport, particularly cricket. It was typical of him that, on the outbreak of war in 1914, he learned that recruits were wanted for the RAMC . Partly no doubt from a desire for adventure, but also because he wanted to do his bit, he offered himself – he was by then exceptionally well-grown, standing six foot tall – and was accepted, although still only fourteen. (He had been a little economic with the truth about his age.) But the Colonel was standing near and asked him his name. There was no escape. 'Falkner, Sir', came the reply. 'Then you must be Jack Falkner's son from Sawston. He and I played cricket together for years. You must be Keith.' So the truth was out, and the fourteen-year-old was told to come again in three years' time. When that time did come, Keith in fact joined the Royal Naval Air Service, obtained a commission as a sub-lieutenant, and qualified as a pilot.

When the war was over, the second phase in Keith's life was beginning. Still a young man of only nineteen, but having become used to considerable responsibility in the outside world, he had to decide what to do next. His main interests were still music and cricket; and he was fully aware that the choice of a career was a very serious matter indeed. He toyed with the idea of a job with cricket; but when he learned that grants were available for study at the Royal College of Music, he applied for entry, with singing as his principal subject, and was accepted. It was a fortunate choice, for as a student there he came under the influence of three remarkable musicians, quite apart from his singing teacher. First there was Sir Hugh Allen, then the Director, who of course he knew well as a New College chorister; second, there was Dr Emily Daymond, a musician of great stature and of extreme personal modesty, who was a close musical collaborator with Sir Hubert Parry, the previous director; and third, Adrian Boult, with whom Keith enjoyed a lasting friendship over many years. Needless to say, he entered fully into the sporting activities of the students, and the fact that he was by far the best cricketer that had ever helped them in their annual struggles against the Royal Academy of Music. In the summer of 1921 his batting average in the RCM team was 65.6.

Keith emerged from his studentship with a strong sense of dedication and responsibility, together with an excellent technical foundation. While a student also he met his future wife, Christabel, herself a fellow student and a pianist and accompanist of great talent. They had a long engagement, as her parents refused to let her get married until Keith was well established in his career and was earning an adequate living. This was an added incentive to Keith to make progress in his chosen calling. From 1922 to 1926 he sang as a lay-vicar in the choir of St Paul's Cathedral, while he gradually built up his reputation as a solo singer and a most sensitive musician. By 1930 he had become recognised as one of the leading bass singers in the country, whether in oratorio or in recital, and was very much in demand. He and Christabel were married in that year, and there began a perfect partnership which survived right up to her death sixty years later. Keith was sought after by Warner Brothers in the early days of sound films to appear in musicals. He had all the charm – appearance, voice and intelligence – and he actually played the lead in three of their films. But he declined the offer to follow a more extended career in Hollywood, preferring to remain in the mainstream of music-making in Britain. By the time the second world war broke out, he had reached the top of the tree as a performing artist. And then it all abruptly came to an end; for Keith was a member of the RAF Volunteer Reserve, and nothing was going to deflect him from doing his bit in yet another war.

It irked Keith somewhat that, owing to his age, he was not accepted for flying duties, so he had to content himself with a ground job. He had hoped then that he might be given a job within reach of the London area, so that he might be able to continue his concert career, even though on a reduced scale. But it was not to be. He was posted to an air-station near Wick, in the far north-eastern corner of Scotland, as the Squadron Leader in charge; and thereafter he had a number of other postings, including Ireland. So singing was out for the duration.

The end of the war presented a problem for Keith. To attempt to resume his career where it had been interrupted, even though he had then been right at the top, would have involved a degree of risk, and certainly a resumption of the grind of one-night stands and constant travelling, besides the problem of getting his voice back into first-class trim: hardly a delectable prospect for his wife and young family. If a suitable job in music of a different kind, without those disadvantages, were to turn up, a change of direction could be attractive. Such an opportunity did in fact occur, for the British Council were anxious to establish a strong centre in Italy, their recent enemy, to promote British language and culture, with music as an important component, as part of the process of rehabilitation of Western Europe. Keith accepted the post of Music Officer, so the family moved to Rome; and no better cultural ambassador could have been found. British artists were enabled to visit Italy, and Italian artists to visit Britain. Christabel became expert in Italian cuisine and many are the tales of Falkner hospitality and encouragement given to British artists.

Keith had done a superb job. But by the end of the decade the British Council were altering their policy, deciding to put more resources into the less well-developed parts of the world, and to reduce those put into Western Europe now that post-war rehabilitation was so well on the way. Another change in direction, with all the accompanying anxieties, was therefore looming up for Keith.

Meanwhile, however, the Music Department of Cornell University in the USA had decided that they should have a Professor of Vocal Music. They were looking for someone more than an academic musicologist, or an expert in voice production; someone rather who could 'promote' vocal music, encourage performance and establish standards. They searched, and in Keith found the ideal candidate. And so, in 1950, another change in direction took place and the Falkner family moved to America.

For the next ten years Keith more than fulfilled the expectations of the University. He resumed concert work, for demonstration was part of the process of education. He encouraged performance, organised and coached operatic work, and created for Cornell a notable centre of musical initiative. He could not resist the temptation of founding a cricket team from among the students and members of his Music Faculty and had the temerity on one occasion to inflict a defeat upon a United Nations eleven. Keith had quite expected to finish his working career in America when the last and most significant change of direction took place.

Some months before Ernest Bullock was due to retire, the Council of the Royal College of Music set about the task of choosing his successor as Director. Keith's name was mentioned among a number, all distinguished musicians. In the course of lengthy discussions and consultations, the appreciation of his qualifications and experience grew in strength – a top-ranking performing artist, a musical ambassador in postwar Europe, and a musical educator at university level in the New World. His sympathetic personality, especially towards the young, was also well known, and he emerged clearly as the best candidate.

His appointment in 1960 as Director was unusual in that it was the first time in getting on for a hundred years that a professional performing artist had been chosen. Nevertheless, it was greatly welcomed. His advent was described by professors and students alike as an opening of the windows. A breath of fresh air was sweeping through the corridors of an institution which, for all its merits, appeared to many to have become stuffy and old-fashioned. To him the first priority was the encouragement of the students and the development of their individual personalities alongside their technical skills, although he used to remind them gently from time to time of the virtues of self-discipline and good manners.

His addresses to the students contained many pearls of wisdom: of the necessity for change but the benefits of the evolutionary approach; on the development of modern music from respect of music of the past; on the difference between sound (something consciously produced) and noise (something without meaning) – his own words are worth quoting:

> We musicians are in a very responsible position. We are the experts who are supposed to know the difference between sound and noise. If we do not praise sound and denounce noise, then no one else will.

It is significant that there was no student unrest at the College of the disruptive kind that was common elsewhere in the early 'sixties. He attributed this to the belief that the RCM students were too hard worked and dedicated to have time to indulge in disruption. But in this I think he underestimated his own influence.

The reputation of the College, both at home and abroad, grew steadily under Keith's direction, and he was an influential member of the Association of Directors of the Music Colleges of Europe. He regarded a widening of the horizons as important. His achievements as Director are well chronicled elsewhere. It was a time of great change, particularly in the mundane field of government funding; but he handled the necessary negotiations with patience and skill. When eventually he retired in 1974, four years after the end of his official span, for the Council were most reluctant to let him go when he was still so vigorous, a small Bach festival was organised in his honour, culminating in a performance of the *B Minor Mass* in Westminster Abbey, conducted by his successor, David Willcocks, with chorus and orchestra from the College. But Keith was not to be found in the seat of honour; he preferred to be with his students up among the basses, making music with them rather than receiving plaudits.

As in his previous spheres of activity, the realities exceeded the expectations, and yet Keith remained the most modest of men, and was incapable of taking personal credit for his achievements. To him the high reputation of the College was due entirely to the efforts of the professors, the administrative staff and the students themselves; but they all knew that it was his personality, his friendliness, his influence and, above all, his encouragement that created the atmosphere in which, to use his own words, 'they could work hard and enjoy what they were doing'.

Keith retired to his beloved East Anglia, but was by no means inactive. He joined the Council of the RCM as a most valued elder statesman, and never breathed down the neck of his successor; for three years he was Co-Director of the Kings Lynn Musical Festival, renowned then for the interest and quality of its offerings; and he produced a book on the voice, in a series designed for the interested general reader as well as the young student and professional, masterminded by Yehudi Menuhin. Typically, Keith's book consisted of a series of essays on various aspects, including one or two by himself, but mainly by experts of his acquaintance whose contributions he judged would be of greater value than any that he might make. He enjoyed the company of his friends and, right up to the year of his death, was a regular visitor to Haddo for June Gordon's oratorio weekend, where he would meet a number of his former colleagues and friends, and where, except for the last couple of years or so, he would join with the basses in performances of quality and deep sincerity. They loved him, and he loved them.

And so we are gathered together today to remember a splendid musician, an inspired educator, and a most lovable friend; and to offer our thanks for his life and for the encouragement that he gave to so many. One is almost tempted to think of Sir Hugh Allen, up there in the organ loft, and perhaps of Keith himself slipping in to join the basses in that wonderful last chorus of the *St John Passion* which we are about to hear.

Sir Keith Falkner

DAVID FANSHAWE

Sir Keith Falkner has had a profound influence on my life, both as a student at the RCM (1965-69) and in my career as a professional musician. We first met in March 1965, in the Director's Office at the College. I was aged 23, and attempting to enter College to study composition. Having had one interview, I was surprised to be sent down to the Director for a second. In my ignorance of College ways, I naturally assumed they were having one last look at me to see if there was anything worth salvaging before throwing me out! On the contrary, I soon learnt that the second interview actually meant one had been accepted, or passed the Entrance Exam (not that I took one), and was now being referred to the Director, as a possible candidate for a Foundation Scholarship. In my early autobiography *African Sanctus* I describe the scene:

So, firmly convinced of my failure, I told them exactly of my plight – and what a plight it was!

'I very much want to come to College to study composition with John Lambert,' I said. 'If you accept me, I shall then have a good chance of getting a County Grant and won't have to go on working as a part-time male model in Canterbury Art School. If I don't get into College I shall continue my studies privately with Mr Lambert but will waste a lot of time being a male model, hitch-hiking up and down to London for my music lessons.'

Dr Gordon Jacob at this point looked up, quite speechless, and dropped his glasses on the desk.

'You what?' he said.

'Male model for life classes at Canterbury Art School,' I replied and proceeded to give the distinguished company a demonstration of what I did for a living. In fact, I nearly decided to take my trousers off there and then, knowing full well what my fate was going to be, but instead I spoke of my fears at having to take the 'written paper' in the afternoon. We talked for a short while and then they asked me to play another of my piano pieces, which only looked impressive because it happened to be published.

'Are you sure you want to come here?' asked Sir Keith.

'Quite sure,' I replied, and then went on to apologise, saying that I would be incapable of doing *any* harmony and theory without the aid of a piano and therefore didn't think I could take the theory paper at all. So wishing them a 'Good morning' I slipped out of the door.

Miraculously, 48 hours later, in my shed in our garden in Kent, I received a red letter from Kensington. It was handed to me by my father, who assumed that the College authorities had made a mistake; he immediately telephoned the College Registrar, John R Stainer, to advise him of their error, only to have it confirmed that I had indeed been: 'awarded *Foundation Scholarship* tenable at the College, from September next'. Now that letter of acceptance from the RCM changed the emphasis of my whole life. It was perhaps, Sir Keith's single and resolute faith in my potential as a composer that ultimately helped to reassure my parents, who came from a Service background, that their eldest son had a future in music. They were mighty relieved!

Those brilliant years at College in the 1960s, skilfully guided by our administrators, were filled with vibrant cacophony! It was quite amazing: trombones in the loos, sopranos in the towers, endless choruses in the 99, The Opera School and at least five orchestras all pounding away in the Concert Hall, like an engine room of music, preparing College for an invasion of the musical colonies. All this served liked a weighted anchor, from which I would eventually steer my own individual 'Star-Path' composing, exploring and ultimately recording the world and its indigenous music. It was after one of my early journeys to the Holy Land, in 1966, that Sir Keith commented in his opening address:

> Thank you for your warm welcome. I trust we are all delighted to be back in College and ready for the new academic year. . . Since we separated for the summer vacation we have all pursued our individual ideas for a holiday; my wife and I buried ourselves in rural Suffolk and came back, like you I hope, full of energy for the New Year. The student who lived with the Bedouin in the desert, rode camels and toured Israel and Jordan, thereby 'acquiring a much better knowledge of the Bible' deserves special mention. I hope David Fanshawe has brought back a film of his holiday so that we may have the pleasure of seeing it at College . . .

I loved my time at the RCM, despite being invariably late back from the holidays. Thankfully, I was allowed to *be* a composer and it was agreed that I need not take exams. Being a bit dyslexic, I wouldn't have understood the questions, let alone know how to compose the answers! As for the 'film' of my holiday, in those days, I confess I only took a notebook and endless coloured slides, but Sir Keith encouraged me to present my travels in the Recital Hall, with slides and tapes – can you imagine? Sometimes there were only about six people in the audience, of which two, usually in the front row, comprised the Director and his endearing wife, Lady Christabel. Their presence totally remedied the poor attendance and rows of empty seats.

In fact, I cannot remember a College concert, formal or informal, where Sir Keith and Lady Falkner were *not* present. Interestingly enough, they had both been students together at College and she was his accompanist. They were indomitable, setting us students a lifelong example and willing us to go on and do our best. No matter what our first studies were, we *all* felt supported and I remember witnessing soloists, suffering terrible nerves and traumas, being soothed by the Director himself, off stage. Somehow, Sir Keith always managed to find the right words of encouragement for students. Unfortunately, we never knew him as a celebrated performer, one of the country's leading bass-baritones between the wars, but we certainly benefited from his personal understanding and vast international experience. He was a wise and great Director, mentor and friend, in spite of the generation gap.

I would now like to quote one more example of Sir Keith's generosity and philosophical approach to his former student. In 1967 I was absolutely distraught, fearing for my place at College, when I was admitted to the RAF Hospital in Al Muharraq, Bahrain, suffering from jaundice. There was absolutely no way I could make it back to College on time, so I wrote to the Director, in a pall of yellow guilt, and within days received his consoling reply:

21st September, 1967.

Dear David,

We are all extremely sorry to hear of your predicament. Mr Lambert has just shown me your letter written on Monday last the 18th. If you have jaundice it will be no use me telling you not to worry. I know only too well from experience that you will think this is the end of everything. You must now do what the Doctors tell you and have a complete rest, forget all your projects and get better. I am sure you need not worry about anything here about your further study. Arrangements will be made to postpone things until you are really better.

This is a very hasty note. I have five minutes before the post. We shall hope to have good news of you soon. Meanwhile take it easy and count your blessings. You have a lot. I was delighted to have your letters en route during the past weeks which I found extremely interesting.

All good wishes,

Yours sincerely,

Keith Falkner

What a wonderful letter to receive in Bahrain, and how relieved I felt. No doubt the Director posted it himself, in that red letter box outside College in Prince Consort Road. He would have done, because he valued the exercise and a breath of fresh air . .

Making one's way as a composer is always difficult. How much did I, and my fellow composers, rely on the indefatigable support of people like Sir Keith? When I needed a reference, he was always willing to write it, or phone on my behalf; as a young professional I welcomed his advice. He acted positively and helped launch so many careers. He and his wife bothered to attend several of my premières, both in and outside College: *Fantasy on Dover Castle*, *Two Chesterton Songs*, *Requiem for the Children of Aberfan*, *Salaams* at the Queen Elizabeth Hall in 1970, and *African Sanctus* in Worcester Cathedral in 1978.

In 1989 I decided to dedicate my piano work *Romanza Burlesque* to Sir Keith and Lady Falkner. I visited them at their home in Suffolk several times and throughout my career remained in touch. Each time I went abroad, I used to phone from Heathrow, or Gatwick, announcing: 'Sir, this is David Fanshawe speaking, I'm just off to South Sudan. . . ' (Hong Kong, Tahiti, Fiji, Sydney or wherever).

'Oh really?' he'd reply. Immediately, one could sense his interest and enthusiasm in support of one's endeavours. 'Do write, we'd love to hear more. . .'

I think these were the last words he spoke to me in 1994.

Every student needs a good and positive example. Sir Keith's example is undoubtedly the way I would like to try and live my life now. I believe we are still in touch.

He was a wise and great Director, mentor and friend, in spite of the generation gap.

Thank you, Sir.

Exercus

KEITH FALKNER AT CORNELL, 1950-1960, an article summarising Keith's years at this institution, appeared in the Royal College of Music Magazine, Vol 56, by Donald Jay Grout, with contributions from John Kirkpatrick and William Austin.

Early in 1950 the Department of Music decided to add to its staff a professor of vocal music. Through a series of fortunate circumstances, and with the mediation of Dr Serge Koussevitzky and Professor Archibald Davison, we were able to bring Keith Falkner to Ithaca. He was appointed Visiting Professor of Music in July of 1950. Cornell had never had a voice teacher on its regular staff and the new venture was regarded with misgivings by some. But the experiment very quickly proved itself a success. In 1952, Mr Falkner became Associate Professor and in 1958 full Professor.

It is neither possible nor desirable to list all the contributions Mr Falkner made to music at Cornell. He organised or coached performances of operas and similar productions to a degree never before known in our department. Gilbert and Sullivan, of course ... but also Menotti's *Amahl*, Vaughan Williams's *Riders to the Sea*, Locke's masque *Cupid and Death*, Purcell's 'Masque of Night' from *Fairy Queen*, Britten's *Noye's Fludde* and many others. In all these was evident not only Mr Falkner's musicianship but also his extraordinary ability – reinforced by his own example – to make people work hard and stay happy while doing so.

His own performances stand out unforgettably: his reading of the narrative in Honegger's *King David*, his singing of Schumann's *Dichterliebe* cycle with John Hunt, of the Christus in Bach's *St Matthew Passion*, and many, many more.

Mr Falkner launched the *Cornell Music Review* and was its editor for three years. It was owing to him also that we had the privilege of receiving Ralph Vaughan Williams as guest professor, conductor and lecturer in the Autumn Term of 1954.

One of Mr Falkner's first acts after coming to Cornell was to organise a Commonwealth Cricket Club from among students and faculty in the University. This group, I understand, had some difficulty in finding other teams in the United States against whom to play. There was one match, if that is the correct term, against the 'United Nations' (fortunately, the line-up 'Commonwealth' versus 'United Nations' had no political significance). I remember the event, not because I was present but because Keith came out to Skaneateles Lake for one of our long walking tours the very next day – and this was the only time within memory that at the end of twenty miles of walking he was more completely exhausted than I was. On such occasions the only way to keep up with him was to get him well tired out the day before.

The ties that have grown up in these ten years of our association – ties of professional respect and personal affection – are not easy to break. Not every Music Department has the good fortune to find a teacher of singing who is at the same time an artist of first rank, a musician of broad understanding, a colleague wise in council, and a human being of integrity and humility. What the present Chairman of the Department, William Austin, wrote about Mr Falkner's production of *Noye's Fludde* in January 1960 would apply equally well to everything he did: 'His energy, foresight, tact and persistence provided most of the binding force to co-ordinate the diverse contributions. His teaching ensured the parts of the solo singers. His speaking, as the Voice of God, gave the performance its moments of great intensity and beauty. At a time when he might understandably have relaxed a bit, in preparation for the new job he is taking on in England in July, he has exerted himself to the utmost, and made Cornell an incalculable gift ... It was, said William Austin later, a perfect example of his way of combining his many contributions to a very moving event ... '

Discography Critique

WAYNE TURNER

Whilst Keith Falkner's records are fairly representative of his art, one must regret that HMV did not allow him to perpetuate much of his greatest work. For instance, it is a pity that Butterworth's *A Shropshire Lad,* Somervell's *Maud,* Vaughan Williams's *Songs of Travel* were never recorded by him and that his Christus has never been generally available. Many solo songs which he made his own were never committed to disc and a lamentable absentee is Bach's solo Cantata *Ich habe genug.*

However, there is plenty to admire in what does exist: the amazing breath control, the mastery of florid technique in Bach and Purcell airs, the 'cello-like line in the *St Paul* aria and the exquisite grace of one of the *Maud* songs.

C 1670 *Elijah*: 'Thanks Be to God'.

Part of a set of four records (C1668/71) of choruses from *Elijah,* sung by the Royal Choral Society. Falkner sings only the recit, leading into the chorus of the same name and declaims the brief passage with firm tone and an appropriate sense of exaltation.

C 1875 *Judas Maccabaeus*: 'Arm, Arm Ye Brave' (Handel).

A fine, stirring account of an oft-recorded aria. Other splendid artists have done justice to the aria, but none equal Falkner in the slower middle section, which shows phenomenal breath-control on the word 'Strengthen'.

St Paul: 'O God Have Mercy' (Mendelssohn).

This is lovely singing, with a fine legato and an appeal for mercy which is quite moving.

C 1940 *Messiah*: 'The People that walked in Darkness' (Handel);
        Solomon: 'What Though I Trace Each Herb and Flower'
        (Handel);

Again a beautiful legato, resembling a string instrument in the flow of sound. The *Messiah* excerpt shows the even quality throughout the singer's compass; *Solomon* incidentally, was originally a role for castrato voice.

B 2917 *Salt-Water Ballads*: 'Port of many ships', 'Trade Winds', 'Mother Carey' (Keel) with orchestra.

Frederick Keel's colourful settings of Masefield's poems are sung with conviction, clarity of enunciation (especially in the patter-like rapidity of 'Mother Carey''), and as usual, lovely tone. John Shirley Quirk's singing of 'Trade Winds' sounds deadly dull compared to this performance. Nowhere is the breath control more apparent than in the final 'blowing'. Westminster issued in 1957, in the USA, a very lovely account of the three songs in which the singer was that very English bass Richard Standen.

B 3105 'Had a Horse' / 'Shepherd: See thy Horse's Foaming Mane', arr Korbay.

Hungarian folk-songs which are given vivid interpretations; virile masculine singing in the first, a menacing tone in the 'Grievous bodily harm' mood of the second. J B Richards, in his Norman Allin article for the *Record Collector*, whilst praising the latter's account of the second song, prefers Falkner's performance, referring to it as 'brilliant'.

B 3175 *The Playbox*: Rocking Horse; Golliwog; Clockwork Train; Toy Band; Teddy Bear; Jack-in-the-Box; Humming-top; Noah's Ark; Bagpiper; Wooden Soldier. (Gerald Williams)

A group of original songs for children. They are charmingly sung by Sir Keith, whose enunciation, so important in this kind of thing, is crystal clear throughout.

B 3321 *Ezio*: 'Droop not, young lover' (Handel);
'King Charles' (White).

The Handel aria, originally known as 'Se un bell' ardire' and composed in 1732 for the bass Antonio Montagnana, has a low E, splendidly smooth runs and the singer makes the most of the words and captures the whimsical mood. Falkner's performance is far superior to the one which is included in an LP disc of Handel arias sung by Forbes Robinson. Maud Valerie White's setting of one of Browning's cavalier poems is given an appropriately dashing performance. The numerous crescendi are skilfully managed, of course, but some may prefer Norman Allin's bluffer approach (Columbia 2693).

B 4531 *The joyful Aeolus*: 'How Jovial is My Laughter' (Bach
　　　　Cantata 205);
　　　　St Matthew Passion: 'Twas in the Cool of Eventide' (Bach).
　　Here is Bach singing at its very best. The calm serenity of the *Passion*
arioso is maintained throughout and only makes one wish that the aria
which follows, 'Make Me Clean, My Heart, from Sin', was not included.
The florid bravura aria from the secular cantata, a popular concert choice
for Sir Keith, is a lesson in the singing of runs, each note clearly
articulated. The breath control is, as always, remarkable, with a
wonderfully calculated crescendo on the long-held word 'stand' near the
end. The *Gramophone* reviewer of the day gave this a deservedly
favourable notice.

B 3658 *A Princess of Kensington*: 'Four Jolly Sailormen' (German);
　　　　Tom Jones: 'On a January Morning' (German) with orchestra.
　　Good singing, from a purely vocal point of view, with a ringing high
F at the end of the Squire's song (Tom Jones), but this song needs,
perhaps, a 'Zummerzet' accent; the jocular approach is right and Falkner
makes the most of the words. The sailor's song needs a touch more
vulgarity, in the best sense of the word, to give it character.

B 3991 'Come Landlord, Fill the Flowing Bowl' (trad);
　　　　'False Phillis' (anon, arr Lane Wilson).
　　The drinking song has Sir Keith with male chorus. It has little to
distinguish it, apart from a splendid solo voice, from a host of similar
items, issued at this time by HMV and usually sung by Stuart Robertson
and the BBC Men's Chorus. The reverse side is a little gem, one of many
17th/18th-century ballads arranged by Henry Lane Wilson (1871/1915),
himself a bass-baritone of no mean distinction. Falkner sings delightfully
and makes the most of this charming little ballad.

B 4072 *Fringes of the Fleet*: 'Fate's Discourtesy', 'The Sweepers'
　　　　(Elgar).
　　Patriotic songs from a group of four, written by Elgar to words of
Kipling and first sung in public by four baritones and chorus (including
Charles Victor) in 1917. These two are easily the best of the set. Falkner
sings the first with firm, virile attack and drive. The second song, the last
of the set, is a splendid one, describing a day in the life of five
minesweepers. Falkner's tonal variety and sensitivity to words help him

to fully convey the contrasts in this fine song, which seems strangely neglected nowadays.

B 8618-9 *Mayfair Melody*: 'San Diego Betty', 'Without the Moon', 'Wings', 'A Song Doesn't Care' (Dyrenforth & K Leslie-Smith).

These songs are from a 1937 film and were recorded on the set. They are somewhat typical of the British 'musical' of the period. There is a great deal of charm and nostalgia in 'Without the Moon' and this song has some lovely mezza voce singing from Falkner, who, like Peter Dawson, is able to make songs in the lighter vein (though by no means trivial) sound better than they are. 'San Diego Betty' is a light-hearted sailor's song in shanty style, but there is a most anaemic male chorus.

B 8064 *A Shropshire Lad*: 'Is My Team Ploughing' (Butterworth);
A Shropshire Lad: 'The Street Sounds to the Soldier's Tread' (Somervell), Gerald Moore, piano.

The weird dialogue between the 'lad' and his dead comrade's ghost is vividly portrayed and the horror of the last reply, 'Never ask me whose', is chilling. This is a fine virile baritone song, richly and resonantly performed here, with the dynamics well calculated and a further example of Keith Falkner's breath control in the phrase 'Soldier, I wish You well'.

B 8095 *Maud*: 'Birds in the High Hall Garden', 'O Let the Solid Ground' (Somervell);
'In Summertime on Bredon' (Peel) Gerald Moore, piano.

The Peel song is probably the best setting of an oft-set poem (Somervell, Butterworth, Vaughan Williams, Hamilton, etc); it is simple, unpretentious, yet evocative. Falkner's tone here is lovely, melting in the soft passage beginning 'But when the snows at Christmas'. There is a restrained anguish in the final phrase 'I hear you, I will come'. 'Birds in the High Hall Garden' is one of the finest examples of Keith Falkner's art; this is a delightful song and he sings it with genuine affection and attention to detail, apart from substituting a crochet for a quaver at one point. He obtains an exquisite effect from 'I kissed her slender hand ... Maud is not seventeen but she is tall and stately'. This is No 5 in the cycle and is followed by the impassioned 'O Let the Solid Ground' (No 4); this is sung with fine ringing tone and excellent rhythmic drive. Moore is superb in these songs. This cycle has thirteen songs in it, but in its first performance only twelve were sung, No. 6, 'Maud has a Garden' being omitted. Plunket Greene being superstitious, refused to sing a cycle with thirteen songs in it! Sir Keith told me that he himself sang the song at Somervell's request, though rarely in a complete performance of the cycle.

HDL 13.   *Alexander's Feast*: (Handel) with Scheunemann, soprano; Chabay, tenor; Cornell University Chorus and Orchestra, conducted by Robert Hull (4 LP sides).

The great bass-baritone aria in this work is 'Revenge, Timotheus Cries' and, as one would expect, it receives a splendid performance: the florid passages quite thrilling and the slow passage beginning 'Behold a Ghastly Band' full of variety, colour and meaning, sung with a steady legato. Over twenty-five years separate this, the last of Falkner's commercial recordings, from his first, and the voice shows no trace of age, but retains freshness and ease of production. The other air for this voice is 'Bacchus Ever Fair and Young' with horn accompaniment, leading into a male chorus.

Victor 14635/61 *St. Matthew Passion* (Bach) with J Vreeland, soprano; K Meikle, contralto; J Preibe, tenor; F Lechner, bass; Harvard Glee Club, Radcliffe Choral Society, Boston Symphony Orchestra, conducted by Koussevitzky, now on AH-202-203.

Falkner is in fine voice and his interpretation of Jesus's words will most probably never be equalled. He conveys the sublime mood beautifully. Few have caught the mood of exaltation at 'sitting at the right hand of God', nor the agony of 'Eli, Eli, lama sabachthani', as he has.

HMV D 922/6 *Hugh the Drover:* (Vaughan Williams), for cast see record listing, conducted by Malcolm Sargent.

Sir Keith has little to sing in this, his first recording. The glory belongs to Tudor Davies in the title role of what is an abridged performance.

HMV C 3748/50 English Madrigals: (Bennett, Farmer, Farnaby, Gibbons, Morley, Pilkington, Vautour, Weelkes, Wilbye: see list for titles) given by The Golden Age Singers (Margaret Field-Hyde, Isobel Baillie, sopranos; Gladys Windmill, contralto; Rene Soames, tenor; Keith Falkner, bass).

These three records form part of anthology of 24 sides (HMV C 3739/50), some 17 other madrigals being sung by the Cambridge University Madrigal Society under Boris Ord. The remaining ten were performed by The Golden Age Singers, the guiding spirit being the soprano, Margaret Field-Hyde. Falkner sings the bass lines and his distinctive, mellow tone, while being easily audible and distinguishable, blend beautifully with those of his colleagues, these being model artists for ensemble work of this type.

ROX 134   'The Aspiration: How long, Great God' (Purcell)
            'If Music Be the Food of Love' (Purcell, 2nd setting). Both accompanied by John Ticehurst (harpsichord) and Bernard Richards (cello). Issued in the USA on Columbia 11099D.
ROX 135   'I Love and I Must' (Purcell)
            accompanied as above (Am. Col. 11100D).

Along with the Bach excerpts and the Somervell songs, these are the finest examples of Keith Falkner's recorded singing and would be quite sufficient proof of his outstanding worth and class. The first item, with words by Morris, is a typical 'scena' for solo voice, consisting of an extended recitative, full graphic word portrayal and followed by a florid, though rather short, aria. Falkner matches this with colourful word-painting himself and demonstrates Plunket Greene's adage that every word has its own particular shade of colour. He shows, too, that the English language can be made to sound beautiful and expressive. This type of Purcell piece, of which 'Ye Twice Ten Hundred Deities' (from *The Indian Queen*) and 'Let the Dreadful Engines' from his incidental music to *Don Quixote* are dramatic extensions, demand almost every aspect of the singer's art: legato, feeling for words, vocal range, coloratura (in the original sense), perfect intonation, breath-control, advanced musicianship, as well as the more subtle skills such as the calculation of crescendi, morendi and mezza di voce. Breath-control must not only support and sustain the tone, but must enable the singer to cope with long, intricate, ornamental, almost instrumental phrases with which this kind of music abounds. Falkner's singing fulfils all these demands.

Colonel Heveningham's paraphrase of Shakespeare's verses was Purcell's second of three settings. It is a lovely andante melody and the baritone's tone, variety of dynamics and shading, in addition to the line he draws, convince one that this is the finest of the three. His artistic phrasing, sense of poetry and delicate mezza voce singing are always in evidence in this love song. 'I Love and I Must' is a type of 'nonsense' song, calling for vocal agility, smooth line and constant variety. Sir Keith, as one would expect, was the ideal Purcell singer and is in his own element here. Indeed, this singing serves as a model for this particular style. The reverse consists of two catches, 'I Gave Her Cakes and I Gave Her Ale' and 'To Thee and to a Maid', sung by the Purcell Singers.

FB 186 'Drums of Peace' (Fraser); 'Bridgebuilders' (Fraser).

These two songs were first published in 1936 for the Oxford Group (Moral Rearmament). The first is mainly choral, though Sir Keith's tones can be distinguished. The music is not memorable. The second song is much better and slightly reminiscent of Quilter's 'Non nobis, Domine' vein. It has Falkner singing in fine style and with bright attack.

* * *

The above review, done originally in 1970 for *The Record Collector*, included all items that were known to exist of Keith Falkner's recordings. Since then, some others have come to light. One was his first solo record, made in April 1928 for HMV. The company decided against issuing it as it would have 'little commercial value', a strange view, it seems, when in 1930 recordings of similar 'commercial value' were issued, eg, the Blow song, performed by the light baritone John Goss, a singer of only average attainments. The Blow song, 'The Self-Banished', to a poem by Waller, has two verses and there is room on this 10-inch disc for only one verse. The song is a very beautiful one, demanding, and in this case receiving, a suave legato line which allows the words to speak for themselves. There is no better version of this fine song than this one. The two Parry songs show great expressiveness in the feeling for the words, a light touch and dynamic range. 'Follow a Shadow' is not as well known as its partner, 'Love is a Bable', a really splendid song which deserves its popularity.

Here is the young artist, singing without inhibitions and with drive and virile attack.

Adlonni Series: *Dichterliebe* (Schumann).

Over 25 years separate this 'private' recording and the one above. Many who know Falkner's, either from recital hall or records, agree with this writer in stating that this is the best example of his work as a singer, along with, of course, the 1937 Christus under Koussevitzky. Here is the mature, experienced artist still in vocal prime with a voice at the service of mind and heart. Here is what is meant by control – breath-control, yes – but complete control of the voice so that it does exactly what he wants it to do. He is completely 'inside' this cycle; so, too, is his accompanist and one can see why Keith Falkner valued John Hunt's work so highly. The cycle may not be the greatest of its genre but it could be claimed that for sheer beauty it is difficult to surpass. The beauty of the music, the high romanticism of the Heine verses, plus the ideal one-half-of-a-programme length, make it popular with singers and audiences alike. The cycle has been recorded many times and this recording equals the best, these being by Gerhard Husch and Hans Hotter. In fact, this is lieder singing in what may well be called the 'old' style, where singers simply sang the music on the page, observing, of course, all the changes in dynamics and tempi. There is, from Husch, Hotter and Falkner, plenty of expression, colour and shading nuances as well as power and the most moving mezza voce where required. This is not the style of Lieder singing which has, since the 1950s, become the accepted and expected one, wherein an over-intellectual approach results in the analytical dissection of almost every word and where the line is bumped about with sudden explosions, irritating mannerisms, enforced darkening of lower notes which wobble in consequence and even containing, at times, what sounds suspiciously like crooning.

One might say that although the German is excellent it is nevertheless an 'anglicised' German; there is no doubt that this is an English singer. Some critics have maintained that there is always a restraint in Falkner's singing, that the emotion is too much under control: then let them hear the final heartbreak of 'Ich grolle nicht'. From the first lyrical entry of 'Im wunderschönen Monat Mai' to the final resignation of 'Die alten bosen Lieder' Keith Falkner is in his very best form: the voice, darker, deeper than his earlier recordings, is superb throughout, a prime example of the bass-baritone voice being used with skill, vocal artistry and sensitivity. Personally, this writer, and a few others who know his singing, find the voice even finer than ever before.

Adlonni A H Series: Another 'private' recording was made at the same time at Cornell with John Hunt. This was of a few English songs by Vaughan Williams, Armstrong Gibbs, Eugene Goossens and Herbert Howells, plus seven folk-song arrangements. In 'The Exile' (Gibbs), Keith Falkner is at his very best in the anguish of the de la Mare verses, from the hushed pianissimo to the outcry of the last phrase. 'Mally-O', a setting by Howells of anonymous Jacobean verses, is sung with great drive and a vital rhythm, showing excellent breath-control throughout, in a demanding song. The folk-songs reveal charm, as well as a warm enthusiasm for the songs, all of which are full of character, in particular, 'I will Give My Love' and 'Seventeen Come Sunday'. The latter, plus the Britten arrangement of 'Oliver Cromwell', reveal plenty of humour, a quality which he got little chance to show in other recordings.

Elgar: *The Dream of Gerontius.* A private recording of a 1935 BBC transmission of a performance from the Three Choirs Festival, with Heddle Nash and Keith Falkner. (John Davies of Adlonni Co., Pwllheli). As will be seen from the text, a superb critique was written by Frank Howes, though it was not a work for which Falkner had deep affection.

Ralph Vaughan Williams: *Sancta Civitas.* Fortunately, Falkner's last public performance was recorded. This was in Oxford with the Oxford Bach Choir and Orchestra directed by the late Sydney Watson, in November 1960. Despite having catarrh, occasionally evident in high passages, this is a very sensitive, well sung, beautifully enunciated performance. The Falkner sound, a highly individual one, is unmistakable, as always, and his warm feeling for this music comes across to the listener. The busy life of a college principal made him decide that this would be his final appearance in a public performance. The singing here makes one regret this decision for there is clearly plenty of voice left! The choral singing is splendid.

In 1971 HMV issued, on their 'Golden Voice' Series, an LP comprising some of Falkner's 78 rpm recordings. The series included eminent British singers of the past such as Clara Butt, Heddle Nash, Eva Turner, Gervase Elwes, Walter Widdop and Isobel Baillie. The sleeve-notes were written by the former bass singer David Franklin (1908-73), and his tribute to Falkner was a warm one:

This record brings back, very vividly, all the admiration I had for him ... good-looking, always immaculately turned out, with great dignity on the platform, he sang – it's an odd word to use of a singer but I'm sure it's the right one – fastidiously. It was a fine and virile voice. He had a good line, as steady as a rock, and with no suspicion of the sort of vibrato that comes when singers unwisely overload their voices. His intonation was impeccable, his control flexible and unobtrusive. He had beautiful diction, and he used words intelligently and with sensitive understanding. In a word ... he had taste. He was the very model of an English singer.

On specific songs, Franklin continued: 'The Purcell songs, vintage 1935, have a fine sense of style. The words are beautifully declaimed, the phrases firmly supported and controlled'. Of the Handel arias, he wrote: '... the long, wandering phrases controlled with consummate ease and pouring out of inexhaustible breath, these were the products of his fine technique and his great artistry'. Of the English songs recorded in 1940, Franklin wrote: 'The voice seems inexhaustible, the tone pours out with strength and with variety, the words are beautifully modelled and he sings with musicianship and sensitivity'.He concluded:

> ... in 1967 he was knighted. It's a pity that he didn't get a knighthood while he was still singing. Obviously, Sir Keith is a good administrator but there are lots of good admin. chaps. There was only one Keith Falkner, baritone, and he deserved a knighthood to himself.

Sir Keith had this to say of his own recordings:

> All the time one is thinking that one could have done it so much better; one is rarely, if ever, satisfied and is left with a sense of disappointment, even of frustration. I'm sure, for example, that if I'd had more time to study them, those three Purcell songs would have been better. However, 'How Cold This Clime' comes out well. The only one I'm pleased with is the aria, 'What Tho' I Trace' from Handel's *Solomon* ... it has a violin line. Listening, very recently, to the transfer of the pre-War *St Matthew Passion* recording is giving me much pleasure.

Discography: Chronological Order

HMV

September 1924:

    D 922/926. *Hugh the Drover* (Vaughan Williams) with Tudor Davies, Mary Lewis, Constance Willis, Frederic Collier and William Anderson. Conductor: Malcolm Sargent.

April 1928: (unissued).

    'The Self-banished' (Blow). 'Follow a Shadow', 'Love is a bable' (Parry).

October 1928: B 2917.

    Three Salt-water Ballads (Keel): 'Port of many Ships', 'Trade winds' and 'Mother Carey'.

February 1929: B 3105.

    'Shepherd: See thy horse's foaming mane', 'Had a horse' (Korbay).

– 1929: B 3175.

    The Playbox (Williams): 10 songs: 'Rocking horse', 'Golliwog', 'Clockwork train', 'Toy band', 'Teddy bear', 'Jack-in-the-box', 'Humming top', 'Noah's Ark', 'Bagpiper' and 'Wooden soldier'.

April 1929: B 3321.

    'Droop not, Young lover' from *Ezio* (Handel) with orchestral accompaniment, conductor George Byng, and, 'King Charles' (White) with piano.

– 1929: C 1670.

    'Thanks be to God' from *Elijah* (Mendelssohn), with the Royal Choral Society.

February 1930: C 1875.

    'Arm, arm, ye brave' from *Judas Maccabaeus* (Handel); 'O God, have mercy' from *St Paul* (Mendelssohn).

April 1930: C 1940.
'What tho' I trace' from *Solomon* (Handel) and 'The people that walked in darkness' from *Messiah.*

– 1930: B 3581.
'T'was in the cool of Eventide' from *St Matthew Passion* (Bach); 'How Jovial is my laughter' from *The Joyful Aeolus* (Bach Cantata 205).

April 1931: B 3658.
'Four jolly Sailormen' from *Princess of Kensington* (German), and 'On a January morning' from *Tom Jones.*

– 1931: B 3991.
'Come Landlord, fill ... ' (Anon) with MV Choir, 'False Phyllis' (arr Lane Wilson).

June 1931: B 4072.
'Fates discourtesy', 'The Sweepers' from *Fringes of the Fleet* (Elgar).

– 1937: B 8618/9.
Four songs from the film *Mayfair Melody* (Leslie Smith): 'Without the moon', 'San Diego Betty', 'A Song doesn't Care' and 'Wings'.

June 1940: B 9064.
'Is my team ploughing?' from Butterworth's *Shropshire Lad* Cycle. 'The street sounds to the soldier's tread' from Somervell's *Shropshire Lad* Cycle.

– 1940: B 9095.
'In Summertime on Bredon' (Peel), 'Birds in the High Hall Garden' and 'O let the solid ground' from Somervell's *Maud* Cycle.

April 1947: C 3748/49/50.
English Madrigals, with the 'Golden Age Singers' (Margaret Field-Hyde, Isobel Baillie, Gladys Windmill and Renc Soames): 'Flora

gave me the fairest flowers' (Wilbye), 'Sweet Suffolk Owl' (Vautour), 'Dainty fine bird' (Gibbons), 'Lady, the birds quite fairly' (Weelkes), 'Care for thy soul' (Pilkington), 'April is in my mistress' face' (Morley), Fair Phyllis I saw' (Morley), 'Now is the gentle Season' (Morley), 'Simkins said that Sis was fair' (Farnaby), and 'Thyrsis, sleepest thou?' (Bennet).

LP HMV *Golden Voice* Series, HMQ 1238. from 78s listed above: 'Droop not, young lover'; 'Arm, arm ye brave'; 'What tho' I trace'; 'The people that walked in darkness'; 'O God, have mercy'; 'Fate's discourtesy'; 'The Sweepers'; 'Birds in the High Hall Garden'; 'The street sounds' and 'O let the solid ground'; 'Is my team ploughing?' 'In Summertime on Bredon'; the two Korbay songs; the *Three Salt-water Ballads*, plus the three Purcell songs, listed below, for Columbia.

COLUMBIA

September 1935: ROX 134.
   'The Aspiration: 'How long, great God'; 'If music be the food of Love' (2nd setting) (Purcell).

September 1935: ROX 135.
   'I love and I must' (Purcell) coupled with the Purcell Singers, with John Ticehurst, harpsichord, and Bernard Richards, cello.

September 1938: FB 1486.
   Two Oxford Group Songs (Fraser): 'Bridgebuilders' and 'Drums of Peace', with MV Choir.

VICTOR – USA

– 1937: 14635/14661.
   St Matthew Passion (Bach). Boston, with Boston Symphony Orchestra, Serge Koussevitzky conductor and J Vreeland (soprano), K Meisle (contralto), J Preibe (tenor), F Lechner (bass) with Falkner in the Christus role. Now on Adlonni AH 202/3.

LP HANDEL SOCIETY

– 1952: HDL 13.

Alexander's Feast (Handel). Cornell University Choir and Orchestra conducted by Robert Hull, with L Scheunemann (soprano) and L Chabay (tenor).

PRIVATE

Cornell, 1954:

Dichterliebe Cycle (Schumann), accompanied by John Hunt, piano. Now also on Adlonni.

Cornell, 1954:

'The roadside fire' (Vaughan Williams), 'The Exile' (Gibbs), 'All day I hear the noise of many waters' (Goossens), 'Mally-O' (Howells), plus folk-song arrangements: 'The Ash Grove', 'Billy Boy', 'Rio Grande', 'The star of the County Down', 'I will give my love …', 'Seventeen come Sunday' (arr Sharp), 'Oliver Cromwell' (arr Britten). Adlonni.

November 1960:

Sancta Civitas (Vaughan Williams), with the Oxford Bach Choir and Orchestra conducted by Sydney Watson.

Cornell, 1967:

Façade (Walton): verse speaker.

INTERVIEWS, TALKS: *Television/Radio*

28 January 1968:

Interview with Bernard Keefe.

1 March 1970:

70th Birthday Tribute, with Frank Howes.

– 1970:

Interview on career, with Madeau Stewart.

– 1972:

The Real Parry: Discussion on Sir Hubert Parry, with Sir Adrian Boult, Herbert Howells and Keith Falkner.

20 July 1974:

Guest on BBC's *Desert Island Discs* with Roy Plomley. With No 8 being first choice, the selections included:

1. Excerpts from Evensong at New College, Oxford, including a Drayton Motet and Psalm 139.
2. Schubert: 'Die Krähe' (The Raven) from *Winterreise*, with Heinrich Rehkemper (baritone).
3. Schubert: *C Major Symphony*, with LPO conducted by Sir Adrian Boult.
4. Britten: 'The ride to Rome' from *The Rape of Lucretia*.
5. Verdi: 'Salce, salce' from *Otello*, with Gwyneth Jones.
6. Brahms: *Variations on a theme by Paganini*, played by John Lill.
7. Messaien: excerpt from Quartet, *For the End of Time*.
8. Bach: excerpt from *B Minor Mass*.

22 October 1975:

BBC-TV. *Face the Music* guest with Joseph Cooper, Joyce Grenfell, David Attenborough and Richard Baker. Falkner successfully answered the two questions posed on Handel's *Ezio* (his own recording) and Britten's *Cantata Academica*.

May 1981:

Radio and newspaper interview in Albuquerque, New Mexico, about career. Former illustrated with several recordings.

28 February 1982:

Reading: A tribute to Sir George Grove during the Thanksgiving Service for the RCM Centenary, Westminster Abbey.

28 May 1991:
BBC Radio 4 programme. Interviewed with Roy Henderson by Richard Baker. Illustrated with several recordings.

1992: Interview on Radio Suffolk.

Selected Index of Musicians

Alcock, Sir Walter (1861-1947).
Organist, Chapels Royal. Organist
Salisbury Cathedral 1916-1947. *22*

Allen, Sir Hugh (1869-1946). Organ
Scholar, Christ's College, Cambridge,
1892, later St Asaph and Ely
Cathedrals. Organist New College,
Oxford, 1901-18. Director of RCM
1918-37. Oxford Heather Professor of
Music 1918-46. Outstanding musical
scholar. A guiding force of powerful
personality and influence in British
music-making. *13, 15, 16, 20, 21, 24,
28, 31, 42, 44, 53, 92, 97, 99, 112,
165, 171, 173, 182, 198, 199, 203*

Allin, Norman (1884-1973). English
bass, a true basso profondo. Beecham
Opera Co/BNOC 1916-29. Principal
roles: Covent Garden, Glyndebourne
Festival, Carl Rosa Opera. Prof RAM
1935-60, Prof RCM 1938-42. *26, 98,
112, 162, 172, 179, 190, 211*

Armstrong, Sir Thomas (1898-1995).
Sub-organist Manchester Cathedral
1922-33; organist Exeter Cathedral
1928-33; organist Christ Church,
Oxford, 1933-55. Principal RAM
1955-68. Composer of songs and
church music. *21, 45, 101, 109, 112,
132*

Baillie, Isobel (1895-1983). British
soprano famous for boy-like purity of
her voice. Autobiography *Never Sing
Louder Than Lovely* encapsulates her
approach to singing. Renowned for the
remarkable longevity of her vocal
career. Much beloved by English

oratorio audiences. *40, 47, 76, 81, 93,
94, 185, 186, 194, 214, 218, 221*

Bairstow, Sir Edward (1874-1946).
Organist/choirmaster York Minster
1912-46. Conductor of many Northern
societies and festivals, a musician of
great influence in the North. Composer of church music and songs. *38, 61,
185, 187*

Baker, George (1885-1975). English
baritone. Studied at RCM and Milan.
Enormously long career, mainly as a
concert singer 1909-66. Vast record
output, often under pseudonyms. In
his mid-70s, Sargent used him for
patter comedy roles in G & S
recordings. Author of *This Singing
Business* and *The Common Sense of
Singing. 38*

Baker, Dame Janet (1933-). English
mezzo-soprano, had highly successful
international career as singer of lieder,
English and French song, oratorio and
opera. Autobiography *Full Circle,*
1982. *124, 125, 164*

Balfour, Margaret (1892-). English
contralto. Some operatic work but best
known as a concert and oratorio
soloist, notably at Three Choirs
Festivals during the inter-war years.
187, 188

Ball, Michael (1946-). Student at RCM
during Keith's tenure, subsequently
composer of orchestral, brass band and
choral music. *126*

Barbirolli, Sir John (1899-1970). English
conductor long connected with Hallé

Orchestra (1943-70). Not unlike Eugene Goossens in coming from a family of foreign musicians. Began as a cellist, at one time the youngest member of the Queen's Hall Orchestra. Married the oboist Evelyn Rothwell. *64, 74, 92, 100, 105*

Bellezza, Vincenzo (1888-1964). Opera conductor at the NY Met 1926-35. Rome Opera from 1935. *64*

Boult, Sir Adrian (1889-1983). Conductor of CBSO 1924-30, BBC Symphony Orchestra 1931-50. *21, 30, 31, 33, 34, 37, 40, 41, 64, 80, 92, 97, 98, 105, 106, 110, 122, 124, 126, 174, 181, 182, 184, 185, 195, 198, 199, 224*

Boyce, Bruce (1910-). Canadian baritone. Studied at Cornell. Made his début at a concert for Eleanor Roosevelt at the White House in 1932. Came to England 1934. From 1940-45 served in Army. Joined New London Opera Co and Covent Garden in the 1950s. BBC radio singer and lieder interpreter. Later taught at RAM, retiring to South of France. *73, 81*

Brewer, Sir Herbert (1865-1928). Composer, organist Gloucester Cathedral 1896-1928. Directed various Three Choirs Festivals, 1896-1928. *25*

Brown, Wilfred (1921-1972). English lyric tenor known for his work in English song and oratorio. Made several recordings of English song, in particular Finzi's *Dies Natalis*. *86, 89*

Brunskill, Muriel (1899-1980). English oratorio and operatic contralto. British National Opera Company 1920-27. Covent Garden 1930s. Tours of USA, Canada, Australia, New Zealand and Holland between 1931-57. *36, 37, 40, 187*

Buck, Sir Percy (1871-1947). Organist, Wells and Bristol Cathedrals, 1896-1901. Also Director of Music at Harrow and Professor of Music in Dublin. Composer of songs and church music. *53*

Cantelli, Guido (1920-1956). Italian conductor. Studied at Milan Conservatory, début in 1943. Turned attention to opera in 1956. Appointment as Musical Director of La Scala came a few days before his death in a plane crash. *68*

Casella, Alfredo (1883-1947). Composer, conductor, pianist and author - champion of all that was new in the art. Pupil of Fauré. Piano master-classes at Santa Cecilia. Christabel studied with him. *68*

Colles, H C (1870-1943). English music critic/musicologist . Studied at RCM. Critic for *The Times* 1905-43 (chief critic from 1911). Lectured at RCM from 1919. Several books, eg, on Brahms. Editor *Grove's Dictionary of Music*, 3rd and 4th editions. *53*

Coward, Sir Henry (1845-1944). The most famous choral conductor of his time. Founded Sheffield Music Union 1876. Conducted choirs at Leeds, Glasgow, Preston and Newcastle. *178*

Coxon, Joan. English coloratura soprano. Well known in the inter-war years in lieder and English song recitals. *185, 186*

Cranmer, Arthur (1888-1954). English bass-baritone. Sang in the long-running production of *The Immortal Hour* (Boughton) in the early 1920s. Better known in oratorio. Author of an excellent book on singing. *99, 188*

Crooks, Richard (1900-1972). American tenor. Opera roles in Hamburg and Berlin, 1927-30. NY Met 1933-46. International concert artist, enjoying enormous popularity. *48, 187, 188*

Dallapiccola, Luigi (1904-1975). Composer and pianist. Extensive output includes operas *Volo di Notte* (1940) and *Il Prigioniero* (1950). *64, 67, 69*

Darke, Harold (1888-1954). Taught at RCM 1919-69. Composer of church music. Organist, St Michael's, Cornhill, 1916-66, and founder/ conductor of St Michael's Singers. Acting organist of King's College, Cambridge, 1941-45. *22*

Davies, Sir Henry Walford (1869-1941). Composer, musicologist, writer, conductor and pedagogue. Popular BBC broadcaster on music. Variously organist St George's, Windsor, and Temple Church, London. Composer of a once-popular oratorio *Everyman*, much church and vocal music. *44*

Davies, Tudor (1892-1958). Welsh tenor. British National Opera Company 1922-29. In première (1924) of *Hugh the Drover* (title role) with Keith. Sadler's Wells 1931-41; Carl Rosa Opera 1941-46. Well known in oratorio and as a teacher. *21, 26, 187, 214, 220*

Daymond, Dr Emily (1866-1949). One of the 50 foundation scholars when RCM opened in 1883. First Director of Music at Royal Holloway College 1887. Founded the *RCM Magazine* 1906. Founded The Society of Women Musicians 1911, being its first president, and the RCM Loan Fund for students. Also founded the RCM

Union. Great friend of and amanuensis for Sir Hubert Parry. Keen non-militant supporter of the Women's Suffrage Movement. *24, 25, 171, 172, 173, 182, 199*

Denison, John (1911). Horn player BBC, LPO and City of Birmingham Orchestras. Music Director, The Arts Council, 1948-65 . General Manager, Royal Festival Hall, 1965-70. *90*

Dent, Edward J (1876-1957). English musicologist. Professor of Music, Cambridge, 1926-41; first president of the International Society of Contemporary Music 1922-38; President of International Musicological Society 1931-49. Translator of many operas. Published works on Scarlatti, Handel and Busoni. Much respected throughout Europe. *62*

De Sabata, Victor (1892-1967). Conductor and composer. Famous for his performances of Verdi and Wagner. *68*

Desmond, Astra (1898-1973). English mezzo-soprano, notably in oratorio at Three Choirs Festivals, where she sang mainly in Elgar works, often under the composer himself. Was fluent in several languages, notably the songs of Grieg and Sibelius. *38, 179, 187*

Dickson, Joan (1921-1995). English cellist. Studied at RCM and with Fournier. Début 1953. Many Proms followed. Teacher at RSA and RCM, also appointed director of instrumental studies at Purcell School. Publications include works on teaching. Awarded Cobbett Medal for services to chamber music. Several works written for her. *71*

Di Stefano, Giuseppe (1921). Italian operatic tenor, one of the best of his day. Often partnered Callas. Had highly successful international career. *64*

Dohnanyi, Ernst von (1877-1960). Hungarian pianist and composer. Many international tours as a concert pianist from the late 1890s onwards; later better known as a composer. *30, 31, 32, 182*

Dossert, Deane. French singing teacher with whom Keith studied briefly. Author of *Sound Sense for Singers* (1932). *171, 175*

Dyson, Sir George (1883-1964). English composer/administrator. Director of Music, Winchester, from 1934, having been music master at Marlborough, Rugby and Wellington. Composer of many choral works, including *Canterbury Pilgrims* and *Quo Vadis?*, orchestral music, choral pieces, church music and songs. Director RCM from 1937-1953. *39, 61, 92, 130*

Eadie, Noel (1901-50). English operatic lyric/coloratura soprano. Sang with BNOC, Sadler's Wells and Covent Garden. *36*

Easton, Robert (1998-1987). English basso profondo, outstanding in the concert world 1926-60. Sang professionally into his 80s. Covent Garden 1935-39. Proms from 1926. Also an outstanding golfer. *26, 181, 141, 187, 190*

Eisdell, Hubert (1882-1948). English lyric tenor. In oratorio, a splendid Bach tenor; in concerts, a famous interpreter of Quilter, who wrote many songs for him. Vast recording output.

Singing professor at Peterborough Conservatory, Canada, 1938. *187, 188*

Evans, Nancy (1915-). Studied privately with John Tobin and Maggie Teyte. Recorded first *Dido* performance for the Purcell Society; Glyndebourne 1938; Covent Garden 1939. During war years Music Section, ENSA. 1946 Glyndebourne sharing role of 'Lucretia' with Kathleen Ferrier. 1949 created role of 'Nancy' in Britten's *Albert Herring*. Associated with Aldeburgh Festival from 1948. Co-Director with Peter Pears of Singing Studies for the Britten/Pears School, later its Director. Married first, Walter Legge (daughter Helga); second, Eric Crozier.

Farrington, Joseph (1882-1960). English bass-baritone. Vicar-Choral at St Paul's Cathedral for many years. Principal with BNOC 1921-29, notably as Wotan and Mephistopheles. In 1940 revival of *The Beggar's Opera. 23*

Fenby, Eric (1906-1996). English musicologist. Amanuensis to Delius 1928-34. Music adviser, Boosey's, 1936-39. Professor RAM from 1964. Published *Delius As I Knew Him* (1966) and *Delius* (1971). *53*

Fielden, Thomas (1882-1974). Taught at RCM 1921-47. Known as 'Fielden of Charterhouse', where he was Director of Music. Several publications on piano technique. *22, 110*

Flagstad, Kirsten (1895-1962). Norwegian opera singer, one of the greatest dramatic sopranos, especially as Isolde and Brunhilde. Sang at Bayreuth, NY Met and Covent Garden, 1934-51. *47, 162, 176*

Flegg, Bruce. English tenor. Studied with Grenzebach and Yves Tinayre. Occasional soloist with Dr Darke's St Michael's Singers during the 1930s. Architect (ARIBA). Gold Medal, Society of Architects. A distinguished water-colour artist. Deputy Director of Music, British Council. Music and Fine Arts Officer, Vienna. Coach/ private teacher. Artistic adviser, Waterford Festival. *82, 174*

Fox, Douglas (1892-1978). Brilliant pianist who lost his right arm in action, Flanders 1917. Carried on with his career. Director of Music, Bradfield College, 1918-30. Director of Music, Clifton College, Bristol, 1931-57. *171, 172*

Garcia. Family of famous singing teachers: Manuel (1775-1832); Manuel (1805-1906); Gustave (1837-1925); Albert (1875-1946), who taught at RCM, GSM and TCM. *Albert, 21, 22, 26, 44, 135, 171, 173; Manuel, 149*

Ghedini, Giorgio (1892-1965). Composer, and editor of old Italian music, eg, Carissimi. *68*

Gigli, Beniamino (1890-1357). World-famous tenor in Italian opera, especially Puccini roles. *64*

Goossens, Sir Eugene (1893-1962). English conductor and composer. Member of the famous musical family. Conductor of Beecham Opera until 1920; Rochester (USA) SO from 1923; from 1931, Cincinnati SO, then Sydney SO (Australia), and Director of New South Wales Conservatorium in 1947. Composer of operas, eg, *Judith* and *Don Juan de Manara*,

orchestral music and songs. *64, 65, 67, 70, 72, 80, 105, 181, 189, 217, 223*

Green, Martyn (1899-1975). Light baritone and patter-song virtuoso with D'Oyly-Carte in G & S comedy roles, 1930-52. Later, in USA, worked in films, TV and New York stage, including *The Ice Man Cometh* (O'Neill). Lost a leg in a lift accident in 1959, thereafter playing seated roles. Author of *I Have a Song to Sing*. *21, 23*

Greene, Harry Plunket (1865-1936). Irish bass-baritone. The most famous song recitalist of his day. Noted for outstanding interpretative gifts rather than for a great voice. Became very influential teacher and, apart from his *Interpretation in Song*, wrote a book on Stanford. Son-in-law of Sir Hubert Parry. Many songs dedicated to him. Gave first performances of song-cycles such as *Maud* (Somervell), *Songs of the Sea* (Stanford), etc. Pupils included Keith, Henry Cummings, Robert Easton. *24, 147, 153, 157, 164, 171, 173, 174, 214, 215*

Grenzebach, Ernst. Famous Berlin singing teacher. Pupils included Lauritz Melchior, Alexander Kipnis, Max Lorenz, Victoria Sladen and, briefly, Keith. *171, 174*

Grout, Donald Jay (1902-1987). American musicologist and author: *A Short History of Opera* and *A History of Western Music*. *76, 79, 80, 85, 90, 101, 114, 126, 208*

Groves, Sir Charles (1915-1992). Chorister, St Paul's Cathedral, and student RCM. Accompanist, later internationally known conductor: BBC NSO 1941-51. Royal Liverpool PO 1963-77, appointed Conductor

Laureate. English National Opera 1978-9. *23, 28, 175*

Gurney, Ivor (1890-1937). One of the finest of English song composers, also a poet. Wounded, gassed and shell-shocked at Passchendaele 1917. Died in an asylum. *21, 38, 40, 80, 82*

Hammond, Dame Joan (1912-). New Zealand-born soprano. Sang in Europe and Australia between 1936-60, notably Covent Garden, Vienna State Opera, Bolshoi, Sadler's Wells. A fine sportswoman. Retired to Australia. Autobiography, *A Voice, A Life. 185, 186*

Harty, Sir Hamilton (1879-1941). Irish conductor and composer of orchestral works, songs and cantatas. Conductor, Hallé Orchestra 1920-33. *43*

Head, Michael (1900-1976). English song composer. Also self-accompanied baritone recitalist. Studied at RAM. *26*

Henderson, Roy, (1899-). Baritone and teacher. Well-known as a song interpreter. Frequent soloist at Covent Garden, Glyndebourne and Three Choirs Festivals. Teacher of Kathleen Ferrier. *26, 81, 98, 124, 128, 130, 134, 141, 178, 179, 184, 189, 225*

Hess, Dame Myra (1890-1965). One of the greatest pianists of her era. Well known for her concerts at the Victoria and Albert Museum and the National Gallery during the 2nd World War. *28, 32, 37, 49, 52, 80, 82, 92, 150, 176*

Hiscock, George (1895-1966). Twice round the world in windjammers. Gave up singing for the stage. Later became Librarian at Christ Church, Oxford. *22, 23, 91*

Howells, Herbert (1892-1983). English composer: large-scale works including *Hymnus Paradisi, Missa Sabrinensis,* much church music, many songs, orchestral and organ works. RCM Professor of Composition from 1922. *21, 40, 46, 49, 65, 70, 81, 99, 103, 112, 120, 124, 128, 132, 217, 218, 223, 224*

Howes, Frank (1891-1974). Music critic for *The Times* 1925-60. Lecturer RCM 1938-71. Published *Man, Mind & Music,* and books on Vaughan Williams, Walton, etc. *38, 70, 73, 98, 159, 218, 223*

Hunt, John (1905-). Solo pianist and accompanist. Studied with Arthur Schnabel (Berlin). Visiting Professor of Piano, Cornell University, 1952-53. Professor RAM, 1955. Tokyo, 1959. *53, 78, 79, 80, 82, 176, 193, 208, 217, 223, 232*

Husa, Karel (1921). Composer/conductor. Studied in Prague and Paris with Honegger and Boulanger. Winner Czech Academy and Boulanger composition prizes. Cornell 1954 to present. Finally able to return to Prague for his country's recognition following the Czech 'reformation' in 1989. *87, 95, 113, 121*

Ibert, Jacques (1890-1962). French composer. Directed French Academy in Rome (Villa Medici) and Paris Opera. *69*

Jacques, Reginald (1894-1969). English conductor/lecturer. Lecturer Queen's College, Oxford. Conductor of Bach Choir 1932-60. Professor at RCM 1937. Ran CEMA from 1940-45.

Founded Jacques Orchestra; published many song-books. *105*

Jarred, Mary (1899-1993). English contralto. Hamburg State Opera 1929-33; Covent Garden 1933-39, especially in *The Ring*. Also sang at Sadler's Wells. Successful career in oratorio and as concert singer. *44, 45, 184, 187, 194*

Jones, Trefor (1901-1965). Welsh tenor. Shared in 1924 première of *Hugh the Drover* whilst a student at RCM. Sang in many productions of operetta and musicals. Distinguished soloist at Three Choirs Festivals. *44, 45, 184, 187, 194*

Jones, Parry (1891-1963). Welsh lyric tenor. Returning from a US tour, 1915, survived the *Lusitania* disaster. Beecham Co. and BNOC 1916-29; Covent Garden 1925-53. *187*

Kirkpatrick, John (1905-1991). Pianist and teacher. Specialized in works of Edward McDowell and Charles Ives. Official biographer and editor of Ives's music. *73, 75, 76, 83, 86, 176, 208*

Kodály, Zoltan (1882-1967). One of Hungary's greatest composers. Wrote operas, masses, a *Te Deum*, large number of songs and choral works. Drew from folk-song and traditional music for his inspiration. *45, 46, 95*

Koussevitzky, Serge (1875-1951). One of the greatest conductors of his time. Began musical career as a virtuoso double-bass player. Conductor of Boston SO 1924-49. *37, 46, 65, 77, 131, 162, 166, 181, 195, 208, 214, 216, 222*

Krips, Josef (1902-1973). Viennese conductor. Variously opera conductor at Dortmund, Karlsruhe, Vienna State Opera, between 1925-38. Conductor LSO 1950-54. Reorganised post-war Salzburg Festivals. *84, 184, 185*

Labette, Dora (1898-1984). English lyric soprano, best known in the oratorio/concert world, but was 'Lisa Perli' in Beecham's well~known *Bohème* production at Covent Garden. Opera successes in Berlin, Dresden and Munich. Recorded several Delius songs accompanied by Beecham. *185, 186*

Lambert, Constant (1905-1951). Pupil of R O Morris and Vaughan Williams at RCM 1926. While still a student, received a commission from Diaghilev for the Ballet *Romeo and Juliet*. Works include *Rio Grande* and *Summer's Last Will and Testament*. Published *Music Ho!: a study of Music in decline*, Faber 1934 (3rd edition, 1966). *21, 70, 71*

Lauri-Volpi, Giacomo (1892-1979). Italian tenor and something of a rival to Gigli, though he was more a dramatic tenor. Published *Voce Paralleli* 1955. *64*

Leslie-Smith, Kenneth (1897-). Scots-born composer of light music. Best known for the song *Always*. Wrote much film music. *45, 213, 221*

Ley, Henry (1887-1962). On RCM staff. Organist Christ Church, Oxford, 1909-26. Music Director, Eton, 1925-45. Composer of church music. *27, 93*

Licette, Miriam (1892-1969). English lyric soprano. Beecham Opera Company and BNOC 1916-29. Sang

frequently at Covent Garden 1919-38.
Founded an opera school in London.
41

Lierhammer, Dr Theo (1866-1954).
Famous Austrian teacher, baritone and
throat specialist. His pupils included
Erich Kunz, Otto Edelman and Keith.
171, 174, 183

Lofthouse, Dr Charles (1895-1974).
Director of Music, Westminster
School. Professor at RCM. Conductor,
University of London Music Society.
Continuo, The Bach Choir 1921-39.
81, 89

Lush, Ernest (1908-1988). One of the
finest of English accompanists. Joined
BBC as permanent accompanist in
1928. Well known for the BBC's *Men
about Music* programmes with Owen
Brannigan. *46, 81, 176*

McArthur, Edwin (1907-1987).
American accompanist/conductor and
composer. Studied at Juilliard.
Accompanied Flagstad, Jeritz,
Swarthout. Conductor Harrisburg SO
from 1950. Composed incidental
music for *Rip van Winkle*, many
songs. Professor, Eastman School of
Music. *176*

McPherson, Charles (1870-1927). Scots
organist and composer. Chorister St
Paul's Cathedral. Studied RAM. Sub-
organist St Paul's 1895-1916;
organist/choirmaster St Paul's 1916-
27. *136*

Mackie, Neil (1946-). English tenor who
has sung widely in Europe and the
USA; particularly associated with
operas by Peter Maxwell Davies.
Professor at RCM from 1985, Director
of Vocal Studies since 1993. *128, 130*

Malipiero, Francesco (1882-1973).
Composer. Director, Conservatorio of
Venice. Edited a complete edition of
Monteverdi. *64, 68*

Marchant, Sir Stanley (1883-1949).
English organist, teacher and church
composer. Organist/choirmaster, St
Paul's Cathedral 1927-49. Principal
RAM 1936-49. *22*

Mayr, Richard (1877-1935). Austrian
bass. Début at Bayreuth in 1902, later
joining Vienna Court Opera
(subsequently the State Opera). Often
sang at the Festivals of Bayreuth and
Salzburg. *174*

Molinari, Bernadino (1880-1952). Italian
conductor, frequent guest in Europe
and the USA. *64*

Moore, Gerald (1899-1987). English
internationally known accompanist
from the early 1930s. Many
recordings. Author of *Singer and
Accompanist* (1953), *The Unashamed
Accompanist* (1957) and *Am I Too
Loud?* (1962). *76, 119, 175, 213*

Mullinar, Michael (1895-1973). Welsh-
born accompanist. Studied at RCM,
pupil of Vaughan Williams. Composer
of songs. Also prepared piano
reductions of RVW's works. Worked
as accompanist under Boult at
Birmingham for many years, often
accompanying Keith. Professor of
Accompanying at RCM until 1965.
38, 41, 86, 175, 177

Nash, Heddle (1894-1961). Outstanding
English lyric tenor. Italian opera
companies 1923-25; BNOC 1925-29;
Covent Garden 1929-47;
Glyndebourne Festivals 1934-38; Carl

Rosa 1941-46; NY City Opera 1957-58. *26, 179, 187, 188, 189, 194, 218*

Natzka, Oscar (1905-1951). New Zealand bass. Came to Britain in 1937 and appeared at Covent Garden between then and 1947, notably as Sarastro. Joined New York City Opera. Suffered a stroke while performing as Pognor in *Meistersinger*, dying a few days later. *44*

Newton, Ivor (1892-1981). Fine English accompanist. Played recitals for Chaliapin, Melchior, Teyte, Henderson, Kipnis, Piatigorsky, etc., and Keith. Published *At the Piano*, 1960. *47, 97, 176, 186*

Nicholson, Sir Sydney (1875-1947). English organist and composer. Manchester Cathedral 1908-18: Westminster Abbey 1918-27: founder and director RSCM 1927. Wrote a comic opera, *The Mermaid*, a boys' opera, *Children of the Chapel*, and much church music. *22*

Noble, Dennis (1899-1966). English baritone, famous in opera and oratorio, also popular concert artist. *26, 180*

Ord, Boris (1897-1961). English organist, composer and harpsichordist. Studied at RCM under Parratt. Organist at King's College, Cambridge, 1929-54, and composer of church music. Lectured at Cambridge 1936-54. *21, 215*

Orr, Charles Wilfred (1893-1975). Gloucestershire composer, his 35 settings of Housman being arguably the best of all. *93*

Parr, Gladys (1892-1988). English contralto. BNOC, Sadler's Wells, Covent Garden, 1923-47. At Aldeburgh Festivals 1947-58, creating roles in *Albert Herring* and *Noyes Fludde*. *41*

Parratt, Sir Walter (1841-1924). English organist and teacher. Organist/choirmaster, St George's, Windsor, 1882-1924. Prof RCM 1908-18. *22*

Pears, Sir Peter (1910-1986). English tenor. Creator of many Benjamin Britten roles from 1944, eg, in *Peter Grimes, Rape of Lucretia, Albert Herring, Billy Budd, Gloriana*, etc. Britten wrote many songs for him. Closely associated with establishment and growth of Aldeburgh Festival from 1946. *61, 65, 67, 74, 106*

Petrassi, Goffredo (1904-). Composer of wide range of orchestral, operatic and chamber music. Influenced by Stravinsky and Hindemith, later serial methods. Eight concertos for orchestra. Professor, Santa Cecilia, Rome. *64, 67*

Phillips, Frank (1901-). English baritone and BBC announcer. Won Rose Bowl at Blackpool Festival 1923. First Prom 1926. Mainly heard in concerts and oratorio. Gave up singing in the 1930s to become well-known announcer and newsreader. *178*

Piatigorsky, Igor (1903-1976). Russian cello virtuoso. Berlin PO 1924-28, then embarked on a highly successful solo career. Went to USA in 1939. Taught at Curtis Institute, Philadelphia. *186*

Pizzetti, Ildebrando (1880-1968). Italian composer of many operas, eg, *Murder in the Cathedral* and *L'Oro*. *64, 67*

Poulenc, Francis (1899-1963). French composer of music in all genres, but particularly songs, choral and piano music. *94*

Previtali, Fernando (1907-1985). Director of RAI and Santa Cecilia Academy. *66*

Radford, Robert (1874-1933). English bass, the best-known of his time. Sang in oratorio, notably at Three Choirs, Norwich and Leeds Festivals. Beecham Co and BNOC 1916-29; also a director of the latter. Sang at Covent Garden and taught at RAM. *189*

Reeves, George (1895-1960). Professor RCM 1917-19. Accompanist for Calve, Agnes Nicholls, Dorothy Silk and Campbell McInnes. *176*

Reith, Lord John (1889-1971). Administrator. The first General Manager of the BBC, 1922-29. From 1927-38, Director-General BBC. Government posts during the 2nd World War and important positions with aircraft industry. With the BBC he raised the level of interest, nationally, in the world of music. *171*

Riley, Stanley (1901-). Studied RCM. BBC Singers, 1927-61. St Paul's Cathedral as Vicar Choral 1923-30. Gentleman of the Chapel Royal 1948-70. Since leaving the Chapel Royal has sung in the Guards Chapel. *23*

Roberts, John Varley (1841-1920). Well-known Oxford 'character'. Author of a book on boys' voices. Organist, Magdalen College, Oxford, 1882-1920. *16, 165*

Robertson, Stuart (1901-1958). English bass-baritone. Vicar Choral St Paul's Cathedral, 1923-30. Three Choirs

Festivals, Bach Choir, operetta and musicals. Appeared in films with his sister, Dame Anna Neagle. Many records for HMV 1926-38. Served in RCN 1940-45. *21, 23, 178, 212*

Rubbra, Edmund (1901-1986). English composer of symphonies, other orchestral music, songs and choral music. *21, 88, 91, 93*

Sargent, Sir Malcolm (1895-1967). Conductor with particularly high reputation as choral conductor. Liked to be known as Britain's Ambassador of Music. *21, 36, 37, 40, 43, 64, 65, 105, 106, 188, 214, 220*

Scott, Charles Kennedy (1876-1965). English choral conductor. Conductor of Philharmonic Choir, Oriana Madrigal Society and Bach Cantata Club. Published books on choral training and conducting. *39*

Serafin, Tullio (1878-1968). Italian opera conductor. Rome Opera 1934-43 and again from 1962. Worked at the Met, Covent Garden and Chicago Opera. Conducted Italian première of *Peter Grimes*. *63*

Shore, Bernard (1896-1985). Viola player and member of BBC SO 1930-40. Professor of Viola RCM from 1959. Author of *The Orchestra Speaks* (1937) and *Sixteen Symphonies* (1947). *21, 78, 141, 176*

Silk, Dorothy (1884-1942). English soprano distinguished as interpreter of Bach and early music. Regular soloist at Three Choirs Festivals and often shared recitals with Keith. *37, 38, 42, 185, 186, 188*

Smith, Cyril (1909-1974). English concert pianist. Studied at RCM.

Proms from 1923. Duet partnership with wife, Phyllis Sellick, from 1941. Stroke paralysed his left arm whilst on a Russian tour in 1956, yet he continued his career, playing three-handed arrangements with his wife. Professor at RCM 1934-74. Autobiography *Duet for Three Hands*, 1958. *45, 99*

Sokol, Thomas. Professor of Music, Emeritus, Cornell University. Director of Choral Music, 1957-95. Choral Director at Berkshire Music Center and Chorus Master under conductors Boulanger, Husa, Leinsdorf, Munch, Ormandy, Stokowski and Tilson Thomas, to name a few. Conducted in 25 countries; broadcasts on BBC TV and TV Moscow, among others. Chairman of Department of Music, Cornell, 1985-62. *5, 87, 88, 94, 111, 124*

Stevens, Horace (1876-1954). Australian bass-baritone. Lay Clerk, Melbourne Cathedral, before Great War. Served with ANZAC 1914-18. Began professional solo career 1919. A regular performer at Three Choirs Festivals 1921-34. BNOC 1921-29, notably as Wotan, Sachs, Prince Igor and Mephistopheles. Taught at the Melbourne Conservatory 1938-54. *25, 38*

Stiles-Allen, Lilian (1899-1986). English concert soprano. Had long career as teacher: one of her pupils was Julie Andrews. *185, 186*

Suddaby, Elsie (1893-1981). English lyric soprano with long, distinguished career in oratorio, a regular soloist at Three Choirs Festivals. *25, 39, 44, 47, 81, 179, 185*

Sumsion, Dr Herbert (1899-1995). Organist/choirmaster Gloucester Cathedral, 1928-67. Director of Gloucester Three Choirs Festivals, 1928-37, and after Second World War. Composer of much church music. *21, 46*

Supervia, Conchita (1895-1936). Spanish mezzo. A coloratura mezzo, almost alone then in being able to sing Rossini's roles, which had been written for her vocal category. A much-praised Carmen.

Tagliabue, Carlo (1898-1978). Italian baritone, sang at La Scala for 25 years. Became a teacher following retirement in 1958. *70*

Tauber, Richard (1891-1948). Austrian-Jewish tenor. Conducted and composed operetta. Equally well known for his Mozart and operetta performances. Singer of enormous popularity. *48*

Tertis, Lionel (1876-1975). Viola player with many London orchestras and string quartets, also soloist. Many works written for him.

Thalben-Ball, Sir George (1890-1987). Australian-born organist, and composer. At RCM from 1919. Famous recitalist and organist Temple Church 1923-81. *21, 22, 33, 99*

Thurston, Frederick John (Jack) (1901-1953). English clarinettist, principal of BBC SO 1930-46, and other orchestras. *21, 168*

Tinayre, Yves (1895-). French baritone and teacher. Concert début in 1919 at Queen's Hall. In 1930s became a celebrated recitalist in the UK, France and Belgium, specializing in early

French music. Several BBC broadcasts. In 1939 sang in New York and settled in USA. Several recordings for HMV, Pathé and Lumen. *171*

Titterton, Frank (1882-1956). English tenor with highly successful career in oratorio and concerts for some thirty years. *41*

Toye, Francis (1883-1964). English music critic and author of books on Verdi and Rossini. Director of British Institute in Florence 1936-9, in which city he lived from 1946. *40, 69, 70, 74, 91, 93, 111, 171, 174*

Turner, Dame Eva (1892-1990). One of the greatest dramatic sopranos of all time, internationally known for her portrayal of Puccini's *Turandot*. Sang at La Scala and Covent Garden. *185, 186, 218*

Vaughan Williams, Ralph (1872-1958). Prolific composer in all forms, including six operas, nine symphonies and many choral works. Believed a composer should 'make his art an expression of the whole life of the community'. *16, 21, 23, 24, 35, 36, 38, 69, 70, 76, 80, 81, 82, 84, 85, 86, 87, 89, 92, 93, 99, 106, 124, 132, 165, 166, 178, 179, 187, 196, 208, 210, 213, 214, 217, 218, 220, 223*

Visetti, Alberto (1848-1928). Opera conductor and composer. Settled in London and taught singing at RCM from 1883, also at Guildhall and Trinity College. One of his most famous pupils was Clara Butt. *21*

Walter, Bruno (1876-1956). Austrian conductor, specialist in the works of Mozart, Wagner and Mahler, the last-named a personal friend. Salzburg Festivals during inter-war years. Went to the USA and worked with New York PSO for many seasons. As pianist, accompanied Kathleen Ferrier in her Edinburgh Festival recitals. *181*

Watson, Sydney (1903-1991). English organist, conductor, composer. Organist New College, Oxford, 1933-38; Master of Music, Winchester 1938-45; Music Director, Eton, 1946-55; Lecturer/organist Christ Church, Oxford, 1955-70. Professor at RCM 1946-71. Composer of much church music. Conducted Keith's last public performance. *99, 218, 223, 239*

Weeks, Gilbert Marcy (1903-1970). Great friend of Keith's at Cornell University. Founded Cornell Friends of Music. Absorbed with music, painting and literature. *76, 80*

Westrup, Sir Jack (1904-1975). English musicologist, Heather Professor of Music at Oxford. Music critic for the *Daily Telegraph* 1934-40. Lecturer RAM 1938-40. Editor *Monthly Musical Record* 1933-45. Lecturer King's College, Newcastle-on-Tyne, 1941-44. Lecturer Oxford University from 1944. Producer of many operas. Edited *Master Musicians Series*. *41, 72, 90*

Whinyates, Seymour (1892-). Violinist with the Whinyates String Quartet 1929-39, British Council head of music 1946. *61, 71*

Widdop, Walter (1892-1949). English dramatic tenor who sang Wagnerian Heldentenor roles and oratorios with great success. BNOC, 1923-29; Covent Garden, 1928-48. *26, 36, 189, 218*

Willcocks, Sir David (1919-). English organist and conductor. Director of Music King's College, Cambridge, 1957-63; conductor of Bach Choir 1960-98; Director of RCM 1974-84. *116, 118, 119, 132, 195, 202*

Williams, Harold (1893-1978). Outstanding Australian baritone in the concert/oratorio scene 1926-52. Well-known in opera with BNOC and in oratorio, also at Three Choirs Festivals, etc. Fine sportsman, notably in cricket and golf. *26*

Wilson, Sir Steuart (1889-1966). English lyric tenor, teacher and administrator. BNOC, 1922-27; General Administrator, Covent Garden, 1949-55. Notable soloist at Three Choirs Festivals, especially as Gerontius, and as Evangelist with the Bach Choir. *25, 37, 38, 40, 44, 67, 81, 184, 188*